Pioneers of the Hardwood

Indiana and the Birth of Professional Basketball

PIONEERS
of the
HARDWOOD

Todd Gould

INDIANA UNIVERSITY PRESS   BLOOMINGTON & INDIANAPOLIS

This book is a publication of
Indiana University Press
601 North Morton Street
Bloomington, Indiana 47404-3797 USA

http://www.indiana.edu/~iupress

Telephone orders 800-842-6796
Fax orders 812-855-7931
Orders by email iuporder@indiana.edu

The paper used in this publication meets the minimum
requirements of American National Standard for Information
Sciences—Permanence of Paper for Printed Library
Materials, ANSI Z39.48-1984.

Manufactured in the United States of America

Library of Congress Cataloging-in-Publication Data

Gould, Todd, date
    Pioneers of the hardwood : Indiana and the birth of professional
basketball / Todd Gould.
        p.   cm.
    Includes bibliographical references (p.   ) and index.
    ISBN 0-253-33373-3 (cloth : alk. paper). — ISBN 0-253-21199-9
(pbk. : alk. paper)
    1. Basketball—Indiana—History.   I. Title.
GV885.72.I6G68   1998
796.323′09772—dc21   97-38268

1 2 3 4 5   03 02 01 00 99 98

To the memory of my grandfather

Homer C. "Hurley" Gould

1906–1996

Throughout the years the Old Coach imparted two
sound pieces of advice to me:

— *Always keep your eyes on the ball.*

— *Until the final whistle sounds, never stop playing as
hard as you can.*

I have always found these words to be profound guidance
Whether it's basketball, or any other endeavor in my life.
Thanks, Hurl!

And to

Melissa

My Forever Partner

Your unending faith in my abilities inspired and
encouraged me more than you will ever know.

Contents

Preface

In February 1993, *Pioneers of the Hardwood* premiered as a statewide television documentary produced by station WFYI-TV in Indianapolis for the Indiana Public Broadcasting System. The one-hour program on the history of professional basketball in Indiana earned critical acclaim, garnered an Emmy Award nomination, and was the highest-rated locally produced show in Indianapolis public television history.

Many sports fans believe that the Indiana Pacers were the first professional team in the Hoosier state. As a sports enthusiast and history buff, I knew that several other teams once existed. But even I was surprised to discover the rich heritage the pro game has in Indiana—a legacy that dates back to 1913. As the producer of the program, I spent three years sifting through thousands of microfilm news stories, hours of old film footage, and many telephone and live interviews with former players, coaches, and fans who shaped the early years of professional basketball.

As a television producer, I always love a good story. This project naturally appealed to me. As I researched, wrote, directed, and produced the show, I found a tremendous respect and admiration for these men and their accomplishments. Typically after a producer finishes an assignment, he moves on to the next project. But I found that I just could not let go of this enthralling and colorful piece of Indiana history. "Somebody should write a book about this," I thought.

Months later I once again found myself trudging through piles of documentation and losing myself in the excitement of old basketball games. Naturally I could not have found much of the research I needed without the assistance of several helpful "investigators." Special thanks goes out to Judy McGeath, the interlibrary loan coordinator at the central branch of the Indianapolis–Marion County Public Library. Cheerfully and diligently, Judy tracked down dozens of rare old newspaper microfilms from around the country. Many of the book's most enlightening and humorous news quips are the result of Judy's efforts. As well, John Selch and Darrol Pierson at the Indiana State Library newspaper archives deserve a big round of applause for traipsing through the musty corridors that house many of the state's oldest and rarest newspapers.

On the national level, Wayne Patterson at the Naismith Basketball Hall of Fame in Springfield, Massachusetts, furnished research and photographs to help bring this story to life. Kudos also to Bill Himmelman, president and historian of Sports Nostalgia Research in Norwood, New Jersey. On several occasions, Bill provided me with extremely rare facts and figures on Indiana's roundball pioneers.

Back in the Hoosier state, Dale Ogden at the Indiana State Museum supplied many of the photographs you see throughout the book, as well as detailed information on the state's earliest pro teams. The Indiana State Museum has a wonderful permanent exhibition in its sports wing with fascinating insights on many of the clubs featured in this book. When spending time in downtown Indianapolis, the Indiana State Museum is a worthwhile visit.

I would also like to thank each and every one of the players, coaches, broadcasters, and family members who gave so generously of their time to talk with me about a special time in their lives. Their accomplishments were not only colorful but often historic. It was an honor and a pleasure to speak with every one of them. I would like to extend additional thanks to Carl Bennett, former manager of the Fort Wayne Pistons. Carl acted as a historical consultant of sorts by enduring a seemingly endless string of phone calls from me to verify significant moments in the game's history.

When I began this project, I had written many television scripts, but I knew nothing about writing a book. In fact, I had no personal computer or typewriter at the beginning of this project. I wrote the first two chapters completely in longhand. Finally a dear friend of mine, Tim Rohrman, felt sorry for me and lent me a laptop computer. I am not sure this project would have come to fruition had it not been for Tim's generous loan.

As far as writing itself went, I turned to Pam Renner, an enthusiastic and gifted writing consultant in Dallas, Texas. Pam is one of those people who can criticize your work and make you thankful and happy about every single criticism. When personal doubts lingered as to my ability to produce this book, Pam was always there to push me, cheer me on, and make me a better writer.

My family certainly played a big supporting role in the creative process. Writing a book on top of a regular job meant many, many late hours in front of the computer. My wife, Melissa, not only had the tolerance to endure these long sessions but never lost faith in my abilities. This book is dedicated to her for giving me her heart and her patience. As well, she gave me another source of inspiration during the final months of the editing process. That inspiration was our newborn son, Nathaniel Robert. When he grows up, he will see my name on the book cover. But I hope he will understand that this project was a team effort between Dad and Mom.

Special thanks also to the rest of my family, my parents and my in-laws. Their encouragement and support were a beacon of hope during the long and lonely writing process.

Finally a word of appreciation for my other family—the folks at public television station WFYI in Indianapolis. General Manager Lloyd Wright, Station Manager Alan Cloe, Executive Producer Michael Atwood, and a whole group of highly dedicated professionals nurtured my idea for the original *Pioneers of the Hardwood* documentary and gave me an important statewide forum for its broadcast. Neither the documentary nor this book would have been possible without their vision and support. A portion of the proceeds from this book will go to the WFYI production fund to support local programming endeavors and help preserve the enlightening, educational value of public television in the Hoosier state.

A total of six years went into this book project. It has been truly one of the most rewarding accomplishments of my life. After completely immersing myself in pro basketball lore for more than half a decade, I *still* find this story fascinating. I hope you do, too.

Basketball really had its beginning in Indiana, which remains today in the center of the sport.

—Dr. James Naismith, inventor of basketball, from a 1936 speech in Indianapolis

Introduction

COLUMBUS, INDIANA, 1916— The temperature was well below freezing on this winter night, but citizens inside City Hall were plenty hot. Inside, public officials and local citizens stood and shouted. But instead of sitting through a political debate or town hall meeting, they wildly cheered as two basketball teams squared off in a game played in the wide hall on the second floor.

A local group, the Columbus Commercials, pitted their skills against the Indianapolis Em-Roes, one of the most successful touring teams in the Midwest. The excitement grew as the Em-Roes entered the playing area from their first-floor dressing room in the mayor's office.

Admission to the exhibition was one nickel per person. Curious spectators watched from a narrow balcony that encircled the playing floor. Others crowded around the floor, just inches from the action. Amid a swelling wall of screaming fans, the players took the floor. An official tossed what appeared to be an oversized brown medicine ball with laces into the air. The battle began.

The score remained low, but the action was intense. The partisan spectators obviously felt their team was not getting enough favorable calls from the referee. They shared their displeasure by chucking hat pins, bottles, and lighted cigarettes at the vigilant official. Unruly crowds often prompted referees to carry a revolver in their back pocket to help them escape an onslaught of disgruntled locals after a ball game.

During the contest most spectators closely watched Em-Roes shooting ace Al Feeney. He led the team in scoring at six points per game. His performance in Columbus was a sight to behold. His two-handed set shots seemed to form a perfect arc on their way to the basket.

Opposing players tried to stop

Feeney from scoring by pushing him to the floor. Feeney retaliated by pushing back, and a fight ensued. The Columbus fans were incensed. At halftime, a group of local hooligans waited angrily in the hall for Feeney to return to the dressing room.

Weary from his scrap in the first half, Feeney, as well as the rest of the Em-Roes, descended the flight of stairs to the Mayor's office and were met by an angry mob. It was a race to the dressing room as the players narrowly escaped the pack of rabid fans. Feeney slipped away as a spectator tore the jersey from his back. Police cleared the scene and, after an hour or so, notified the Em-Roes that it was safe to come out and finish the game. Feeney, bloody and shirtless, entered the playing floor for the second half and led his team

to a dramatic victory. At the end of the game, law enforcement officers escorted the Em-Roes out of town. For their winning efforts, Feeney and his teammates each received five dollars.

The Indianapolis squad hustled home to get some rest before they went to work at their regular jobs at local factories and schools the next day. The Em-Roes would be on the road again in two days when they travelled sixty miles to Rushville for another game. The schedule was demanding, and the crowds were tough in this whirlwind, semiprofessional basketball circuit. But there was something about the game that kept players like Al Feeney on the court and on the road. Perhaps it was pride, or the thrill of competition, but without a doubt, each player possessed a burning passion for the game.

This account is based largely on a 1964 retrospective from the *Indianapolis News*. The article captured the intensity of one of Indiana's most exciting and colorful professional basketball rivalries, between the Indianapolis Em-Roes and the Columbus Commercials. The encounter typified the rough-and-tumble world of the nation's first professional basketball teams. These men were dedicated. These men were ornery. And these men loved the game.

There was little glamour or pageantry in their story. Life on the road was long and arduous. Yet, under these primitive conditions, the forefathers of professional basketball in Indiana forged a remarkable legacy as unlikely and magical as a last-second shot that spelled a championship.

The history of basketball is very special. It is the only competitive sport with its origins native to the United States. It was a purely invented sport that dawned literally overnight. The game was born out of necessity. Many of its first rules still remain in use today.

Neither money nor fame motivated basketball's first professionals. Instead it was their unquenchable desire to play that brought the game to a new level. When many of the game's first proponents turned a disapproving eye toward the sport, athletes used their own ingenuity and resources to keep their beloved pastime alive. The origins of professional basketball were not romantic or mythical but practical.

Yet many times throughout its history, the sport displayed a compelling and dynamic character that paralleled storybook legend. In no area of the country was this more evident than in the Midwest and particularly in the basketball hotbed of Indiana.

Many sports fans in the Hoosier state believe that the history of professional basketball in Indiana began in 1967 with the debut of the Indiana Pacers in the old American Basketball Association. On the contrary, more than six decades before the Pacers ever dribbled one of those odd red-white-and-blue balls up the floor, a primitive professional basketball heritage had taken root in the Midwest.

While "play-for-pay" ball enjoyed a rich legacy on the East Coast, many of the most significant contributions to professional basketball developed in small rural cities sprinkled throughout the Midwest—places like Sheboygan, Akron, Fort Wayne, Davenport. Indiana sports fans thrilled to the sights of professional basketball as early as a decade after James Naismith invented the game. Hoosier towns such as Fort Wayne, Whiting, Evansville, and Anderson were all sites for "big league" basketball during the game's early years.

Indiana is best known for its strong legacy in high school and college basketball. The story of the early days of the professional game in the Hoosier state is less known. But perhaps no other state has had a greater influence on the genesis of professional basketball than Indiana. A Hoosier team participated in the first national professional league, and the first radio and television broadcasts of professional games featured squads from Indiana. The development of the 24-second shot clock, formalized "big-league" contracts, and air travel to visiting cities, all commonplace in today's professional basketball world, were shaped, to a large extent, by coaches, players, and fans in Indiana and throughout the Midwest. The Hoosier state was also the scene of one of the biggest scandals in United States sports history. Its influence still can be seen in both college and professional basketball today.

This is the chronicle of a game and the men who played it. It is not a saga of money and fame but rather a story of character and heart. At times it becomes living drama, scandalous and suspenseful. At other times it reflects the epic events of our nation's history. But mostly it represents a colorful side to our human nature. For better or worse these American athletes overcame remarkable challenges to create one of the most exciting and best-loved athletic institutions in the country.

Pioneers of the Hardwood

> A team would come into town and give an exhibition in the local gymnasium or armory or barn. There was just something mythical or romantic about it—players living out of suitcases, driving from town to town for meals and half the ticket money that they could get from spectators. That was the life of basketball's barnstormers.
>
> —Ron Newlin, former director, Indiana Basketball Hall of Fame

1. Dividing Up the Nickels

In the autumn of 1892, a young Presbyterian minister from Crawfordsville, Indiana, enrolled in the Young Men's Christian Association Training School in Springfield, Massachusetts. His name was Nicholas C. McKay, and he was a native of England. McKay served as general secretary of the Crawfordsville YMCA. He was interested in studying and implementing a new physical education program in his midwestern organization.

McKay's instructor was James Naismith, an energetic 31-year-old who sported a thick, bushy mustache. For nearly a year, Naismith trumpeted the virtues of a new recreational pastime he had created the previous winter. This new game required that McKay and his classmates divide into two equal teams, as Naismith threw a soccer ball into the area of play. Each team's objective was to successfully pitch the ball into a makeshift peach-basket goal hung from the railing above the gymnasium floor.

The activity proved to be popular among members of the group. Naismith received many requests to reprint the original rules of his game so that similar contests could be staged in YMCAs throughout the country. Nicholas McKay was, no doubt, impressed by this new competition—a game Naismith simply called "basket-ball."

Within a year McKay returned to Indiana and introduced basketball to the citizens of Crawfordsville. Here the phenomenon known later as "Hoosier Hysteria" took root. Curious townsfolk scurried to the Crawfordsville gymnasium on Main Street to steal a peek at this new and unusual recreational sport.

Making some minor adjustments to Naismith's original concepts, McKay improved on the peach-basket goals. He summoned a local blacksmith to forge two iron hoops, which he then secured to the balconies above the gym floor. Coffee sacks were draped below the iron rims to catch each successful goal.

James B. Griffith, a student at nearby Wabash College and an active member of the Crawfordsville YMCA, was often a participant in McKay's initial basketball practice games. In a 1944 article in the *Crawfordsville Journal-Review,* Griffith recalled: "In the first game, which McKay staged between a bunch of fellows who were interested in gym work at the old 'Y,' the thing I remember most vividly is having a pair of bruised knuckles the next morning, caused by knocking the ball out of the coffee sacks each time someone tossed a goal. Being just about the tallest and slimmest kid on the floor, it became my job, right off, to jump up each time a goal was made and knock the ball out of the sack, ready to be tossed up again as play was resumed."

Throughout the country, basketball's popularity grew steadily, but in Indiana, interest in the game exploded. Fans seemed to have an eerie obsession with the game—an enthusiasm that surpassed spectator support for clubs in the rest of the country.

To understand why this was so is to understand the nature of Indiana's agricultural society at the turn of the century. Ron Newlin, former director of the Indiana Basketball Hall of Fame, explained: "Actually, with all the different sports that were taking shape at that time, it makes sense that basketball was taking root in Indiana. Football took root in Ohio, because Ohio is a state . . . with small cities, which had the masses to put together 20-man teams. Indiana was filled with small towns, where each little school may not be able to get 11 boys together to play football. But anyone could put five boys together to play basketball. And since Indiana was an agricultural state, planting in the spring and harvesting in the fall, winter was the time people had for games and spectator sports."

Within six months after McKay's return to Crawfordsville, YMCA groups throughout the state were featuring the game of basketball as an integral part of their physical education programs. By March 1894 the stage was set for an official competition of this new winter pastime between two teams from neighboring towns.

Breaks School is a three-story brick building five miles north of Crawfordsville. Its bell tower stands majestically over a landscape of corn and soybeans. More than a century has passed since the sounds of clanging school bells and the steady clopping of horse-drawn buses filled the air. The wind whistles through its skeletal remains—faint whispers of a bygone era. But in March 1894 Breaks School was alive with excitement. It was the 16th, a very special day. Several boys from the physical education class gathered at the downtown YMCA to meet some young men from the Lafayette YMCA in a new athletic competition.

Newlin set the scene at the Crawfordsville YMCA: "The playing floor took up the entire room. There was a running track above the floor where you would have watched the game. There was a potbelly stove in one corner, so you probably would want to avoid chasing a ball into that corner. Just as so frequently the spectators would be in the balconies behind the basket watching the game, the hometown fans would help out a little bit by reaching through the railing and swatting away the other team's shots or guiding the home team's shots into the basket. In later years backboards were not created so much to give players something to bank the ball off of as it was to prevent spectators from goaltending."

Dale Ogden, sports historian and curator of history at the Indiana State Museum, added: "The out-of-bounds lines would have been the walls or the doorway. You went out-of-bounds when you went out the door into the next room. The baskets were hung from balconies. If your shot went over the basket, the ball went into the crowd in the balcony. [The ball] simply went wherever it was shot—out the window, into the crowd or vestibule, wherever!"

What this first game lacked in style, it made up for in excitement. The final score was Crawfordsville 45, Lafayette 21—a remarkable point total in an era when a team's total score averaged below two digits.

The *Crawfordsville Journal-Review* reported on the contest: "Basketball is a new game. But if the interest taken in the contest tonight between the YMCA teams of Crawfordsville and Lafayette is any criterion, it is bound to be popular. There was a large crowd present, and at every good play, the yells and applause were deafening. The two [teams] were an athletic-looking body of young men, and the play was fast and furious." The article continued, as the reporter from the *Journal-Review* penned arrogant praise for the hometown boys: "Every one of the Crawfordsville boys played his position to perfection. If a return game is played in Lafayette, as is expected, they should easily duplicate the score."

In more sportsmanlike fashion, the *Lafayette Journal* also reported on the contest: "Our boys put up a good game and are not discouraged. A reception was given our team after the game, and the Crawfordsville boys proved themselves to be perfect gentlemen and splendid entertainers."

In its first few years, Naismith's game underwent many changes. In 1894 the Overman Wheel Company manufactured the first official basketball, made of a rubber-inflated center and a laced, leather exterior. By 1895 officials awarded opposing players free throws when a foul was committed. And by 1898 players legally advanced the ball by dribbling.

Most of these early changes had a positive impact on the game. The greatest stimulus to the growth of professional basketball, however, had nothing to do with streamlining Naismith's rule book. Rather it was the game's alarming rise in popularity and its intense competitive nature that pushed basketball to a new level.

Luther Gulick, Naismith's mentor, grew concerned about the rising number of unsportsmanlike incidents in YMCA gymnasiums. "The game must be kept clean," he wrote in an 1897 article in *Association Men*. "It is a perfect outrage for an institution that stands for Christian work in the community to tolerate not merely discourteous and ungentlemanly treatment of guests, but slugging and that which violates the elementary principles of morals. It hurts the religious life of the Association; it hurts the influence of the Association on the community; it hurts the personal influence of the general secretary and physical director of the Association; it injures the character of the men who play. If the fact were generally known, it would influence the financial support of the Association."

Dr. Gulick was concerned that his young Christian athletes were behaving in "un-Christianlike" ways. His writings shook associations across the country. Many YMCA directors, already unsure of what to make of this strange new phenomenon, immediately banned the game from their physical education programs.

Yet the game's popularity continued to grow. Basketball soon outgrew the YMCA's ability to control it. Only five years after Naismith's brainstorm, the game of basketball advanced to a whole new level. By 1896 the game's first professionals had taken to the floor.

The Trenton, New Jersey, YMCA team was very popular with the local citizens. But when Dr. Gulick warned that unsportsmanlike conduct among basketball's participants might have a demoralizing effect on YMCA groups around the country, the Trenton YMCA panicked. Its officers immediately banned the game from their athletic program. But the local team was determined to continue playing the game they loved. They rented the Trenton Masonic Hall for an exhibition and asked spectators to donate their spare change to help cover rental costs.

Flamboyantly dressed in velvet trunks, long tights, and fringed stockings, the Trenton club put on a spectacular display of athletic ability in a thrilling and victorious exhibition on November 7, 1896. At the conclusion of the game, the players were surprised to discover that after they paid their rental costs, there was actually money left over. They divided the surplus equally among the team members. Each player earned $15 for the evening's performance, with one extra dollar given to the organizer and team captain, Fred Cooper.

The record books show this contest to be the first play-for-pay game in basketball history. Professional basketball did not develop from fabled sportsmen, avid spectators, or shrewd businessmen. Several stubborn young men who enjoyed the game simply refused to stop playing when the local YMCA vetoed use of their home court. Trenton's success with a semiprofessional game sparked a new revolution in basketball.

The term *semiprofessional* is often used for these early pioneers. During the formative years of play-for-pay ball, every player had a regular 40-hour-per-week job. These folks played ball essentially for fun. Any money made on the contest was just an added bonus. The game never was established as a full-time profession until after the Second World War.

Most of the early semiprofessional teams toured from town to town. They loosely organized contests with the local townsfolk. One of the earliest and most successful teams of this era was New York's Original Celtics. For nearly 30 seasons, the Celtics posted phenomenal records, including a 193–11 mark in 1923. As an encore, they topped themselves the following year with a 204–11 record.

Through the years, the Original Celtics enjoyed the skills of many fine players. The team leader was Nat Holman, "Mr. Basketball," a tough-minded son of Jewish immigrants, who later coached City College of New York to NIT and NCAA titles in the same season.

Henry "Dutch" Dehnert was the large man in the middle. He was quick and strong with a body that resembled a refrigerator. He was credited with the development of a new move known as the pivot play, which he mastered. To execute the play, he posted his big body near the goal, facing away from the basket. When he got the ball, he either tossed it quickly to an open teammate or faked a pass and turned to the goal for an easy basket. This move, while commonplace today, was revolutionary during the early days of professional basketball.

Then there was Joe Lapchick, the tall, awkward kid who developed his lanky physique into a finely tuned scoring machine. His influence on professional basketball would be felt for many years, first as an all-star with the Celtics, then as the highly successful coach at St. Johns University, and eventually as coach of the New York Knicks on the professional level.

The Original Celtics were more than terrific basketball players. They were also shrewd businessmen. Holman, Dehnert, and the rest were so skilled in their ability to control the score of a game that they could play a contest to an intentional tie by the end of regulation time. Before agreeing to play the overtime session, they would call a meeting with local promoters at center court amid the screaming fans. There they would negotiate for more money just to finish the game. If an agreement could not be reached, the contest simply ended in a tie, much to the disappointment of the hometown fans.

By playing all their games on the road, touring clubs like the Celtics expected to encounter fervently biased hometown fans. Often the local referees reflected this hometown partisanship. Touring clubs generally referred to these officials as "homers." When the Celtics sensed they were receiving an unfair number of foul calls from a homer, they reverted to their secret play, known as the "referee press." Lapchick described this infamous play, in which two Celtic teammates simultaneously collided with the official and created a violent "Celtic sandwich." This gave the official a less than subtle reminder to keep his calls fair and honest or another "accident" might occur.[1]

Back in Indiana, basketball blossomed into a popular pastime in many small farming communities in the state. In Darlington, a little town near Crawfordsville, schoolchildren formed their own crude version of the game. On a wide, outdoor court, kids tossed a makeshift ball at trees, used as goals. When the ball hit the tree below the first limb, an exuberant youngster scored one point for his team.[2]

On the high school level, the game flourished and reshaped the way midwestern youths spent their winter hours. In the tiny Hoosier town of Buck Creek, the boys' team had no gymnasium, just an empty business room with a low ceiling. But the small-town squad had a distinct advantage over their foes. They painted a faint line strategically across the ceiling above the basket. When a Buck Creek player fired a shot directly on that line, the ball caromed off at a perfect angle into the basket. Opposing players from bigger, more powerful schools often found it difficult to defend the dreaded "Buck Creek Bank Shot."

In Carmel, just north of Indianapolis, the local basketball squad played its home games at a neighborhood lumber yard. One January night the temperature dropped to a bitter three degrees below zero. Undaunted, the Carmel boys proceeded with their scheduled game in the outdoor arena. That is how the lumber-yard gym earned the title "the Igloo."

In 1911, Crawfordsville High School captured the first state basketball title by defeating nearby Lebanon, 24–17. Crawfordsville's success also extended into the college ranks. The town's tiny Wabash College laid claim to the "national or world championship" of college ball in 1905 by defeating teams from Purdue, Minnesota, Wisconsin, and Illinois.

Amateur basketball had built high excitement for the game in the Midwest. The time and place were right for a new professional basketball revolution in the state. On the south side of Indianapolis, two entrepreneurs went into business together. Lee Emmelman and Walter Roeder established Em-Roes Sporting Goods in 1913. Originally designed as a supply store for hunters and fishermen, Em-Roes evolved into an overall "sportsman's paradise." Two long counters banked the narrow, wooden isles of the downtown store. Behind them towered shelves that reached from floor to ceiling with row upon row of equipment for every sporting need—bicycles, bats, balls, fishing gear, hunting rifles. One of the most popular and unusual-looking balls Em-Roes stocked had a rubber-inflated center and a laced, leather exterior. The basketball was definitely a hot item at the store.

Business was brisk, aided by a new and unusual promotional gimmick. Lee Emmelman was fascinated by the incredible popularity of the state's new amateur sport, basketball. He easily convinced his partner that a touring basketball club, sponsored by the store, would bring widespread publicity to Em-Roes.

The key to the success of this venture was to find players talented enough to attract large crowds. Emmelman scouted the city's top industrial and church leagues. There he discovered two amateur league champions, the Indianapolis Central Christian Church and an industrial team power, the Detch Specials. By autumn 1913 the two melded under Emmelman's direction into one of the Hoosier state's first and most successful play-for-pay teams, the Indianapolis Em-Roes.

High-scoring Harry Schoeneman, starting forward for the team, was the pride of the business boys' class basketball team at the Indianapolis YMCA. The *Indianapolis Times* once opined that "as a basket shooter [Schoeneman] probably is not excelled by anyone in local basketball circles." At a time when tall players were rare, the 6'2" Em-Roes forward towered over opponents. Schoeneman tallied baskets by night and legislative votes by day as an employee of the state government.

Opposite Schoeneman at the other forward position was the team's business manager, Benny Evans. A savvy player with scrawny limbs, Evans was a star for the Central Christian team in the Indianapolis Sunday School League.

Glen Kline, former guard for the Detch Specials, was still attending high school when he joined Emmelman's club. Kline later graduated from law school and worked for the state unemployment compensation department during the Great Depression.

Another former standout with the Detch Specials was Lynn Smith, center and team captain. Smith worked at the Indianapolis Motor Speedway when he wasn't racing down the court for the Em-Roes. The *Indianapolis Times* remarked that Smith "is an ideal center. He pays close attention to the ball, putting it where it will do the most good on the jumpoff and is a basket shooter of some ability."

At one guard position was Oscar "Dutch" Behrent, a lithe, red-headed truck driver who possessed strong ball-handling skills. Behrent traded off at guard with Everett Babb, a two-sport sensation who also starred with the Eastern and Marion Club football team. In 1916 Babb earned a reputation as "one of the best floor guards in the country."[3]

At the heart of the team was floor general Al Feeney. Most spectators knew Feeney as the anchor of Notre Dame's legendary Feeney-to-Dorias-to-Rockne passing combination that defeated Army in a classic football contest in 1913. In that game Feeney hiked the ball to Dorias, who successfully threw one of the first touchdown passes in football history into Rockne's outstretched arms. Feeney was an all-around athlete with remarkable talents on the basketball court as well as the football field. He was one of the team's leading scorers and was, in the words of the *Indianapolis Times*, "a bear on defense. He is a swift, accurate passer and clever in juggling the ball. He plays an exceptionally hard defensive game and for this reason is much feared by opposing players. He is probably one of the best-known basketball players in the country."

In silk shorts supported by a leather belt, knee-high socks, padded knee wraps, and green, woolen jerseys with the store's name emblazoned on the front, the Indianapolis Em-Roes took the floor in paid exhibitions throughout the state and region. Before 1916 only a few select cities in the Midwest had the opportunity to witness the advanced skills of the semiprofessional game. Now the Midwest produced its own play-for-pay teams, and fans responded with a religious fervor. In Fort Wayne, games were played in the old South Side High School gymnasium, called "the Pit" because the balconies were so low that fans could reach through the railing with umbrellas and canes and swat opposing players on the head.

As part of the 1914 New Year's Day athletic card sponsored by the Indianapolis YMCA, the nucleus of the Em-Roes squared off against a team known as the Easterns in a best-of-three tournament to determine "the basketball championship of Indiana." The *Indianapolis Times* reported that the final contest featured "erratic shooting at times, but still was so full of scoring and action as to cause the large crowd of enthusiasts repeatedly to cheer." At this time, team scores that reached a total of 20 points were rare. But in this tournament finale, the Em-Roes stunned the crowd by tallying 39 points and nearly doubling their opponents' total. The *Times* reported: "Throughout the first half the teams were neck and neck. . . . In the final half, [the Em-Roes] displayed the better teamwork, and, by combining that with aggressiveness and accurate basket shooting, ran up fourteen more points, while holding their opponents to but seven." After the tournament, sportswriters around the region referred to the Em-Roes as a team that displayed "one of the state's finest brands of fast basketball."

From 1914 through 1916 the Em-Roes compiled an impressive streak of 122 consecutive victories. As they toured from town to town, many small-town clubs were gunning for the hotshots from the big city. In a 1964 interview with the *Indianapolis News*, Em-Roes player Glen Kline recalled: "In those days our team rode the interurban to and from the games at Columbus. We usually were met at the station on our arrival there by a group of not-too-well-wishing fans who informed us that this was *it* and that we might as well prepare for a licking. And they were never far from wrong, because every game was close and hard-fought. We only escaped on occasion by a few points difference." Kline, a cocky 16-year-old when he first played for the Em-Roes, noted that the games at Columbus "knocked the rough edges off my ego."

But as a grinding stone sharpens an ax, so the abusive crowds honed the Em-Roes to razor-sharp perfection. The Em-Roes rapidly became one of the Midwest's dominant touring teams. In 12 years they won nearly 90 percent of their contests, including 400 wins in their first 425 starts. Spectators gathered in growing numbers to enjoy the traveling club's exciting exhibitions.

The Em-Roes and other semiprofessional teams during this era were known as barnstorming clubs. The term *barnstorming* originated with the great air shows of the late 1910s and the 1920s. The lifestyle of a barnstorming pilot was romantic and exciting. He lived out of his suitcase and traveled from town to town like some enchanted nomad. The life of a barnstorming basketball player was similar. Dale Ogden, sports historian and curator of history at the Indiana State Museum, explained: "As barnstormers, the Indianapolis Em-Roes essentially would play anybody, anywhere, at any time. They played about 450 games between 1916 and 1924, against all comers. They would charge a nickel apiece to get into one of their games, and then at the end of the game, all the players would divide up the nickels."

Emmelman and Roeder were two of the country's first basketball business leaders to recognize the powerful potential in college recruiting. To find a gifted pool of collegiate talent, the two men looked no further than nearby Crawfordsville, the birthplace of midwestern basketball. Wabash College developed a reputation as one of the finest basketball programs in the game's first 25 years, led by two of the country's top talents—Ward "Piggy" Lambert and Homer Stonebraker.

Lambert stood mature and strong, a sturdy 5′6″ tall. His muscles were solid and chiseled, like a piece of wrought iron. In a 1964 retrospect in the *Indianapolis News*, Lambert's teammate, Em-Roes floor guard Glen Kline, noted that "Lambert's great coaching career has been allowed to overshadow his equally great playing ability." Kline declared that Lambert was the greatest player he ever saw.

Homer Stonebraker, standing at just over 6′4″, was as much an oddity as an athlete. In his day it was rare to find basketball players more than six feet tall, so Stonebraker was a virtual giant on the court. He was one of the original inductees into the Indiana Basketball Hall of Fame, and his play was legendary in the state. Other big men during his era were awkward and unskilled; coaches recruited them simply to tap the ball to a teammate and stand aside. Stonebraker was one of the game's first big men to bring true athletic talent to the game.

His skills were in high demand. Throughout the late 1910s and the early 1920s, when touring semipro clubs popped up all over the Midwest, it was not uncommon for the most talented players in the region to play on two different teams during the same season. Stonebraker was such a phenomenal player that at the height of his professional career, he signed semiprofessional contracts with three different squads per season, each team located in a different Indiana city.

Stonebraker's career began in Wingate, a tiny village just west of Crawfordsville. Today a hand-painted sign on the outskirts of town proclaims the village's pride and joy: "Welcome to Wingate, State Basketball Champs, 1913–1914." The Wingate Spartans put the town on the map. And Homer Stonebraker *was* the Wingate Spartans.

In 1913 Wingate did not have its own gymnasium. The team, dubbed the "gymless wonders," played their home games in New Richmond, six miles away. The squad practiced on a rugged, outdoor court. Players tossed the ball through a metal hoop fashioned by the local blacksmith. Their uniforms consisted only of tank tops and baseball pants.

Stonebraker possessed a remarkable intelligence and natural instinct for the game. Singlehandedly he brought his team to a new level of play. As Leland Olin, Stonebraker's teammate at Wingate, recalled, "We had a secret code for all center jumps. The way Homer would brush his hair, walk into the circle, or move his eyes determined where the tip was likely to go. Most teams never caught on to this deceptively simple system."[4]

Wingate made headlines throughout the state with what seemed to be astronomical scores. They thrashed Waveland 75–7 and pounded Cayuga 85–9. Their biggest win came at the hands of hapless Hillsboro, which suffered a 108–8 drubbing at the hands of Stonebraker and crew. In the Hillsboro contest, Stonebraker alone scored 81 points.

In *The Cavalcade of Basketball*, author and statistician Alexander Weyand listed several of the country's most outstanding players in 1916, including an "unusually gifted" junior center from the Midwest by the name of Stonebraker. During the 1916 season at Wabash College, Stonebraker earned third-team All-American honors. The next season he moved to second-team All-American. To Emmelman and Roeder, and to any basketball fan during the 1910s, Homer Stonebraker represented the future of the game.

Emmelman and Roeder took big risks by investing in an unproved athletic business venture. But Em-Roes Sporting Goods Store became an established institution in the city and region, and the gamble of owning a semiprofessional basketball team paid off, not only for the two Indianapolis entrepreneurs but also for the play-for-pay game in the Midwest.

We looked forward to coming to Indiana to play, because we always knew that we'd have a good ball game in Indiana. Indiana was much like New York City in that it was a hotbed for basketball. Many of the nation's premier players were coming out of Indiana. It was one of the top basketball states in the country at that time.

—William "Pop" Gates, Hall-of-Fame member of the all-black barnstorming squad, the New York Renaissance

2. The Golden Age

The Original Celtics brought their barnstorming tour to the Great Lakes region in the winter of 1922. In impressive fashion, the Celtics dominated most of the exhibitions. By the end of February, the Celtics totaled 97 wins versus only five losses. Playing an array of local church league and industrial "all-stars," they easily defeated teams of comparatively inferior talent. They steamrolled their way through the Midwest at a seemingly unstoppable pace. Then they reached Fort Wayne, Indiana.

As early as 1914, fans in Fort Wayne had turned out in large numbers and paid 15 to 25 cents to watch city league championships at the old Concordia College gym. Known as the Summit City, Fort Wayne became a basketball stronghold in the Midwest. Several national touring clubs had made it a practice to stop in Fort Wayne on their way through the state for an exciting evening of hoops that guaranteed large profits.

In 1919 a new semiprofessional basketball team formed under the guidance of team manager and cigar store owner Clarence "Dink" Alter. For three years Alter managed the St. Mary's Saints basketball squad in the Fort Wayne independent, amateur circuit. The idea of organizing a semiprofessional club first came to Alter when he was stationed at Camp Jenicart, near Bordeaux, France, during the First World War. While he was "over there," Sergeant Major Alter met a fellow Hoosier, Sergeant Homer Stonebraker.

Alter knew of Stonebraker's hardwood accomplishments before the war, while he was still the manager at St. Mary's. Sight unseen, he attempted to secure Stonebraker's services for the Saints in 1916. Both entered the war before Stonebraker replied to Alter's offer.

In the Army "Dink" Alter was in charge of personnel in Europe, where he processed men for debarkation. One day as he looked down his list, his eyes fell upon the name Homer Stonebraker. When the lanky, young giant approached his desk, Alter identified him immediately. The two carried on a lengthy discussion that centered on Indiana and basketball. Stonebraker left Alter's office with the promise that if Alter started another team in Fort Wayne after the war, he would join.

In 1919 private citizen Alter reorganized the St. Mary's team in Fort Wayne. He never forgot the conversation he had with Stonebraker that day at military headquarters. Stonebraker now lived in nearby Hartford City, where he worked for an insurance company and coached the high school basketball team. When Alter came calling, his old Army buddy jumped at the chance to play semipro ball again. Stonebraker became Alter's first recruit.

Stonebraker helped Alter draft the finest talents in the region, including the most exciting backcourt duo in the Midwest,

"Moose" Cochrane and Francis "Bake" Bacon. The *Fort Wayne Journal Gazette* once described Cochrane as "a bear under the basket. His hard defensive play makes it difficult for the opposition to score. . . . Local fans will be glad to know the big fellow will be in [Fort Wayne] togs this season." Bacon, a superb athlete who starred in football as well as basketball, was St. Mary's floor leader, known for his speedy dribbling and all-around floor work. The *Journal Gazette* boasted of Bacon's ability to "boost his mates total of points with an occasional looper from far down the court."

Other starters included Ralph Miller, a transplant from the West, who honed his skills in an upstart Pacific Coast league, and Tillie Voss, a local football hero. Together these young players were enthusiastic, talented, and fun to watch.

The outstanding lineup Stonebraker assembled was more than Alter and little St. Mary's could handle financially. Alter knew that in order to bankroll the team, he needed outside support. He approached M. J. Grace, chairman of the local Knights of Columbus, who entered into the project with great enthusiasm. Grace dubbed the team the Fort Wayne KCs, or "Caseys," as the sportswriters penned.

The team focused its promotional efforts on the past successes of Stonebraker. The *Fort Wayne Journal Gazette* heralded "Stoney" as "one of the new cogs in the local K.C. scoring machine, too well known to local caging fans to need introduction." Building high expectations for the gentle giant, the article continued, "His long shots will be featured in nearly every game for the Caseys. The big fellow was in Fort Wayne recently and told friends here that he was ready for a big season." One national publication, *Holiday* magazine, called Stonebraker "a roundball Bunyan in Indiana's court history."

From the beginning the Caseys were extremely successful and wildly popular. Throughout the early 1920s, the team averaged only three losses a season during their long, grueling Midwestern tour. A newspaper columnist in the Midwest dubbed them "the premier basket-shooting aggregation from Fort Wayne, claimants to the mid-western loop title."

The Caseys' most spirited contests came against an intrastate rival, the Huntington Athletic Club. These annual battles were far from good-natured. For a time during the early 1920s, relations between the two Indiana communities were severed as the Fort Wayne–Huntington basketball rivalry festered into open hostilities. Huntington featured the talents of DePauw University scoring ace Murray Mendenhall and two other all-conference collegiate stars featured in the national Spaulding Guide.

As a showcase for the Midwest's top talent, the Casey-Huntington series guaranteed a sell-out crowd. Headlines from local papers, such as the *Journal Gazette*, blared out in bold type: "Capacity Crowd Expected to See Star Cagers Play in Important Series." Many fans from the visiting squads' community packed into their Model Ts and formed an impressive convoy to invade "enemy territory." Attendance records skyrocketed as regional rivalries intensified.

Hilliard Gates, Fort Wayne sports broadcaster, recalls one of Stonebraker's legendary performances in the annual series with Huntington: "They were down by a point, and the opposition took a shot and missed. Homer realized time was running out, and he didn't have time to dribble very much. He just had to let it go at the opposite basket. The ball went over two beams near the top of the roof of the gym! [The ball] sailed over the two beams and went through perfectly and they won!"

Throughout the eastern half of the United States, storefront posters and garish advertisements in newspapers read like circus hype:

BASKETBALL - TONIGHT!

Knights of Columbus, Fort Wayne

vs.

Palace Club, Washington D.C.

500 Reserved Seats on Sale

75 Cents—plus war tax

500 General Admission Seats on Sale

50 Cents—net

TWO TEAMS OF LEADING BASKETBALL STARS!

The Big Game Starts at 9 O'Clock

One basketball aficionado took particular interest in the success of the Caseys—Jim Furey, manager of New York's Original Celtics. The *Fort Wayne Journal Gazette* reported: "Manager Furey of the Celts was so impressed with the Caseys' play at Washington and Hagerstown that he started talking about plans for a series between the two clubs. . . . Local fans are hoping the negotiations to bring the Celts here are successful, as the famous entertainers are always a great drawing card."

For weeks Clarence Alter negotiated with the manager of the Shamrocks. Furey demanded $2,500, plus travel expenses, to come to Fort Wayne. Alter balked. No Caseys game ever cleared more than $800. The contract with the Celtics would be one of the biggest business gambles he had ever taken. But obviously for Alter the potential for a huge promotional blitz with two of professional basketball's best teams was far too appetizing to pass up. Furey finally agreed to forgo the travel expenses. Alter signed the contract for $2,500, and the two titan clubs were set to clash in March 1922 at the Concordia College gymnasium in Fort Wayne.

Word hit the newsstands in Fort Wayne on February 18: "Champion Celtics to Appear Here: Manager Alter Wires 'OK' to World's Title Claimants for Games on March 7 and 8." A wave of excitement swept the city and electrified the dull gray wash of Indiana winter. "The subject of their coming has been on the lips of every follower of the game hereabouts for some time past," the *Journal Gazette* reported. "Further announcements will be awaited with undue interest." The article continued to build the upcoming series to epic proportions: "The Celtics seem eager to test the skill of the renowned Caseys. . . . [Such a series] would be the greatest basketball attraction ever staged in the middle west, as it presents two of what are unquestionably the ranking quintets of the country matched against each other in a battle that would go a long way to deciding the caging supremacy of the world, now claimed by the Celtics."

Because the Casey organization put up $2,500 to bring the fabled champions to town, ticket prices at the Concordia College gymnasium soared to an alarming $1.50 for a general admission seat. But as local press continued to hype the series as "the basketball classic of classics," the price seemed to matter little to the fans. Thousands of enthusiastic spectators swarmed the ticket office. Written ticket requests from the entire region cluttered Alter's desk as well. Both games sold out in two days. "Never in the history of the caging sport has such a widespread interest been aroused, and it appears that everybody is going to be present," the *Journal Gazette* noted.

Not only was fan interest for the series high, but the two-game clash soon swelled to prominence in the national press as well. The *New York Evening Mail* waxed melodramatic: "Kipling's East is East and West is West and never the twain shall meet, already shattered and bent out of logical proportion by intersectional baseball and football clashes, will be refuted this week in professional basketball, when the Original Celtics of this city, claimants of the national championship, meet the Fort Wayne (Ind.) Knights of Columbus, middle-west title holders, in the biggest intersectional event of this sort ever undertaken."

By March 7 the excitement had reached fever pitch. On a blustery cold night, lines of spectators filed into the small Concordia College gym, where chilled bodies bathed in the hot anticipation of the evening's main attraction. A record crowd of 3,500 crammed into the tiny arena. Three hundred extra seats were brought in at the last minute to handle the overflow crowd. Spectators were soon within inches of the playing area. The air was thick with the smell of popcorn, hot dogs, and nickel cigars. The old wooden bleachers bowed under the collective weight of the capacity crowd. Several clever, young lads climbed the back walls and perched themselves on the rafters overhead to get a better view of the floor below.

Fans from across five states gathered at the crowded gym. Many stood along the back, shoulder to shoulder. Each strained his head to catch a glimpse of the main attraction. At one end of the floor, local band director Charles Schweleter and his volunteer orchestra added to the festivities with a variety of toe-tapping melodies.

Soon it was game time. The Celtics were first to enter the playing floor. The crowd cheered and jeered wildly. Questions abounded. Could their local underdogs compete with the mighty Celtics? As usual, the Celtics were the center of attention. They calmly conducted their pregame rituals amid a swelling wall of hysteria closing in around them.

The Caseys were next to step onto the floor. The cheers grew deafening. Homer Stonebraker led his team out of the locker room and into an adoring sea of mayhem. As the Caseys began to warm up, the Celtics paused to scout their opponents. While most of the players limbered up with the standard two-hand set shot, the Caseys' giant leader actually took his warmup shots underhanded. Apparently the Celtics sized up their tall rival a bit too hastily. They returned to their pregame routine with mistaken overconfidence.

Celtic Joe Lapchick recalled: "Our best guard was Chris Leonard, known as 'the Dog' or 'the Leech,' because he played his opponent so tight from one end of the court to the other. Stonebraker shot underhand from a distance of 50 feet, and he was always ready to let it fly. Leonard let him shoot from the latter distance unmolested. After all, who can shoot from 50 feet underhand and hit? But this guy was really good. He could make them from out there!"[1]

From the game's onset, it was all Stonebraker. The Fort Wayne captain set the tone for the contest when he successfully let one fly from nearly three-quarters court in the game's opening minutes. "Lucky throw," one Celtic player sneered. Within minutes, however, the New Yorkers learned that luck had little to do with Stonebraker's success. By halftime the big fellow had connected on three other long bombs that left the hapless Celtics shell-shocked.

The Caseys' defense was equally devastating. "Moose" Cochrane and "Bake" Bacon successfully shut down Celtic star guard Nat Holman. They allowed the dynamic playmaker only one point the entire evening. The Caseys also stopped legendary Celtics center Dutch Dehnert. The master of the pivot play did not score a single point.

In the final tally, Stonebraker shot five for six and scored all but one of his team's field goals. Adding another six points from the foul line, he totaled a game-leading 16 points. Fans in Fort Wayne that night witnessed one of the rarest sights in professional basketball that season, an event that occurred only 4 percent of the time throughout the entire year—the "World Champion" Celtics lost, 21 to 17.

The city erupted in ecstacy. Within the joyous celebration,

there was little doubt who was the most elated. "Do dreams come true?" asked the *Journal Gazette*. "Ask Captain Stonebraker, who was the happiest man in the city last night. 'Stoney,' who, as a basketball star and leader, has few equals, realized the greatest of all tests lay in the coming of the Celtics, and earnestly prayed for victory. The Fort Wayne captain appeared last night with smiling countenance and to his teammates and friends was supremely confident. He told them that he had dreamed of the game and that the K.Cs were going to win by a score of 21 to 18. When the struggle ended, 'Stoney's crew' were returned the victors and the score was 21 to 17. 'That dream came pretty close to coming true,' said the Fort Wayne player, who is likewise confident that his team can repeat tonight."

With the taste of victory still on their lips, the Caseys prepared for the second of their two-game series with the Celtics the following night. Both teams squared off at center court with the Celtics bent on revenge. Profiting from their experience the night before, the Celtics engulfed Stonebraker with unrelenting defensive pressure. The Fort Wayne giant did not score a single field goal the entire game. He tallied only nine points, all from the foul line.

In impressive fashion the Celtics proved why they were known as the world champs. The *Journal Gazette* summarized the contest: "Playing the most dazzling brand of basketball ever seen here, the Original Celtics of New York City turned the tables in decisive fashion on the K of C's last night in the second and final clash of the series at Concordia gym, winning by the score of 48 to 23. From the first whistle the Celtics went in to win. Their supreme air of confidence gone, having been shattered by the defeat handed them the previous night, they realized that reputation alone availed them nothing. It was up to them to deliver against the hardest-fighting . . . quintet the easterners had ever encountered, and they brought into action every phase of the brilliant scoring machine of which they were a part."

The two-game series ended in a tie, one game apiece. For basketball fans throughout the country the Caseys' split with the Celtics legitimately ranked them as one of the nation's top basketball powers. The reputation of Stonebraker and his team now preceded them in barnstorming contests through the eastern half of the United States. And at home, the Caseys captured the interest and enthusiasm of a state gone basketball crazy.

The success of the Caseys over the Celtics apparently caught the eye of many of the nation's first sports executives. One such person was Joe Carr, president of the National Football League. Carr watched the development of semiprofessional basketball with great interest. For years Carr had hoped to organize the nation's top professional basketball squads into a structured league. Early attempts to form pro leagues on the East Coast failed. But Carr planned to widen the base of his organization to include top touring clubs from the Midwest.

By 1925 Carr announced plans for the new American Basketball League, the first league with a truly national focus. Practically every franchise in the league represented a large metropolitan area. Laundry tycoon and pro football magnate George Preston Marshall owned the Washington Palace Five. Baseball star Henry Heilmann bankrolled the Brooklyn Arcadians. And George Halas, owner of football's Chicago Bears, ran the Chicago Bruins franchise. Other clubs in major markets included the Cleveland Rosenblooms, the Boston Whirlwinds and the Detroit Pulaski Post Five.

Caseys manager Alter traveled to Cleveland to meet with Carr to discuss Fort Wayne's possible entry in the league. Alter explained that a Fort Wayne civic association was willing to contribute $1,000 to purchase a franchise with the new league. But league officials questioned how a small city like Fort Wayne could stay competitive with the larger and more financially stable ABL markets. Carr cast the deciding vote. The ABL would indeed welcome one small-city team into its national cast. The Caseys were now among the country's elite. Big league basketball had come to Indiana and the nation.

The era known as the Roaring '20s baptized Americans into all that seemed good and fun in life. Heroes reigned as the country celebrated the daring accomplishments of Charles Lindbergh and the Hollywood antics of Charlie Chaplin. Women won the right to vote, which vaulted them through a series of social changes and continued to transform their roles in society.

Dale Ogden, curator of history at the Indiana State Museum,

set the mood of the era: "The 1920s was a very special decade in American history. . . . You had a lot of people looking for interesting new things, interesting experiences. People were looking for excitement, and one of the ways they could generate this excitement artificially was in athletic competition. So you had this big boom in athletics, particularly professional athletics."

The decade was called the Golden Age of Sports. The 1920s saw the rise of boxing legend Jack Dempsey and gridiron great Harold "Red" Grange. And in baseball, there was New York's Babe Ruth. In his first season with the Yankees, he amassed a record-setting 59 home runs. Babe Ruth captured the hearts and imaginations of sports fans across the nation. His thunderous hits symbolized a boom in professional athletics.

The New York district of Harlem was the scene of a unique and exciting cultural revolution known as the Harlem Renaissance. Black immigrants traveled from all parts of the globe to experience this time of great social change. One such immigrant was Robert Douglas, a native of St. Kitts, Jamaica. Douglas arrived in Manhattan at age 16 with no job and little money. Taking a doorman's job at 84th Street and Columbus Avenue, he worked twelve hours a day for four dollars a week.

After work one night in 1905, one of Douglas's fellow employees invited him to watch a basketball game in the dusty attic of a five-story building on 59th Street. In an article in the *Amsterdam News*, Douglas later reminisced: "We had to walk up five flights of stairs to the gym. I thought it was the greatest thing in the world. That's when I started with basketball. You couldn't keep me off the court after that!" Douglas began slipping away from his doorman's job to start a Caribbean athletic club that sponsored cricket and basketball teams. He also played with an all-black amateur basketball team, the Spartans, which competed in limited, inner-city contests.

By 1922 Douglas was playing and coaching for the Spartans in the amateur Metropolitan Basketball Association. Eventually Douglas formed an alliance with businessman William Roche, who had constructed a new meeting hall and ballroom in the heart of Harlem, the Renaissance Casino and Ballroom, which played host to the city's elite black performers in the worlds of dance, music, and the arts. Roche agreed to move out the tables and wheel portable goals onto the dance floor, so that Douglas could provide pre-show basketball exhibitions for the throngs of people waiting to dance the night away. Roche also agreed to sponsor Douglas's team if the club took the name "Renaissance" as a constant advertisement for the Casino. The team became known as the New York Renaissance, or simply the Rens. To the sports world, it was the first all-black professional basketball team. To the music world, it was the oddest warmup act in history.

Within three seasons Douglas had assembled a seven-man nucleus that became one of the most dominating basketball teams in the game's history. The club featured the talents of Clarence "Fat" Jenkins, a two-sport sensation who also starred in the Negro National Baseball League, and Eyre "Bruiser" Saitch, another two-sport phenomenon who was ranked sixth on the U.S. Negro tennis circuit.

Other outstanding players were "Wee" Willie Smith, "Tarzan" Cooper, John "Casey" Holt, James "Pappy" Ricks, and Bill Yancey. Hall-of-Famer John Wooden remarked that Yancey was "the greatest outside shooter I ever saw. I remember once before a game, he laid out nine spots on the floor, all from a distance of today's three-point line, and he'd shoot from each spot. He'd hit from all nine spots, then turn around and hit nine more coming back the other way, all without a miss. . . . Yancey used a two-hand set shot and got that shot away very quickly. I don't think there's anybody in the game today who could shoot any better or more accurately." Yancey was another multitalented athlete. For several years he starred at shortstop and right field for the New York Black Yankees baseball team.

By 1924 the Harlem team was drawing the attention of white spectators as well as black. Most fans, particularly in the Midwest, had never seen a black basketball team play. The Rens were a curiosity, especially at their extraordinary level of play. Within the dimensions of the basketball court, color lines seemingly blurred in the Rens' fast and furious pace. "By showing respect, Bob Douglas said we'd earn respect," recalled team member William "Pop" Gates. "We were so widely known that everybody was watching us. So Bob didn't want anybody acting up or making the team look bad. He didn't want any blemishes on our reputation."

The barnstorming circuit was extremely difficult for the Rens. When Douglas decided to mainstream his team into the white professional tour, a volcano of bigotry and hatred erupted among the white basketball community. Death threats followed the team as it traveled from town to town, particularly in Indiana and other midwestern and southern regions dominated by the Ku Klux Klan during the 1920s.

Team member Johnny Isaacs recalled: "We played one team in Bedford, Indiana. It was one of those rough games where bodies were bumping up against each other a lot. And one of their guys slammed against Puggy Bell, one of our teammates. It was an accident, but it made the fans angry. Several people, including a county police officer, jumped over the railing and began kicking Puggy in the shins. There was a lot of pushing and shoving going on. It was rough."

As the Rens traveled through Indiana, they generated widespread interest among Hoosier basketball fans. Gates recalled: "Most games were sold out, because many of them were advertised weeks in advance. Bob Douglas and [manager] Eric Illidge were arranging games throughout Indiana and the Midwest through the Chambers of Commerce in each of the towns we played in. So each of them had a lot of time to advertise that the Rens were coming to town." Isaacs stated: "We were always impressed by Indiana. We mostly played in high school gyms there. And those high school gyms were larger that most of the college gyms in New York City. Most folks back east couldn't believe it when we told them about the popularity of the game in Indiana."

Racial prejudice was not the only difficulty the Rens faced on the road, as Isaacs related: "I remember once we traveled to Bloomington, Indiana. Eric Illidge had a schedule on a little piece of paper that said 'Bloomington.' So he assumed it was Bloomington, Indiana. But unfortunately for us, it was Bloomington, Illinois. Well, we pulled into the gym in Indiana and got dressed to play. I went out early to check on the crowd, and there was nobody around. I saw this young boy, and I asked him when the game was supposed to start. He asked, 'What game?' I knew there were a bunch of cars parked outside the arena. I assumed that they were there for the game. But the boy told me, 'Oh, no. There's a magician here in town tonight.'

"So I ran down and told the team that there was a mistake. That's when Illidge realized that we were supposed to be in Bloomington, *Illinois*. Boy, were the guys angry! We had to jump into the bus quickly and drive 400 miles over to Illinois for the game. We stopped at a roadside phone and called the promoters in Illinois and told them we had an accident, and we were running late. We didn't even get into town until 11:00 that night. And would you believe it?! The people were all there still waiting for us. We were so tired and angry, but we still played a great game that night. . . . The worst part of all was that we had no place to stay in Illinois that night, so we had to drive all the way back to Indianapolis to stay. In all, we must have traveled nearly 1,000 miles that day."

Rens player "Bruiser" Saitch recalled that team members sometimes slept in jails during their Midwestern tour "because they wouldn't put us up in hotels. Standard equipment for us was a flint gun; we'd spray all the bedbugs before we went out to play and they'd be dead when we got back. . . . We sometimes had over a thousand damn dollars in our pockets and we couldn't get a good god-damn meal."[2]

Pat Malaska, an all-American at Purdue University and an outstanding semipro player whose teams toured with the Rens, recalled: "They had some difficulty in getting places to stay because most folks didn't want to house the blacks. But on the court they were pretty well respected, I'd say. They were a clean bunch. They weren't dirty ballplayers. People liked them. People liked seeing them play. I'd say, all in all, they were very well respected." But clearly they were respected more on the basketball court than in Indiana restaurants and hotels.

By the fall of 1925, the country's top touring teams had abandoned their nomadic ways and joined Joe Carr's new American Basketball League. The ABL was the first league to promote exclusive written contracts to keep players from jumping from team to team. Carr also promised a strict enforcement of league rules, which banned gambling by players, managers, and spectators.

Any owner or player who consorted with gamblers risked automatic forfeiture of the entire franchise. The league encouraged college graduates to test their skills in the new semipro circuit but warned that the ABL would levy stiff penalties against any club that signed a player before his college eligibility had expired.

As Fort Wayne club owner Alter filed his new league charter, he changed the name of the team from Caseys to Hoosiers. The new name better represented Indiana's entry into big league basketball. And the association with the popular Indiana University squad by the same name appealed to the loyalties and passions of amateur basketball fans in the state.

Along with the new name came a spiffy new look for the team. The club was now in the national spotlight. The dull wool Knights of Columbus jerseys gave way to shiny silk shirts and shorts. Each jersey sported the name Fort Wayne, along with two flags crossed majestically over the chest. One was the flag of the city of Fort Wayne. The other was the United States flag, a symbol of the team's new national status.

Travel during the league's winter season was treacherous as clubs toured through snow and ice in trains and unreliable automobiles. Moreover, weekday job commitments restricted play to weekends only. Therefore league officials limited the number of games scheduled for their inaugural season. Carr divided the schedule into two mini-seasons, a 16-game fall season and a 14-game winter tour (a far cry from today's 82-game schedule).

Although teams were restricted by the total number of games, they expected a competitive contest each night out as they faced the best squads from around the country. The schedule guaranteed a good show for the fans. Attendance numbers in Fort Wayne and other ABL cities routinely averaged close to 3,000 a night. The excitement and competition grew intense as several ball clubs vied for top honors in league play. During each mini-season in 1925–26, the Fort Wayne Hoosiers finished in the middle of the standings.

Brooklyn won the first season championship, Cleveland the second. The league staged a five-game championship series for the two clubs, with Cleveland winning the title in three straight games. Attendance figures for the series inspired league executives. Nearly 10,000 spectators a night enjoyed the American

League's first "World Series." Certainly no one got rich from the new league. Yet Carr's initial success encouraged the owners. The league struggled and survived its inaugural year.

For the Fort Wayne Hoosiers and their star Homer Stonebraker, the ABL provided a perfect national spotlight to showcase the Midwest's greatest talent. Stonebraker's spectacular play earned him the respect and admiration of fans throughout the country. Stonebraker, however, was growing weary. He was only 27, but life on the road was taking its toll. Perpetual roughhouse play and an intense barnstorming schedule proved too much for the Fort Wayne captain. The following season, he limited his playing time to make way for younger talent. But without Stonebraker's court leadership the team quickly tumbled to the bottom half of the league standings. Fort Wayne fans looked to the future of their team with uncertain hope.

The Fort Wayne association felt that the addition of one star performer would give the Hoosiers the needed strength to cope with the best of the league. ... Fort Wayne's basketball prospects were given a considerable boost ... when it was announced that Benny Borgmann, one of the greatest stars in the east, had been secured to play with this city's club in the American League.

—*Fort Wayne Journal-Gazette,*
December 18, 1926

3. The Unanimous Choice

In the mid-1920s, New York's Metropolitan League featured some of the biggest names in semiprofessional basketball. Leading the league in scoring at an astonishing 11.8 points per game was Bernhardt "Benny" Borgmann, former University of Notre Dame standout and star of the Kingston (N.Y.) Colonials. For a brief stint, Borgmann had toured with the famed New York Celtics and shared the court with Nat Holman, Joe Lapchick, and "Dutch" Dehnert.

Borgmann's talents were always in high demand. He was a virtual basketball chameleon. On one East Coast swing, he joined the Celtics for a week of sell-out performances. Then, the following week, he donned another club's uniform to play *against* the very same Celtic squad. No matter what jersey he wore, he displayed a fierce competitiveness rarely seen in the East Coast circuit. Borgmann scored 53 points in one three-game series against the Celts in 1925.

After dominating the Eastern leagues for many seasons, Borgmann decided in 1926 to showcase his talents in the American Basketball League. On December 18, ABL president Joe Carr and the city of Fort Wayne got an early Christmas present when the New York scoring ace signed a contract with the Hoosiers. Borgmann was coming back home again to Indiana. He arrived in Fort Wayne just days before a two-game showdown with the famed Celtics. The league advertised the series as "the greatest basketball attraction in the universe."[1] The two contests, while perhaps falling short of such a grandiose billing, were nonetheless exciting. The New Yorkers ruined Borgmann's ABL debut by winning both games by narrow margins. But the two games in Fort Wayne were sell-outs, which encouraged ABL officials. The league now had legitimate drawing power in the Midwest.

When Borgmann moved to Fort Wayne, the Hoosiers were a woeful 3–6 in league play. So manager Clarence Alter turned the job of managing and motivating the club over to his newest recruit. On January 6, 1927, Alter announced that Borgmann was succeeding Ralph Miller as captain of the team. Miller, a two-sport phenom, planned to report to the Indianapolis Indians baseball training camp later in the spring. According to the *Fort Wayne News-Sentinel* the idea to appoint Borgmann captain came "at the suggestion of Miller himself. . . . Miller expressed the belief that a man should be named to succeed him. Borgmann was the unanimous choice of the players, and although reluctant to accept, finally was prevailed upon to take the assignment."

The move symbolized not only a change in leadership for the Fort Wayne club but also a change in the style of play. Miller and Homer Stonebraker, two of the game's earliest professionals, had created an inside game in which players patiently worked and reworked the ball into the big men for easy baskets. The pace was slow and deliberate. Borgmann brought a new style and a new attitude to the league. He was short. He was fast. And he let his shots fly from virtually anywhere on the court at any time. Borgmann's intense, frenetic play closely resembled the fast-paced style of the New York Rens. Most league teams and fans were not accustomed to this type of basketball. Borgmann's play was exciting.

A week after being named captain, Borgmann burned Washington for 17 points. Clarence Alter made the trip to the nation's capital to watch his new star. Alter was one of two familiar faces on the Fort Wayne bench watching Borgmann's performance with great interest. The other was Homer Stonebraker. Once the biggest drawing card in the Midwest, Stonebraker now sat passively as the future of his team and the game itself unfolded on the court before him.

But the big fellow was not ready to bow out just yet. The following night, before a crowd of Indiana congressmen and other Washington dignitaries, Stonebraker stepped onto the court to play side by side with Borgmann. The *Fort Wayne Journal Gazette* reported on the contest on January 18: "The game [last night] marked the return of Homer Stonebraker, the visitors' veteran forward, who fittingly celebrated the event by being high point man of the game with three goals from the field and four from the free throw line. He was closely pressed for scoring honors by Benny Borgmann, the Hoosier captain, who had a total of nine points to his credit."

Three days after Stonebraker's outstanding performance, Alter announced regrettably that he had released Stonebraker from the team. He reasoned to the press that he needed to make room for two new stars from New York's Metropolitan League. News of Stonebraker's release blanketed the sports page of the *Fort Wayne News-Sentinel*. "Stoney's release marks the passing of the most widely-known and one of the most popular players in the middlewest," the paper stated, terming Stonebraker's career as "meteoric."

Midway through the 1926 season, the Cleveland Rosenblooms stood in first place. The Fort Wayne Hoosiers fell to sixth place, with a record of 8–13. Without the services of the city's favorite son, Stonebraker, Fort Wayne fans turned anxious eyes to Stoney's speedy successor. Suddenly the responsibility for the franchise's financial success fell solely and squarely on the shoulders of 5′9″ Borgmann. Only 35 days into his tenure with the Hoosiers, the league rookie from New York now had to prove his mettle.

While Borgmann revolutionized the style of play in Fort Wayne, another revolution of sorts was taking root at Wendell Phillips High School in Chicago. In 1926 Phillips caused quite a stir by winning the city high school basketball championship, the first all-black team to do so. After graduation, the nucleus of this group formed a team that represented the Giles Post of the American Legion. Dick Hudson, an ex–football star, organized several paid exhibitions that pitted the Giles Post against other talented African American squads in the area.

Hudson swung a deal with the management of the Savoy Theater and Ballroom to play Saturday night exhibitions. Somewhat like the Renaissance Casino management in New York in its arrangement with Robert Douglas's Rens, the Savoy Ballroom managers agreed to sponsor Hudson's squad. Known as the Savoy Big Five, the team often played before packed houses of party goers who came not only to watch the games but also to dance to the spectacular postgame entertainment of bandmaster Cab Calloway and Peg Leg Bates.

Many midwestern promoters refused to schedule games against the Negro club. As a result, the Savoys' appearances were limited. Concerned, Hudson consulted his friend Walter Ball, former all-star pitcher with the Negro Baseball League's Chicago American Giants. The two decided that if the team had a white promoter and manager, it might book many more contests and bring in more money. The two paid a visit to the business district on the South Side of Chicago. There they made a proposal to a pudgy, odd-looking little man, Abe Saperstein, a Jewish businessman. He gladly accepted it. For a prearranged fee of $100 and 10 percent of all bookings, Saperstein took his new team on the road. He renamed the group Saperstein's Harlem Globetrotters and supplied them with bright red, white, and blue uniforms created in his father's tailor shop.

Basketball fans today know the Harlem Globetrotters as a touring comedy troupe. But in 1927 and for several years after, the

Trotters played hard-nosed, serious basketball. Led by the greatest African American talent in the Midwest, the team featured Walter "Toots" Wright, Byron "Fat" Long, Willis "Kid" Oliver, Andy Washington, and Al "Runt" Pullins, a sharp-shooting speedster on the court. As a unit, the Harlem Globetrotters were spectacular. Black newspapers such as the *Indianapolis Recorder* heralded the club as "Chicago's pride among basketball tossers."

The Globetrotters dominated their barnstorming circuit. Their first year they won 101 of 117 games, and for the next two seasons they won nearly 90 percent of all their contests. After their third successful season, Saperstein realized that his team's court supremacy angered many small-town patrons who did not enjoy watching their local teams lose by large and often embarrassing margins. Therefore he choreographed several gimmicks and stunt plays to keep the fans interested and entertained. Once the Trotters built a sizable lead, they broke into fancy passing and dribbling displays and other comic routines. Soon their popularity soared with audiences of all races. By the mid-1930s comedy had taken center stage. The basketball court became their theater, as the Harlem Globetrotters gained fame and fortune on the professional barnstorming circuit.

On the American Basketball League stage, Benny Borgmann and the Fort Wayne Hoosiers played out a stellar drama. The sharpshooter answered his team's plea for leadership in spectacular fashion. Joining the team eight games into the 1926–27 season, he forced himself to learn the club's style of play literally overnight. But by the end of January 1927, with only thirteen games under his belt, he had climbed into ninth place in the league's scoring race.

Rarely did any one player in the ABL score in double figures. Borgmann made it a habit. He scorched the Philadelphia Quakers with 20 points in one contest. He averaged 10.1 points per game in his first 13 games. At season's end in March 1927, he held the league's highest scoring average at 11.2 points per game.

Borgmann's influence was apparent in the league standings as well. Fort Wayne climbed to a respectable second-place finish during the last half of the 1926–27 season. The New York Celtics, a new ABL entry that year, captured the second-season crown and went on to defeat the previous year's ABL champs, the Cleveland Rosenblooms, for the 1927 American Basketball League championship.

Fan turnout throughout the season again encouraged league officials. The Celtics' entry into the ABL obviously enhanced the league's credibility and name recognition. One Celtic game in Philadelphia attracted nearly 9,000 fans, while other contests in Cleveland and Washington routinely packed 7,000 spectators in the bleachers. Games in Fort Wayne, the smallest of the ABL cities, attracted a respectable 4,000 fans per contest.

The growth of the semiprofessional game prompted the *Central Press* to run a syndicated article, "Pro Basketball Enjoying Biggest Season," that stated: "Basketball is one new professional sport being tried on a national plan that has a chance to live. So say the men who are carrying the brunt of the financial burden in the promoting of the game. And they are the ones who should know best. From the playing end, the competition could not be keener. Any team in the league is strong enough that on its good nights, it can defeat the leading outfits of the circuit."

The Indianapolis Exposition Building stood at the center of the Indiana State Fairgrounds. Most Hoosiers referred to it as the "cow barn." Each summer, farmers paraded their livestock through this broad, two-story structure. But in March 1927, members of the Indiana High School Athletic Association removed the hog and cattle stalls to clear enough room for capacity crowds. For one thrilling weekend the boys' state basketball tournament invaded the vast arena. Soon a wave of urgent excitement washed over the entire facility.

For the past three seasons the Martinsville Artesians had hovered near the top of the state basketball rankings. In 1925, the club had earned a spot as one of the top 16 teams in the tournament. The following year, they had finished as runners-up to Marion High School. In March 1927, they won it all.

The Artesians and Coach Glenn Curtis had a well-balanced attack. But most of their success stemmed from the play of an outstanding 5'10" junior guard. Sleek and sinewy, his chiseled body glided effortlessly across the court. No single player in the state's history had a better court presence and knowledge of the game.

By his junior year, he had earned his second All-State honor in basketball. He had mastered the fundamentals of the game at an early age. He was a constant scoring threat, and his tenacious defensive play was unsurpassed. He often sported scabs on his knees and elbows, as he sacrificed his body to dive for a loose ball on the floor. His play was always aggressive, but his lifestyle was puritanical—no drinking, no smoking, no swearing.

From his earliest basketball competitions, he was a scoring ace with natural court awareness. He led his grade school and junior high school teams in scoring. And by the time he reached Martinsville High School in 1925, sportswriters throughout Indiana lauded him as "a player of great promise." The *Martinsville Daily Reporter* noted of the young star that "local people swell up like prideful toads at the mere mention of his name—and the greater the friendship, the bigger the swell." Former football star and sports broadcaster Tom Harmon described him as "a king, the idol of every kid who had a basketball, and in Indiana, that was every kid."[2] His name was John Robert Wooden.

Wooden was born on October 14, 1910, the third of six children. He grew up just north of Martinsville in Centerton, Indiana, a tiny farm community with a population of 50. His father, Joshua, ran a large family farm and raised livestock, as well as wheat, alfalfa, and many sorts of vegetables.

Joshua was an accomplished baseball player in his day. But John and his older brother, Maurice, had little interest in the baseball diamond their father carved into a corner of their wheat field. Instead the two boys focused their childhood energies on an old tomato bushel, hung from the hayloft. Using a cheap, rubber ball purchased at the local Five and Dime, John and his brother played raucous games of basketball each night from the time they came home from school until the golden Midwestern twilight silhouetted the two youngsters.

Joshua Wooden once gave John a scrap of paper with a quote from Shakespeare's *Hamlet* scrawled in rough print. On the paper were words of sound advice from a father to a son: "Be true to thyself, make each day a masterpiece, help others, drink deeply from good books, make friendship a fine art, and build a shelter against a rainy day." This was how John Wooden led his life.

"Wooden was an excellent ballplayer," recalled former professional teammate Pat Malaska. "John was probably the best I've ever seen at going under the basket and faking a shot—stopping dead in his tracks and letting the defender run past him. Then he would make an easy lay-up. He moved *all* the time. John was just a very intelligent player and a gentleman."

Much like Ward Lambert and Homer Stonebraker before him, Wooden found himself in the spotlight of Hoosier Hysteria. He recalled: "When you think of basketball, you think of Indiana. Martinsville was a town of 4,800 when I was there. But the gymnasium at the high school seated 5,200! And that was not too uncommon around the state. It just seemed like basketball was such a religion. Almost every youngster aspired to play basketball."

The 1927 state championship was the crowning achievement in Wooden's high school career. The 16-team final in Indianapolis was a pressure cooker of intense action and excitement. Wooden recalls, "We played four games in roughly 25 hours. We played one game on Friday night and three games on Saturday. As you look back at it, that was probably too much. But we didn't think about it at the time. There was just a tremendous interest for [the tournament] throughout the state."

Wooden later enjoyed unparalleled success as an All-American at Purdue University, as a professional player, and as the winningest coach in college basketball tournament history at UCLA. Still, the 1927 Martinsville championship holds a special place in Wooden's heart. "Nothing compares with winning an Indiana high school state championship. I really believe that," he proclaimed through a broad smile. "I had pretty good success playing on and coaching NCAA championship teams. I've been involved in many ways. But there's nothing that quite compares to playing on an Indiana high school team. The Final Four in college basketball—it just doesn't compare with the Indiana high school tournament."

Fort Wayne ushered in several new faces at the start of the 1927-28 campaign. Manager Alter signed up one of the country's top coaches, Frank "Pop" Morganweck, to lead his squad.

Since the turn of the century, Morganweck had organized and coached semiprofessional basketball teams in New York's Metropolitan League.

The press often referred to Morganweck as "the Connie Mack of professional basketball." His gentlemanly demeanor resembled that of the great Philadelphia Athletics baseball manager, and, like Mack, Morganweck had a reputation for building winning teams year after year. He was slender and unassuming, with a balding, egg-shaped head and broad-rimmed glasses. His tailored, three-piece suits gave him the look of a banker or clergyman. During the early 1920s Frank Morganweck headed Borgmann's old club, the Kingston Colonials. In fact, it was Morganweck who "discovered" the talented Notre Dame graduate and lured Borgmann to New York. Now the mentor and his student were together again, this time in Fort Wayne.

Alter also transplanted two other New York natives to the fertile basketball grounds of the Midwest. Bill McElwain, a 5'10" forward from Yonkers, and Joe Griebe, a six-foot guard from the Brooklyn Visitations, had both starred in the New York Metropolitan League. In another successful deal, Alter landed a contract with Washington's "boy wonder," 21-year-old Rusty Saunders, the ABL's leading scorer the previous two seasons.

The 1927–28 ABL season expanded to fifty games, with the top two teams in each division meeting in a three-game playoff series for the divisional title in the spring. Each division champ then played a "best-of-five" series for the ABL championship.

As expected, the Celtics ran away with the eastern division title that year. During one stretch, from December 1927 through January 1928, the Celtics put together a 15-game winning streak that placed them safely ahead of the second-place finisher, the Philadelphia Warriors. The seasoned talents of Joe Lapchick, Nat Holman, Dutch Dehnert, Davey Banks, and Chris Leonard were too much for the rest of the division. In the "best-of-three" eastern divisional playoffs, the Celtics easily eliminated Philadelphia in two straight games.

In the western division, the action was much more intense. Max Rosenbloom's Cleveland club was in a hot division race with Morganweck's Fort Wayne squad. A late-season surge by the Hoosiers put them in first place by season's end. That momentum led the Indiana boys easily through the western division playoffs as Cleveland fell in two straight games.

Fort Wayne's playoff victory set up another heated series with its old rival, the New York Celtics. "The scene for the world's greatest basketball classic, the series for the championship of the universe, will be laid right here in little old Fort Wayne, when the Hoosiers meet the New York Celtics in the first game of the playoff between the eastern and western champions," the *Journal Gazette* noted. "Last fall when the American League season opened, the fondest dream of the most rabid Hoosier fan was that the local team might come through to a world's title; the next fondest dream was that they might at least get a chance to play for the championship. The Hoosiers have made one vision a reality, and they still have a chance to make good the other."

The series pitted a David against a Goliath of sorts. Fort Wayne waged its contests at the old North Side gym, which seated only 3,800 spectators. By contrast, New York played its home games in famed Madison Square Garden. The Garden held more than 18,000 fans and hosted many of the biggest sporting events in the country. The *Journal Gazette* gave a hopeful preview of the series: "The odds will, of course, be all against the Hoosiers, but they still have a chance. The Celts have 'off' nights, just as other teams do. When they are going right, they are unbeatable. If they happen to slump a bit and the Hoosiers keep going, the series may develop into quite a battle before it's over."

The Hoosiers were the underdogs, and their chances of winning grew even slimmer when Borgmann injured his knee eight minutes into the first game. New York gained the momentum and pushed ahead to win the first contest, 30–21. "The Celts were the Celts all the way," the *Journal Gazette* observed. "They practically clinched the victory in the first ten minutes of play while the Hoosiers were trying to get organized and having a terrible time trying to make their shots stick in the net. . . . The Hoosiers, although they came back with a couple scoring flurries that aroused some hope among the 3,500 or more local followers, found the task far too hard."

So Fort Wayne fell behind by one game. But as the *Journal Gazette* stated, the team fought back "like wild men" in game two. Still without their injured leader, several other Hoosier players stepped up their roles, and Fort Wayne turned back the powerful Celtics by a final score of 28-21. During the second half, the Hoosiers' defense was unrelenting; the high-scoring New Yorkers failed to get a single field goal.

New York came back with a game three victory, winning handily, 35-18. The Hoosiers kept the contest close during the first half but ran out of gas during the game's final ten minutes. Borgmann, wearing street clothes, sat on the bench and watched helplessly as his tired club took a pounding from "the haughty Shamrocks."[3]

Game four took place at Brooklyn's Arcadia Hall. Hutner Clothing Company of Fort Wayne, along with Western Union, arranged for reports of the game to be dispatched from New York to Fort Wayne. The wire service sent play-by-play accounts to Fort Wayne's Moose Auditorium, where Gunnar Elliott, coach of Concordia College and an announcer with Fort Wayne radio station WOWO, relayed the wire reports to more than 2,000 fans gathered on the auditorium floor.

The Celtics held the edge in victories and experience, but the Hoosiers were resilient. Just as in a classic heavyweight bout, the two clubs traded quick offensive punches and fierce defensive attacks in game four. The New Yorkers built a sizable lead in the early stages of the game. But Rusty Saunders and Shang Chadwick, the Hoosier center, kept Fort Wayne close in the waning minutes of the second half. In a contest that went down to the wire, New York narrowly escaped the pesky Hoosiers with a 27-26 victory. The *Journal Gazette* grieved: "Fort Wayne's great rally in the second half just failed to overcome the long lead the Original Celtics had established in the first session and the flying Irish won the fourth and final game of the world's professional basketball championship."

The series capped a year of league domination for New York and marked the beginning of a new era in Fort Wayne. After the 1927-28 season the small Indiana city gained recognition as a national basketball power.

But ABL president Carr was not in a mood to celebrate. Attendance figures for Celtics games at Madison Square Garden disappointed arena executives. Semiprofessional basketball, while on the rise, was still far behind boxing, skating, and other Garden events in popularity and ticket sales. Also, New York Celtics owner Jim Furey was serving time in prison on embezzlement charges. As a result the Celtics had no one to bankroll and promote their ABL tour. By season's end Garden officials debated whether or not to evict the world's most famous professional basketball team.

Carr faced another dilemma, too. Lack of teamwork and flagrant fouls ran rampant in league play. Basketball fans seemed to prefer the cleaner college game to pro ball's "thuggery." The ABL's financial roller-coaster sent Carr and his six remaining franchises plummeting into another steep ravine.

In the fall of 1928 the New York Yankees put the wraps on another World Series crown. Then a month after the Bronx Bombers completed their four-game sweep of the St. Louis Cardinals, spectators again packed Yankee Stadium. This time they cheered wildly in a football match between Notre Dame and an undefeated and heavily favored Army team. In a pregame speech, master motivator Knute Rockne asked his squad to play the game in memory of former Notre Dame graduate and All-American halfback George Gipp, who died of strep throat in 1920. In an emotional plea, Rockne summoned his troops to "go in there with all you've got and win just one for 'the Gipper.'" The Fighting Irish beat Army that day, 12–6.

The day following the Notre Dame victory, another sports story shared the headlines with Rockne and his glory: "New York Celtics Broken Up; Players Go to Other Squads." The news blared across sports pages from the New York to the Hoosier state. Professional basketball's most famous club had finally succumbed to financial pressures. Joe Lapchick, Dutch Dehnert, and guard Pete Barry became free agents and joined Max Rosenbloom's Cleveland franchise. Nat Holman and Davey Banks stayed in New York and organized a new ABL franchise, the New York Hakoahs, an all-Jewish club.

The champion Celtics were not the only missing ingredient in the ABL's familiar mix. Carr had overcommitted himself with executive posts in professional football, baseball, and basketball. Because football and baseball were more popular and lucrative, Carr stepped down as head of the ABL. In his place, league owners elected John O'Brien, organizer and president of New York's highly successful Metropolitan League. O'Brien immediately went to work to heal the ailing national league.

The new chief divided the schedule into two mini-seasons, with the two season winners meeting in a best-of-seven championship series. The Cleveland Rosenblooms, with several old Celtic players, battled with Fort Wayne and won the first half-season title by a single game. Fort Wayne turned the tables on the Rosenblooms during the second season and prevailed by one game.

During the championship series, Borgmann was sensational. He poured in 40 points in four games to lead all scorers. But the talents of Lapchick, Dehnert, and Barry proved too much for the Hoosiers. Cleveland took the series in four straight games. Each Cleveland player received $500 as the championship prize. Each Hoosier hoopster collected $380 for the series. The championship purse was an all-time high for the league.

As sensational as news of the ABL championship was to fans in Fort Wayne, another important game captured perhaps even greater attention from the growing legion of Fort Wayne loyalists. On January 27, 1929, the New York Renaissance brought its famous barnstormers to town for a showdown with the Hoosiers. It was the first time Robert Douglas and his club had ventured into the Summit City. Given Indiana's record of Ku Klux Klan activity during the decade, the Rens were no doubt wary of any series played in Indiana. But on this visit Fort Wayne proved to be a gracious host to the visitors from Harlem. "The Hoosiers will go outside the American Basketball League to play the world champion colored club, the Renaissance team of Brooklyn," trumpeted the *Journal Gazette*. "The Renaissance outfit travels almost every night, but plays every Sunday night at Renaissance Hall, New York City, where their games are broadcast. Here they have humiliated the strongest teams, including the world-famous New York Celtics."

During the first contest, the Rens kept the Hoosiers' sharp passing attack in check with tenacious defensive play. Still Fort Wayne hung on for a 34–25 victory. The *Journal Gazette* reported: "The American League leaders played raggedly through a large part of the game, and only the woeful inability of the colored lads to connect with a larger percentage of their shots enabled the home guard to finish on top." Apparently the Rens complained of the "hard backboards and a misshapen ball" used during the contest. The *Journal Gazette* reported: "The colored lads moved over the floor like cats and their basket shooting showed a marked improvement over the preceding night, but the Hoosiers . . . kept the game close in the early stages and won out by virtue of some nifty basket tossing in the second half."

The Hoosiers' victory over the acclaimed World Colored Champions gave sportswriters at the *Journal Gazette* reason to boast that "the Fort Wayne Hoosiers are undoubtedly the Champions of the Midwest." Manager Alter and ABL president O'Brien were no doubt pleased. Attendance figures in Fort Wayne were on the rise. The Fort Wayne Hoosiers and the ABL again looked to the coming season with cautious optimism. But in the autumn of 1929, a dark day on Wall Street signaled the possible dismantling of the structure not only of the ABL but also of the entire American economy.

On October 29, the mayor of Fort Wayne and other officials broke ground on the city's first skyscraper, a new $1,250,000 home for the Lincoln National Bank and Trust Company. Charles H. Buesching, executive vice-president of Lincoln National, announced that the 22-story structure would be the state's tallest. Fort Wayne businessmen rejoiced. In New York City they panicked. The stock market crash catapulted the United States into a bleaker and more desperate era.

John O'Brien and ABL team owners saw the financial plunge as merely a temporary setback, and plans commenced for the 1929–30 American Basketball League season. But ABL team owners grossly underestimated the lasting effects of the economic slump. The Brooklyn Celtics folded under financial pressures. The Syracuse All-Americans, a new league entry in 1929, was next to fall by the economic wayside, in January 1930. Fort Wayne sold Benny Borgmann's contract to the Paterson Whirlwinds. As a result, the Hoosiers fell to fifth place in the league standings. The Cleveland Rosenblooms had another outstanding season, aided by the performances of former Celtic veterans Dehnert, Lapchick, and Barry. Yet even in Cleveland, attendance figures and profits dropped at an alarming rate.

For three seasons, Indiana University, led by Coach Everett Dean, had been one of the top-ranked basketball squads in the country. The success stemmed largely from the play of Branch McCracken, the Hoosiers' muscular, big-boned center. The tall country kid with a broad smile was a product of tiny Monrovia High School. For his size he had lightning reflexes and an uncanny knack for the game of basketball. He led his team in scoring three consecutive years, earning All-Conference honors three times and voted the Big Ten's Most Valuable Player in 1928. He broke the league's scoring record his senior year and was a consensus All-American in 1930.

After his final game at IU, McCracken prepared for a career as a college basketball coach at Indiana Normal College in Muncie (now Ball State University). But as the former Hoosier court leader hung his college jersey up for the last time, Bruff Cleary, promoter of the Fort Wayne Hoosiers pro team, approached McCracken with an enticing offer.

Hilliard Gates, Fort Wayne broadcaster and historian, chuckled as he recalled what happened: "When Branch finished his senior year of eligibility (he hadn't graduated yet), he was called by Bruff Cleary to play for the Fort Wayne Hoosiers at the end of the 1929–30 season. Branch played in one exhibition and played quite well. When the game was over, he went over to Bruff and said, 'Bruff, could I have the money you promised?' Bruff said, 'Fine,' and he handed Branch a check for 50 dollars. And Branch looked at the check, then looked back at Bruff and said, 'I don't want to be paid for the *whole* season. I just want a little advance money, that's all!'"

Fort Wayne was eager to sign the league rookie, even if his coaching responsibilities in Muncie prevented him from playing nearly half the league schedule. "The coming season should prove to be an exciting one for the Fort Wayne professional cagers," the *Journal Gazette* stated. "Branch McCracken, former Indiana University star, will be with the local American League club in its first game of the season. The probabilities are that he will be unable to become a regular member of the Hoosier squad this year, but some arrangements may be made whereby he can be called into service for part of the games at least."

The presence of McCracken and other collegians, such as

Charles "Stretch" Murphy, a two-time All-American from Purdue University, and Lou Spindell from City College of New York, boosted the level of excitement in league play. But in those early Depression days, few fans could afford the 50-cent admission price to league games. The level of talent in Fort Wayne was stronger than ever, yet franchise profits were dwindling.

The Brooklyn Visitations edged the Hoosiers by one game during the first half-season race. At the end of the second season, Fort Wayne tied Chicago for the league crown and forced a best-of-three showdown between the Hoosiers and the Bruins. Alter's boys wasted little time or energy with the Windy City crew. Fort Wayne swept Chicago in two straight to earn the right to play Brooklyn in the league championship series.

The 1931 ABL finals marked the first radio broadcast of a professional basketball game. The Fort Wayne Basketball Association arranged a play-by-play account over station WGL, with pregame interviews beginning at 8:30 P.M. on March 5, 1931. Gunnar Elliott, the man who relayed wire reports of the Hoosiers' 1928 series, called the game from a primitive booth stationed at the end of the Twenty-Third Armory in Brooklyn. The broadcast was unrefined and filled with static, but it was *live*.

Brooklyn took the first two games of the series before the Hoosiers turned the tables on the Visitations. In a close battle before throngs of supporters in Fort Wayne, Alter's club edged past Brooklyn, 24–20. "Last night's game was a spectacular battle," the *Journal Gazette* trumpeted. "The Hoosiers won by giving a sensational display of basket tossing, especially in the first few moments of the game, and by stopping those dangerous lads from the east who have been popping in baskets from all over the floor."

During the final minutes of that third contest, Fort Wayne guard Frank Shimek and Pat Herlihy, high-scoring forward for Brooklyn, tussled for a loose ball near the angry crowd. One middle-aged woman reached out and struck Herlihy on the head with her purse. Herlihy, widely known as a ruffian in the league, did not take this action lightly. He quickly snagged the purse and threw it back at the woman. "Only those in the immediate vicinity knew whether Pat's aim in this instance was true," the *Journal*

Gazette quipped, "but judging from his accuracy on the court throughout the ball game, he must have scored another bull's eye."

The crowds were even greater the following night for game four of the series. Police officers dotted the boundary lines surrounding the court. Each had a watchful eye on the crowd. Bandmaster John Verweire and the Musicians' Union Band provided a festive atmosphere and downplayed the tide of violence that had washed over the gym the night before.

This time the battle *on* the court took center stage. The game went into two grueling overtime periods. The *Journal Gazette* called it "one of the most hotly contested games in an American League playoff series, with both teams fighting like madmen all the way. The nerves of the players and the spectators were drawn to a razor's edge." The Hoosiers captured the fourth game by four points but dropped the fifth the following night in a listless affair before 4,000 disappointed spectators in Fort Wayne.

Needing only one more victory to clinch the series, the Visitations returned home to Prospect Hall in Brooklyn, the site of game six. The *Journal Gazette* gave a gloomy forecast for Fort Wayne: "The Hoosiers are faced with an almost insurmountable task to win the championship. Only a basketball miracle can save them now." Unfortunately for the Hoosiers, no miracle occurred. A rowdy New York crowd thrilled as the Visitations eliminated the Indiana boys by a final score of 24–18. Though Fort Wayne had been favored to win the championship, Brooklyn prevailed, four games to two.

The ABL tournament was the epitome of the league itself. The franchises offered exciting play. But violence and roughhousing tainted the excitement. The 1931 championship series did nothing but add to pro ball's image as a roughhouse sport. But ABL president O'Brien had much more to worry about than the league's image. Nearly 5,000 banks had closed in the past two years. America had slipped deeper and deeper into a financial abyss. The Great Depression claimed many casualties, including farms, factories, and recreational industry. Now it claimed professional basketball as well.

Looking over the disastrous financial records of the past two seasons, O'Brien announced in the summer of 1931 that the ABL would suspend operations for the coming season. The country's first experiment with organized professional basketball was over.

The league brought many significant changes to the game. Dale Ogden, sports historian and curator of history at the Indiana State Museum, explained: "The American Basketball League was the first professional league to institute the three-second-lane rule, which prevented big men from simply standing under the basket and having [teammates] just lob the ball up for them to put in. The ABL was also the first league to mandate the use of backboards. . . . They were also the first pro league to adopt the college prohibition against dribbling with two hands. . . . Perhaps the ABL's biggest contribution was that it was the first league to start treating semipro basketball like a real business. Teams had specific playing schedules, and owners were required to have all players sign contracts for their teams. Certainly all these developments had a far-reaching impact on the game as we know it today. What killed the ABL was not a lack of organization. It was a lack of money."

He was a hard loser. He didn't like to lose. I remember some of the old players said that if they lost, he didn't even want to talk to them. But still, he treated most of them like sons. Most of them recollect that Frank was a good ol' boy.

—Don Kautsky, on his father and
pro team owner, Frank Kautsky

4. The Grocer and the "India Rubber Man"

The 1930s were dark and difficult years for most Americans. The Great Depression devastated the country's economic landscape. One-fourth of the American workforce found themselves on the dole. President Herbert Hoover promised a "chicken in every pot," while Franklin Delano Roosevelt, a Democratic governor from New York, vowed a "New Deal" for all Americans. The decade brought sweeping change to the country. After FDR won the 1932 presidential election, he introduced extensive federal legislation. He poured $500 million in government relief funds into new jobs programs, such as the Civilian Conservation Corps and the Works Progress Administration. He brought aid to the farmers and to the banks, all in an effort to shake up the stagnant economy.

Shakeups occurred on the sports scene as well. Jesse Owens, an

African American sprinter from the United States, set the Olympic world on fire with gold medal performances at the 1936 Games, held in the heart of Nazi Germany. And in the midwestern United States there were shakeups on the high school hardwood. At Butler Fieldhouse in Indianapolis, Washington High School won the 1930 state basketball tournament with a victory over Muncie Central, 32–21. Dave Dejernett, the Hatchets center, led all players in scoring in the final contest with eleven points. Dejernett was tall and talented. He was also African American. His southern Indiana team was the first integrated squad to win a state championship.

On Madison Avenue in Indianapolis stood a small, family-run grocery store. On the lower level of the two-story wooden structure, seven employees worked to serve the residents of the neighborhoods bordering the city's south side. The store front sported a large eagle painted between two windows. Above the second floor the proprietor's name stood out in big block letters, "Frank H. Kautsky—Groceries, Meats."

The store's owner, Frank Kautsky, was a plump little man with a round face and a high forehead. He always wore a three-piece suit, glasses, and a genial smile. A neat bow tie underscored his chubby chin. Frank was an inveterate cigar smoker. Often in the back room of the store, the air was thick with the scent of Kautsky's nickel cigars. The grocer was bubbly and outspoken with a high, squeaky voice. He had a nervous energy about him that always teetered between tense and excited.

Kautsky was born in 1889 to parents of Austrian-Bohemian descent. His father came to America by stowing away on a steamer ship to escape military training when he was 17. Frank grew up on the south side of Indianapolis and ran a dairy farm until he was 29 years old, when he went into the grocery business. He was a successful businessman and a sports enthusiast. He played semiprofessional baseball until 1926 and sponsored his own diamond team throughout the 1920s and '30s. He also dabbled in golf. Whether player or manager, he was intense, demanding excellence from himself and every other member of his team.

One of Kautsky's best friends was Paul "Pete" Bailey. A recent graduate of nearby Indiana Central College, Bailey was nearly 20 years younger than the grocer. But the two men shared a special friendship that centered on athletics. "It was pretty much like a father-son relationship," Bailey recalled. "Frank and I got to be real close. In fact, I not only played baseball for him, but I started driving him around, kinda' like a chauffeur. It wasn't long before I became his right-hand man. His family helped him run the store, and I helped him organize his athletic ventures."

Bailey was an all-around athlete who excelled in basketball as well as baseball and golf. "I used to play anywhere and everywhere," Bailey mused. "Indoors, outdoors, it didn't matter. When I was growing up, I'd play basketball in the haylofts of barns. I played games in churches. Once I played in a gym that had two big iron posts in the middle of the floor. We all had to be careful not to collide into those posts on our fast breaks."

Kautsky was aware that Pete was a prime basketball talent but had never actually seen him in action on the court. In fact, Kautsky had never seen a single basketball game. Bailey was determined to change that. He invited Kautsky to come to Edgewood Grade School, where Bailey was teaching at the time, to watch him in a pickup game with several former college and high school basketball talents. As Bailey recalled: "I think they charged a nickel to get in to the gym that night. And I saw Frank come in with the rest of the [spectators]. I was aware that he knew very little about the game. That night I happened to have a really good game. I think everything I shot at the basket went in. And Frank just got carried away. He got so excited. He loved it. That was a real turning point for him. Before we left the gym that night, he talked me into playing ball and organizing a team for him. That's how we got started with basketball."

That season the Indianapolis Kautsky AC's (Athletic Club) debuted on a statewide amateur independent basketball circuit. "Frank told me to go out and get some players and organize a team," Bailey explained. "'Just take care of it,' he told me. He bought new jerseys, white with blue trim, that said 'Kautskys' on the front. Ol' Frank was really impressed with those, let me tell you. That's when we started playing independent ball in the city."

Bailey recruited two other Indiana Central graduates—his brother, Abe, and Bob Durham, as well as two Butler University graduates, Lefty Evans and Jim Houser. He also drafted Buck Burrows from Indiana University and two former city high school standouts, Jack Hill and Joe Kelly.

On game nights, Kautsky piled his team into his giant Chrysler and drove to various sites around the city. The Kautsky delivery truck often rambled along behind the big car. With the butcher in the driver's seat, the rickety old truck with the Kautsky name on the side bounced and swayed down the road. In the back, dedicated friends and family members sat on milk cartons and tried to keep their seats and spirits upright.

Only about 200 spectators attended these early contests. Kautsky and other promoters often staged gimmicks to attract fans during the lean years of the Great Depression. One special holiday promotion was "turkey night," in which two lucky ticket-holders won free Christmas turkeys. Other contests featured pre-game exhibitions from barnstorming women's clubs, such as the Hoosier Demons and the Real Silk Girls Club.

In December 1931 the Central States Basketball Association announced plans for the city's Gold Medal basketball tournament. The Kautskys found themselves in the championship game against Bond Bread, a former city champion. Bond Bread was the favorite to win the tournament. But in the waning moments of the contest, Bailey and forward Durham paced the Kautskys with a strong scoring surge that boosted the team to a 20–11 victory and the Gold Medal championship. Durham was a first-team all-tournament selection, and Bailey earned second-team honors. Members of the Kautsky team received gold medals in the shape of a basketball for their championship performance.

Two months later, Kautsky entered his club in the state independent tournament, held at the downtown YMCA in Indianapolis. The grocer put his team's new city championship title to the test against the best teams in the state. In the finals they again faced their old rivals, Bond Bread. The two Indianapolis teams battled fiercely through two overtime sessions until Kautskys forward Evans sank a shot that put the grocer's team up for good. Kelly led the team with six points as the Kautskys again eliminated Bond Bread and won the state independent title. When Bailey presented Frank Kautsky with the state championship trophy, the owner's enthusiasm overflowed. He now had a new passion and a new vision. For the next two decades, basketball would be a way of life for the energetic grocer from Indianapolis.

The next year Kautsky's club turned professional. The team held its exhibitions on the second floor of the National Guard

Armory on North Pennsylvania Street in downtown Indianapolis. Bailey recalled: "The idea to start playing pro ball at the Armory came from Abe Goldsmith. Abe had a supply store in town, and he made basketball goals—sold a bunch of 'em around the city. Abe started taking over the business responsibilities of the basketball team. He booked games for us and took care of ticket sales and advertising. Back at that time, they could always get a good crowd into the Armory for our games. Sometimes you couldn't even get a seat." First-floor offices at the Armory served as dressing rooms for the teams. Players and fans both entered the playing floor from a stairwell at one end of the court. During many Kautskys games a player who charged out of bounds for a loose ball often collided with spectators who arrived late.

It was the heart of the Depression, and Kautsky knew that spectators could not afford to pay a heady $1 admission price to see a game, the price charged by many teams in the faltering American Basketball League in 1931. So the grocer slashed ticket prices to 40 cents for reserved seats and a quarter for general admission. And, as the *Indianapolis Star* once noted, "if you didn't have the price, Frank would get you in some way." Frank's son Don recalled: "Back then we didn't charge much. A lot of times, when I was younger, I had to run the grocery store so my dad could run around with his basketball team. Somebody had to stay there and watch the store, because we had to make money. Certainly he didn't make any money with the ball team." It was true that during the team's first four years, Kautsky never made a cent on his basketball team. When a reporter asked him why he continued to support such a pitiful business venture, he answered simply, "I like to see them play."[1]

"It's during a game that he really shows where his heart lies," one *Indianapolis Star* reporter noted of Kautsky. "Practically never sitting *on* the bench, but straddling a bit of atmosphere above it, he lives, dies and is crucified with every play, every basket, every missed pass. When he forgets and wears his hat to the bench, it's a sad article once the game is over. He'll stretch it, pound it, and, on occasions, throw it down and stomp on it."

"Frank was a real funny man," former Kautsky player Pat Malaska said. "I used to get a big kick out of him. He yelled in that high-pitched voice. And if you played well and you won, he was one happy individual. He might even overpay you once in a while. But if you lost, he was something else. He didn't want to talk to you. He didn't want to see you. I don't think he even wanted to pay you."

Bailey recalled: "Frank always got steamed up pretty easy. Bad plays would often get him teed off. It didn't take much to get him going. If he was upset about the way somebody was playing, he might not wait until the end of the game to go and talk to him. He was liable to yell at him right in the middle of the game, right there on the floor. I guess he figured he was paying the bill, and he felt he had the right to talk to his players whenever he wanted. . . . Frank was one of those guys who acted like he had the sole right of way in everything that he did. No one had the inclination to tell him what to do. But I think that's what made him so successful."

With all his idiosyncrasies, Kautsky had integrity. After the American Basketball League folded in 1931, many team sponsors faced great difficulties in getting fans to turn out for games. As a result, owners could not afford to pay their players. But Kautsky always paid his players, often more than he had promised them when they played an outstanding game. "In the early years with the team, Frank used to pay us ten or twenty dollars a game," Bailey said. "It was really something back during those times when we didn't have any money, and Frank would pull us aside after a good game and give us an extra ten dollars or so. That was something else!" And former Kautsky luminary Frank Baird recalled: "We used to laugh. Frank would carry a big roll of bills. We'd refer to it as a head of lettuce. He'd have a big bulge in his pocket. After the game was over, we'd be dressing, and he'd come along and put some money in your hand. And you'd just stick it in your pocket and not look at it. Only after he left did we look and see what we made that night."

Kautsky's own credo reflected his integrity as a businessman and team owner. "The cleaner you play and the more honest you are with the fans, the longer you will last," he once told a reporter from the *Indianapolis Star*. "I just want to have the kind of team that won't make me wear out the seat of my pants fidgeting on the bench. I want to walk around smoking a cigar and know that we're going to win."

During the 1930–31 season, Frank Kautsky fidgeted and smoked his way through his first year as a successful semiprofessional basketball team owner. He had the personality needed to bring fans to the games. But to keep them coming season after season, he knew that he needed top-name athletes to attract large crowds. Kautsky scoured the region for the most highly touted players. In the fall of 1932 he landed one of the nation's best.

On the college hardwood, Coach Ward Lambert guided his Purdue Boilermakers to the Big Ten basketball title in 1932 and the mythical national championship. For years Lambert had cultivated outstanding teams that hovered near the top of the conference standings. And during the past three seasons, his clubs had risen from conference contender to national powerhouse. Lambert's record in the early 1930s stemmed partly from the talents of a tough fireball at guard, John Wooden, the Indiana native who had led the Martinsville High School basketball squad to the state championship in 1927. Wooden received Helms All-American honors in 1930, 1931, and 1932. He led the Boilermakers to two Big Ten championships and helped Lambert clinch his sixth conference title in twelve years.

Wooden was the epitome of what Lambert preached, a model student who graduated in the top one percent of his class. He was intelligent, with a tremendous court presence. He was aggressive and tough. And he played all out, with a reckless disregard for his own body. Wooden often dived for balls that sailed toward the sidelines. His teammates dubbed him the "India Rubber Man" because he seemed to constantly bounce off the floor.

Wooden was more than a tough-minded player. He was a true game tactician. He played and thought like a coach. The 5'11" guard had such a solid grasp of the game and Piggy Lambert's fast-break style of play that by his senior year, Wooden was assisting Lambert by reviewing games with his teammates, breaking down each play, and offering effective critiques and improvements for his team. On the hardwood battlefield, Lambert was the brilliant strategist and Wooden the ultimate field general.

By the time Wooden graduated in 1932, he was one of the nation's hottest basketball properties. Upon graduation he took a high school teaching position in Dayton, Kentucky, on the advice of Lambert. For $2,000 a year, he taught English and coached the Dayton Greendevils basketball squad. As a coach he was just as tough-minded and aggressive as he was as a player. During one practice session, sloppy play infuriated him. He grabbed a basketball from the sidelines and stormed onto the court. "All right, you guys!" he exclaimed. "I'm gonna show you how bad you are." He challenged the entire starting five to try to prevent him from scoring. "Do anything you want to try to stop me," he demanded, then bolted through the entire team, darting and dribbling his way in for an impressive basket. Players forced their bodies against him in a futile attempt to stop the former All-American. As one player recalled: "He didn't pull any punches, and he wanted you to rough him up. But if you got near him, you wound up on the floor. And we were all pretty good-sized guys, too."[2]

His court savvy and strength made Wooden more than a formidable high school coach. Semiprofessional clubs throughout the Midwest lobbied for his services. Former Cleveland team owner Max Rosenbloom hoped to rebuild his basketball dynasty around Wooden and offered him $5,000 for one season. Wooden received several other enticing offers as well. But Wooden, a devout Christian, hesitated to play for professional clubs because most league tilts were scheduled on Sundays. Ultimately his passion for basketball was too strong, and he went to Indianapolis to meet with Frank Kautsky.

"Frank asked me to come up and play with them—explained the whole situation to me—and offered to pay me well in comparison with what others were getting at that time," Wooden recalled. I got fifty dollars a game, plus all expenses. And during the Great Depression that money really helped. I was making more for him than I was in my teaching job. He was a wonderful person for whom to play, a very, very wonderful person. And he really loved sports. You always had your money in cash in an envelope after every game. Sometimes there'd be a little extra in there. He never said anything about it."

With Wooden in the lineup, Kautsky had a true drawing card to attract fans to the Pennsylvania Street Armory. The grocer was elated. "Oh boy, Johnny Wooden!" exclaimed Don Kautsky. "My dad always said he could stop on a dime and give you five cents change. He was just so fast. My dad always thought a lot of Johnny."

Every week Wooden drove more than 120 miles from Dayton,

Kentucky, to Indianapolis to play in Kautsky's Sunday exhibitions. Often the former Purdue great brought along his young charges from Dayton High School to watch the game from behind the bench. It was a primitive era for the professional basketball circuit. Wooden had to bring his own gear, liniment, bandages and tape to each game. "It was difficult," he recalled. "Sometimes I drove all night, went home, got a shower, put on a clean shirt, and went right to school. I taught English at the time, and I often worked on my lesson plans as I traveled. I don't think my teaching suffered because of it, but it wasn't easy."

Wherever the Kautskys played, Frank touted his nationally celebrated guard. As the team toured the Midwest, fans crowded into tiny gyms hoping to catch a glimpse of the great John Wooden. Fellow player Frank Baird, another former Helms All-American, recalled: "One time we went to Pittsburgh, and that little gym there was just jammed. They must have had way, way too many people in there for fire regulations. And the first thing they asked us when we entered the court was 'Which one was John Wooden?' Well, John always had to travel so far, and sometimes he was restricted [from touring with the team]. And I remember the fans being quite disappointed when they found out John couldn't make it. I don't know if John had ever played in Pittsburgh before, but he certainly was a drawing card there."

Kautsky also solicited other top-name talent. Each player was paid $25 to $40 a game. Wooden was the highest-paid member of the club at $50 per contest. During those bleak financial times, Kautsky's offer for a second income was very attractive, and he soon corralled the talents of Wooden's former teammate Charles "Stretch" Murphy, a lanky, 6'7" center whom Wooden called "the most valuable player of his time." Kautsky also recruited Clarence "Big Chris" Christopher, a 6'7" giant from Butler University, and Indiana University All-American and former Fort Wayne Hoosier standout Branch McCracken. By 1932 Kautsky had assembled one of the most talented roundball quintets in the entire Midwest. The Pennsylvania Street Armory soon overflowed with an enthusiastic throng of spectators.

After a month of listless challenges from local industrial and church league teams, Kautsky looked beyond the scope of central Indiana for more formidable competition. He approached Akron,

Ohio, businessman Paul Sheeks, recreation director for the Firestone Tire and Rubber Company and former basketball coach at
Wabash College. Together the two arranged for a series of inter-
state exhibitions. Kautsky and Sheeks realized the potential of a
Midwest barnstorming circuit that featured the best teams from
Ohio and Indiana. They plotted a rough schedule and called
the circuit the National Basketball League. Besides the Kautskys
and the Firestones, the league featured the Akron Goodyears, the
Toledo Crimson Coaches and the Lorain Fisher Foods, all from
Ohio. The Hoosier state presented four more entries, includ-
ing the Fort Wayne Chiefs, the Kokomo Kelts, the South Bend
Guardsmen, and the Muncie Whys.

Kautsky and Sheeks clearly had the strongest teams in the organization. The Firestones, the 1932 National Industrial League
champions, featured the talents of Shang Chadwick, the former
ABL standout with the Fort Wayne Hoosiers. Contests between
the two squads were always high-scoring and close. For one
heated battle, the *Indianapolis News* reported, "an overflow
crowd of more than 4,000 spectators" perched themselves on the
edges of their seats as Wooden put on a spectacular shooting performance, landing eight field goals and five free throws for an
impressive 21-point output. Yet his heroic effort was not enough
to overcome the Firestones. Sheeks's club surged to a nine point
lead by halftime. Wooden's efforts brought Kautsky's team close,
but time expired. The Indianapolis squad fell just a point shy of
a remarkable comeback. The Firestones prevailed, 32–31.

Despite keen competition in league play, the NBL's inaugural
year would be its last. Frank Kautsky's experiment did not with-
stand the economic forces of the Depression. But the National
Basketball League provided some exciting entertainment and
sparked a border rivalry that later formed a solid foundation for
a new, more powerful national league. Kautsky would be back.

During the Depression most semiprofessional teams found
themselves back on the barnstorming circuit. The most popular
of these nomadic clubs continued to be New York's Original
Celtics (regrouped after the ABL split-up and now known as the
Cleveland Rosenbloom-Celtics), the Harlem Globetrotters, and
the New York Renaissance. The Rens were, perhaps, the strong-

est barnstorming team of the era. From 1931 through 1935, Bob Douglas's club compiled 478 wins to only 67 losses. During the 1932–33 season, their record was 120–8. Their success inspired a writer from the *New York Age* to pen: "everywhere the team goes, it is received with enthusiasm and the ovation due a world's championship outfit. Fans crowd around to have a look at the boys and to touch the greatest players in the world."

Indianapolis Kautskys fans greatly anticipated visits from touring clubs like the Rens and the Celtics. When these East Coast barnstormers rolled into Indianapolis, the tiny Pennsylvania Street Armory overflowed with legions of enthusiastic spectators. At times Frank Kautsky rented the 15,000-seat Butler Fieldhouse to accommodate the increased crowds.

In January 1934 the Kautskys faced two big challenges: the Rens and the Rosenbloom-Celtics. The *Indianapolis News* announced the first clash: "One of the strongest net clubs in the country, which holds the undisputed colored championship, will meet the Kautsky A.C's Sunday afternoon, when the Renaissance club of New York plays here. The team has been together a number of years and excels in flashy teamwork to score its points."

"The Kautskys were always considered a tough team," recalled Rens Hall-of-Famer Johnny Isaacs. "I used to listen to a lot of the older guys on our squad. They would always shake their heads when we talked about Indianapolis. 'Tough team . . . tough team,' they'd always say. They had a formidable lineup with guys like Johnny Wooden on their team. And Frank Kautsky could really draw big crowds there at Butler Fieldhouse. We always felt that we were on an important mission whenever we went in to play the Kautskys."

Another Rens Hall-of-Fame star, William "Pop" Gates, remembered the strong professional basketball tradition Frank Kautsky built over the years. "Kautsky, in my opinion, was one of the great innovators in the game of basketball," Gates said. "He arranged to play a series of games with us at Butler Fieldhouse, which was one of the country's most spectacular arenas to play in. He would always bring in large crowds, upwards of 10,000–12,000 spectators. So Frank Kautsky had the ability to attract great interest in the game and draw a lot of fans. He should get a lot of credit for developing the pro game in the Midwest. Frank was instrumental in making pro basketball what it is today. Of course, he had some remarkable talents on his teams, folks like Johnny Wooden and Frank Baird. Kautsky could really recruit some players that played a helluva game. [The Kautskys] always had a reputation for fine basketball talent, and Indiana had a great reputation as one of the top basketball states in the country. We always had good, tough games in Indiana, particularly with Frank Kautsky's teams. Those players really knew their basketball. It was a great state to play in."

In the contest the Rens clearly outclassed the Hoosier team. Wooden, who managed to score seven points, recalled the experience: "Oh my, those Rens. They were a pleasure to even play against. I'd have to be careful I didn't stop playing and start watching them, because they played a beautiful game of basketball." During the second half, the Rens built a 14-point lead. Then they pulled the ball out near center court to eat time off the clock. Their stall tactics featured an impressive display of passing and dribbling.

Even though the Kautskys lost, local fans thrilled to the Rens' dazzling roundball skills. Next day the *Indianapolis News* exclaimed: "Great! That sums up the marvelous passing, ball handling, teamwork and basket scoring ability of the New York Renaissance colored quintet, which Sunday afternoon defeated the Kautsky A.C's 34 to 28 in one of the greatest, if not the greatest, exhibition of basketball ever seen in this city. Words are inadequate to describe the manner in which the visitors whipped the ball around in a flippant way but always to a man who was open while the array of former Hoosier collegiate net stars who comprise the Kautsky lineup were left flat-footed as the Renaissance tossed in baskets. Even Johnny Wooden's clever dribbling was lost as Clarence Jenkins policed the Kautsky star throughout the contest."

The Kautskys had little time to lick their wounds. Three weeks later the Rosenbloom-Celtics paid a visit to the Pennsylvania Street Armory. The *Indianapolis News* was wary: "The fact that the Rosenbloom [Celtics] hold a ten-point decision over the New York Renaissance quintet this season will be enough data for most fans as to the class of the Cleveland club, but in addition the team so far has won fifty-one games out of fifty-four."

This time Kautsky's squad rose to the occasion and played a stellar ball game. The *Indianapolis News* reported proudly: "Those Cleveland Rosenbloom-Celtics walked onto the floor at the Armory Sunday afternoon with 'world champions' inscribed on their warmup shirts. Forty minutes later the score read: Kautskys 37; Rosenblooms 29. With a crowd looking on which had heard of the prowess of the Rosenblooms, the Kautskys gave them a neat lesson in basketball."

Fisticuffs early in the contest between the Kautskys' Clarence "Big Chris" Christopher and the Celtics' Nat Hickey marred an otherwise flawless performance by the Indianapolis squad. "Hickey tried to put Chris in the bleachers," the *News* noted. "Chris was smiling. After all, Chris takes it all in good fun. The fans expect him to be rough. But he never gets unruly. Hickey, however, must have thought that Chris was a cinch. He pushed him into the wall and then took a couple of wallops. Chris, seeing that Nat was serious, swung once. It connected with Nat's right eye. Nat's eye begun swelling immediately. Both were tossed out of the game. Hickey brought the old pro angle into the argument and got the worst of it."

"Stretch" Murphy outscored his stout counterpart, Dutch Dehnert, 10 to 8. John Wooden added seven points and held the speedy Celtics' guard, Davey Banks, to a single field goal. Apparently Wooden's dribbling was so sensational that defensive ace Pete Barry could not keep up. Barry continually fouled the former Purdue sharpshooter in hopes of slowing him down. All seven of Wooden's points came from the free throw line.

Later in the season the Kautskys faced the New York Rens again. This time Indianapolis came out on top. In one season John Wooden and Company proved they had the court savvy to mix it up with the best professional teams in the country. And Kautsky proved his skill as a promoter by bringing the country's greatest basketball talents to the heartland. With the talents of Wooden, Murphy, and other former collegiate all-stars, Kautsky produced a team that brought recognition and respect throughout the eastern United States. This reputation was the cornerstone Kautsky used to build a winning tradition in Indianapolis.

Dr. James Naismith, inventor of
the game of basketball in 1891 in
Springfield, Massachusetts.
(Basketball Hall of Fame photo)

An early outdoor basketball game
in Springfield, Massachusetts, in
1892. *(Basketball Hall of
Fame photo)*

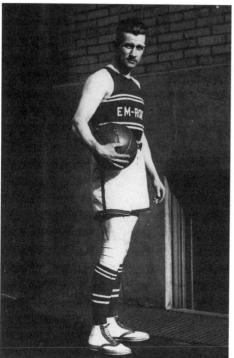

Top left: In 1913, Al Feeney was a court leader for the Indianapolis Em-Roes. He later became mayor of Indianapolis. *(Indiana State Museum photo)*

Top right: Before he coached Purdue University to an unprecedented eleven Big Ten titles, Ward "Piggy" Lambert was a star at point guard for the Indianapolis Em-Roes in 1916. *(Indiana State Museum photo)*

Left: In 1916, Indianapolis Em-Roes center Homer Stonebraker captured the attention of the national news media with his stellar shooting ability. *(Indiana State Museum photo)*

ORIGINAL CELTICS

nny
kman

Dutch
Dehnert

Joe
Lapchick

Nat
Holman

Pete Barry

New York's Original Celtics, with defensive wizard Chris Leonard and Davey Banks (not pictured), dominated semiprofessional basketball's barnstorming circuit during the 1920s. *(Basketball Hall of Fame photo)*

The Harlem Renaissance of the
1930s included Clarence "Fat"
Jenkins, Bill Yancey, John Holt,
James "Pappy" Ricks, Eyre
Saitch, "Tarzan" Cooper, and
"Wee" Willie Smith. *(Basketball
Hall of Fame photo)*

William "Pop" Gates joined the
New York Renaissance in 1939.
He later became one of the first
African Americans to break
basketball's color line
in the 1940s. *(Courtesy
William Gates)*

Bernhardt "Benny" Borgmann of the Fort Wayne Hoosiers led the American Basketball League in scoring in 1926, 1927, and 1929–31. *(Indiana State Museum photo)*

Kautsky's Grocery Store on Madison Avenue on the south side of Indianapolis sponsored one of the nation's most successful semiprofessional basketball teams from 1931 through 1947. Team owner Frank Kautsky is fourth from the left. *(Courtesy Mrs. Betty Gray)*

Paul "Pete" Bailey, organizer and star of the first Indianapolis Kautskys team. *(Courtesy Pete Bailey)*

Team owner Frank Kautsky's family members were big supporters of his clubs. As they traveled to exhibitions throughout the state, they often sat on milk cartons and rode in the back of the grocer's meat truck. *(Courtesy Mrs. Betty Gray)*

John Wooden starred with the
Indianapolis Kautskys and the
Whiting/Hammond Ciesars from
1932 to 1938. *(Purdue University
Athletic Department photo)*

One of Indiana University's most
successful athletes, Branch
McCracken went on to star in the
semiprofessional game in the 1930s
with the Fort Wayne Hoosiers and
the Indianapolis Kautskys. *(Indiana
University Archives photo)*

Action from an Indianapolis Kautskys game
against the Sheboygan Redskins in the
1930s. *(Indiana State Museum photo)*

From 1936 to 1941, the Whiting/Hammond Ciesar Chrysler-Plymouth All-Americans were the pride of the Calumet Region. Team owner Ed Ciesar is second from left. Players include, from left, Vince McGowan, Joe Sotak, Ed Campion, Bill Perigo, Bill Haarlow, Ken Gunning, John Wooden, and Joe Stack. Bill Ciesar, in the pin-stripe suit on the right, was business manager. *(Indiana Basketball Hall of Fame photo)*

New recruits helped the New York Renaissance capture the 1939 Chicago World Tournament. The championship team included "Wee" Willie Smith, "Tarzan" Cooper, Johnny Isaacs, William "Pop" Gates, Puggy Bell, Eyre Saitch, Zack Clayton, and Clarence "Fat" Jenkins. *(Courtesy Mr. William Gates)*

Fort Wayne business entrepreneur and professional
team owner Fred Zollner.
(Courtesy Bob Parker)

Fort Wayne's flamboyant
fireball, set-shot artist Bobby
McDermott, paced the
Pistons to two National
Basketball League champion-
ships and three Chicago
World Tournament titles
during the World War II era.
*(Basketball Hall of
Fame photo)*

The 1946 World Champion
Fort Wayne Zollner Pistons.
Seated: Buddy Jeannette, Bob
McDermott, and Paul "Curly"
Armstrong; second row: Jerry
Bush, Chick Reiser, Bob
Tough, and Charlie Shipp;
standing: Manager Carl
Bennett, John Pelkington, Bob
Kinney, Ed Sadowski, and
team owner Fred Zollner.
(Courtesy Bob Parker)

Ward "Piggy" Lambert
became commissioner of the
National Basketball League in
1946. *(Purdue University
Athletic Department photo)*

The Anderson Duffey Packers
won the National Basketball
League title in 1949. The
championship team included:
front row, Milo Kominich, Bill
Closs, Howie Schultz, Ed
Stanczak, John Hargis; back row,
Ralph Johnson, Jim Walton,
Coach Murray Mendenhall,
Frank Brian, "Bud" Mendenhall,
Jr., and Frank Gates.
(Courtesy Howie Schultz)

"Run-and-gun" Murray
Mendenhall had a successful
professional coaching career with
the Anderson Duffey Packers and
the Fort Wayne Zollner Pistons.
(Courtesy Howie Schultz)

Action at the Wigwam in Anderson heated up in 1948
when the Packers' Frank Brian led the fast-break
attack. *(Indiana State Museum photo)*

When Ward Lambert resigned his post as commissioner of the National Basketball League, league president and Anderson, Indiana, team owner Ike Duffey (seated left) and NBL vice-president Leo Ferris (seated right) hired former Purdue University standout and Sheboygan coach Doxie Moore (seated middle) to the NBL's top position. *(Indiana State Museum photo)*

The Indianapolis Kautskys captured the 1947 Chicago World's Tournament championship. That team included: front row, Gus Doerner, Lowell Galloway, Arnie Risen, Bill Closs, Homer Thompson; back row, Woody Norris, Ernie Andres, Bob Dietz, Leo Klier, and Herm Schaefer. *(Courtesy Bob Dietz)*

In the spring of 1949 the National Basketball League granted five graduates of the University of Kentucky their own franchise. They became the Indianapolis Olympians, known to the league as "the Runnin' Rookies." Seated are NBL president Ike Duffey and team members Joe Holland and Wallace "Wah-Wah" Jones. Standing are NBL commissioner Doxie Moore, Lexington sportswriter and team manager J. R. "Babe" Kimbrough, and NBL vice-president Leo Ferris. *(Indiana State Museum photo)*

The Indianapolis Olympians of the NBA in 1949–50. The starting five were Ralph Beard (no. 12), Cliff Barker, Wallace "Wah-Wah" Jones, Joe Holland, and Alex "the Beak" Groza. *(Courtesy Cliff Barker)*

In May 1949, the National Basketball League and the Basketball
Association of America merged to form the National Basketball
Association, today's NBA. Representatives at that historic signing
were Anderson, Indiana, team owner and NBL president Ike
Duffey, NBL vice-president Leo Ferris, New York Knicks and
Madison Square Garden manager Ned Irish, and Walter Brown of
the Boston Celtics. Standing in the middle is NBA commissioner
Maurice Podoloff. *(Basketball Hall of Fame photo)*

Fort Wayne's Allen County War Memorial Coliseum played host
to the 1953 NBA All-Star Game. More than 10,000 spectators and
nearly 100 media representatives from around the country attended
the festivities in Fort Wayne. *(Courtesy Bob Parker)*

Fort Wayne's fierce front line in 1955 included Mel Hutchins
(no. 10), Larry Foust (16), and George Yardley (12).
(Courtesy Bob Parker)

I think Frank was a good businessman. You wouldn't think he was, seeing as he sponsored a team that wasn't making any money. He didn't make any money, I'm sure of that. But he loved basketball. I thought he was just a fine human being. I enjoyed the years I played for him.

—John Wooden, Indianapolis Kautskys, 1932–36, 1938, on team owner Frank Kautsky

5. A Bunch of Palookas

The small legion of Indianapolis Kautskys followers during the mid-1930s must have breathed a sigh of relief at owner Frank Kautsky's announcement. Earlier in the year, Kautsky scoring ace and former Purdue All-American John Wooden had accepted a new teaching position at Central High School in South Bend. Rumors abounded that Wooden had also signed to play with a semi-professional club in the northern Indiana area. But that autumn Kautsky announced with glee that he had reached an agreement with the Hoosier hotshot. When the Kautskys began their 1934–35 season, Wooden once again was in the starting lineup.

That year Wooden teamed with Bill Perigo, a former Western

State College standout, Marshall Tackett, an All-State guard from Butler University, George Chestnut, a big man with surprising agility from Indiana State, and Clarence Christopher, the Kautskys' captain. The press dubbed them "the speed merchants." Wooden led a lightning attack of fast-break, fire-department basketball. The Kautskys scored nearly 40 points a game at a time when most teams averaged only half that. They even tallied 63 points in a contest against the famed New York Celtics.

With the demise of the National Basketball League, Kautsky's experiment of the previous season, and professional basketball gone back to the ways of barnstorming, the consistency of the league schedule was over. But the demise allowed for greater scheduling freedom in Kautsky's weekly showdowns at the Pennsylvania Street Armory in downtown Indianapolis, and the Kautskys played host to a variety of challenging and entertaining foes.

One colorful opponent was Olson's Terrible Swedes, from Cassville, Missouri. The Swedes featured a squad of giants who averaged more than 6'5" tall. African American teams, such as the Chicago Savoys, the Toledo Brown Bombers, and the Philadelphia Commandeurs, often thrilled crowds with their solid passing attacks and comedy routines by talented athletes such as Jackie Bethards.

Another popular touring team was the Philadelphia SPHAs (South Philadelphia Hebrew Association), an all-Jewish squad led by Eddie Gottlieb, the club's owner-manager. Gottlieb was known as "the mogul." A native of Kiev, Russia, he was one of the era's greatest promoters, also organizing wrestling matches, semipro football contests, and Negro League baseball games. But his crowning promotional achievement was the SPHAs.

While Kautsky's club battled for Midwest title honors, Gottlieb's men ruled the East Coast circuit. When the Eastern League started in 1933, the SPHAs claimed the league championship. They went on to win six other league titles over the next twelve years. Before more than 3,000 fans in the ballroom of Philadelphia's Broadwood Hotel, Gottlieb promised "a fight in every game, guaranteed."[1] In the marbled grand ballroom, spectators sat in posh, upholstered seats and watched as East Coast sensations such as Moe Goldman and Chick Passion charged out on the court and deliberately picked a fight with opposing players.

After each home contest, Gottlieb staged a dance on the ball-room floor. One player on the SPHAs' roster, Gil Fitch, doubled as band leader. After the final whistle, he quickly changed from his basketball uniform into a tuxedo and led the musical festivities. The SPHAs played most of their games close to home. But once a year around Christmas, the team traveled to the Midwest on a barnstorming tour. One of the most heated rivalries took place at Butler Fieldhouse against Kautsky's club.

In anticipation of the SPHAs' arrival, Kautsky recruited an aggregate of new players, including Leroy "Cowboy" Edwards, an Indianapolis native who had won the league scoring title at Oshkosh the previous year. Edwards had a hook shot that was equally lethal from either his right or his left hand. Kautsky also recruited Frank Baird, a Helms All-American guard from Butler University. Baird recalled his first experience with "big league" basketball: "We played against a lot of good ballplayers [in college]. But when you got in the pro ranks, it was a step higher. I thought maybe I knew a lot about basketball. But I learned a lot in a hurry when I went up against some of those veteran pro players. I just got a big kick out of it, because we were playing against the best ballplayers in the country night after night."

It was always a classic East versus West battle when the SPHAs met the Kautskys. In 1934–35, the easterners came out on top. Led by what the *Indianapolis News* called "the smoothest passing combination in basketball today,"[2] the SPHAs handed the Kautskys a 37–27 defeat. One of the largest crowds of the season, more than 3,500 strong, turned out to watch the game at Butler, and that helped inspire both Kautsky and Gottlieb. The contest marked the beginning of an annual rivalry between the two squads that proved very popular among Hoosier hoops fans.

As a group of rambling barnstormers, Kautsky players found life on the road extremely difficult, especially during the icy winter months. Frank Baird recalled: "Many of our trips were Saturday-Sunday trips. We'd hit Oshkosh on Saturday night, then up to Sheboygan for a Sunday afternoon game. Then we'd hustle to get back to our regular jobs on Monday morning. Other trips we'd take to Cleveland and Pittsburgh were quite long. Of course the weather was the big thing. If you'd travel to Wisconsin, you never knew how much snow and ice you were going to run into.

You have to remember, we didn't have interstates back in those days. You had to drive through all these little towns. So lots of nights were quite long."

Former Kautsky player Pat Malaska said: "My first coaching job was in Fairmount, Indiana. I would travel by car from there to Oshkosh or Sheboygan and come back very, very late. Most of the time I barely had enough time to take a shower and get to school. And I did all that for $15 a game." For Malaska, many of his weekend excursions with the Kautskys were humorous. Still others were dangerous. "I remember we had one near fatal accident when we were going south on a tour to Atlanta," he recalled. "We were changing drivers, and I don't know who was driving, but he was unfamiliar with where the lights were on the car. He pushed the wrong button and the lights went out. By the time he hit the brakes, we were within a foot from a giant cliff. We just about went right over the edge. That scared the daylights out of us."

Wooden also recalled the road-weary days on the barnstorming circuit: "Bill Perigo and I were heading to Pittsburgh, and the weather was terrible. Cars were over on the side of the road. It was so icy. And we were late and trying to make up a little time—a really foolish thing to do. Well, we stopped somewhere in northern Ohio and saw we weren't going to make it to Pittsburgh in time for the start of the game. So Bill stopped somewhere to call the folks in Pittsburgh to let them know we were running late, and I went in to get some sandwiches and some coffee. When we got back on the road, Bill said, 'You'll never guess what that fella back at the telephone booth said. I told him where we were going, and he said, "You'll never make it." And I said, "Oh, yes, we will." And he said, "That's what those two fellas down at the morgue thought also!"' So that was a pretty tough time, but we finally made it."

At one point the Kautskys had a 15-game home winning streak broken by a visiting team from New York. After the contest, the Kautskys were scheduled to play the second half of a weekend double-header out of town. The team, dejected by the loss, solemnly packed for their road trip. The loss incensed Kautsky. As he watched his squad load the car for their trip, he turned abruptly to team manager Abe Goldsmith and snapped, "You go on the trip. If you think I'm going with that bunch of palookas, you're crazy."[3]

In November 1935 Kautsky again teamed with his old friend Paul Sheeks, athletic director for Firestone in Akron. The two organized the Midwest Basketball Conference. Indianapolis had two entries, Kautsky's club and the Indianapolis U.S. Tire Company.

C. E. Stoutenber, plant manager for U.S. Tire, had conferred with personnel director E. M. Cushing, found that the plant employed several outstanding net stars, and immediately decided to sponsor a club. It featured several former high school all-stars, including Leroy "Cowboy" Edwards from Indianapolis, Lefty Evans of Logansport, Charley Shipp, leader of Indianapolis Cathedral High School's national Catholic championship team, and Oral Hildebrand, a two-sport sensation who pitched for the Cleveland Indians.

Kautsky again featured the talents of Wooden, as well as Perigo, Baird, and big George Chestnut. Kautsky built a lineup that was sure to draw large crowds. To make games even more attractive, Kautsky announced that he would not raise ticket prices for league contests. Floor-level seats remained 40 cents apiece. A seat in the balcony cost a quarter.

The U.S. Tires and the Kautskys shared the National Guard Armory in downtown Indianapolis for all their home contests. Both played on Sunday afternoons, with each club alternating weeks at home. Each squad also competed in special statewide tours against barnstorming powerhouses such as the New York Rens and the Original Celtics.

"Cowboy" Edwards was the shining star for the U.S. Tires. In one contest against Akron, he poured in 16 points to lead the Tires to a 43–22 victory. Five of his field goals came in rapid succession in the third quarter. The big Indianapolis forward was so impressive, even players on the Akron bench stood and applauded his efforts.

Despite Edwards's heroics, however, the U.S. Tires struggled through their Midwest Conference loop, mustering only five wins. One contest in Buffalo epitomized the team's frustrations. The *Indianapolis News* reported that "the game was interrupted at one point when the boys stopped and started tossing fists instead of baskets. This flare-up was the result of tenseness the entire game, starting when Oral Hildebrand and Buffalo guard Elky Maister almost came to blows and ended when Charley Shipp, Buffalo's Sam Seigel and Maister started a private war in one corner of the floor. Ringside critics gave Shipp the edge."

Kautsky's club, on the other hand, enjoyed its best season, with nine league victories to only three losses. The season was also a personal highlight for Wooden. Fans thrilled as he amassed a remarkable personal record. "I had 99 free throws in a row in competition without a miss," Wooden recalled. "In one game at the Armory I hit my hundredth free throw. Frank Kautsky stopped the game and came out and handed me a $100 bill. That was a lot back then. Well, I was pretty excited, but my wife was really excited. She came down out of the stands and grabbed that $100 bill rather quickly." The Kautsky guard went on to make 34 more free throws in succession.

The new league added structure to the professional game. But league play was still as rough and raucous as ever. Not only did players endure long and bumpy road trips along midwestern back roads, they also banged, crunched, and elbowed against opponents who often left them black and blue. Frank Baird gave one personal example: "We were playing once in Detroit, and we had a two-on-one fast-break play. I had the ball, and one of the Detroit players ran over to block my shot. He didn't mean to, but he ran right over me—hit me hard. I flew up into the seats. The fans were sitting right near the floor on bleacher seats, and when I flew at them, they spread out, and my left arm went right through the bleachers. I caught one of the bleacher seats right on my left shoulder. It drove my shoulder clear out of joint, right up to my chin. Well, they stopped the game, and a nice young man came out of the crowd. He was a doctor. He took me out in the hall. He told me to relax, as he lifted my arm. All of a sudden— *whock!!*—he popped my shoulder hard. I heard it pop back in. Oh boy! The perspiration came off my forehead, and I was just a little bit shaky. The doctor told me to go to the locker-room and get some rest. In two weeks, I was back playing again with the Kautskys."

The championship series that year was a round-robin affair with Frank Kautsky's club, the Akron Firestones, the Pittsburgh

YMHA's and the Chicago Duffy Florals all competing for the league crown. Chicago was the surprise team in the tournament. In the final weeks of regulation play, the Florals had stormed back from third place in the western division to capture a playoff spot, and in the playoffs they faced Sheeks's powerful Akron club. They stunned the heavily favored Firestones with a first-round victory.

Kautsky made some last-minute arrangements just prior to the series with Pittsburgh. In hopes of ensuring victory for his boys, Kautsky signed Cy Proffitt, a former Butler luminary, and Bob Kessler, Big Ten Player of the Year from Purdue. His strategy worked. Kessler led the Kautskys to an easy victory over Pittsburgh to set up a final showdown with Chicago for the league championship.

In the final contest, Kessler was sensational. Still sizzling from his Big Ten tour of duty, he pumped in 23 points to lead all scorers. It was not enough. Paced by Eddie Kolar's 14 points, the Florals surged ahead of the Kautskys in the final minute of play to win the Midwest Conference championship, 39–35.

For Frank Kautsky it was another successful season, capped by another heartbreaking finish. But even with the tournament loss, Kautsky and the other team owners scored a major victory off the court. Big-name talent and low ticket prices attracted fans—sometimes thousands of fans—to semiprofessional games. League schedules were still sporadic, however, and the economic pressures of the Depression hampered the league's early development. Yet the Midwest Conference somehow survived. Newspapers now regularly covered semipro games and lent new credibility to the game. Kautsky and Sheeks accomplished what no other promoters had been able to do. They created the foundation of a lasting institution. Big league basketball was here to stay.

In northeastern Indiana, the basketball-crazed city of Fort Wayne produced the newest addition to the Midwest Professional Basketball Conference. In the fall of 1936, the Fort Wayne General Electrics, a local amateur industrial squad, took to the floor for their first tour on the professional hardwood. With jobs scarce, the ability to play basketball was a tremendous asset for former college and independent players who looked for stable incomes. Corporate teams such as the Goodyears and the Firestones of Akron and the Fort Wayne General Electrics provided extra money for talented athletes. Recruits worked behind the desk by day and on the court by night.

Ray Lindemuth, manager of the GE Electricians, built his club around the talents of several standouts from the Fort Wayne industrial leagues. Scott Armstrong, Lindemuth's top recruit, was a skinny forward, measuring just over 6′4″ and a mere 190 pounds. A former high school star in Fort Wayne, Armstrong went on to shine at Butler. After graduation, he returned to his hometown to continue his basketball career with the GE Electricians.

In one wild contest, Fort Wayne squared off against the eastern division leaders, the Firestones. The *Fort Wayne Journal Gazette* reported it: "The GE club net team was beaten by the Firestones, 40 to 34, in a spirited battle here last night. . . . The Firestones tucked away the victory with a scoring drive in the final period after the first three periods had been a strictly even battle. . . . Not only was the game closely contested from the scoring standpoint, but the players themselves became rather heated up in spots, and the tenseness of the battle finally broke out into open hostilities midway in the second half. After a personal brush between two of the players, nearly all the rest of them jumped into the breach and started swinging. After a brief melee, the disturbance was quelled. None of the players was banned from the game."

By the end of the regular season Fort Wayne had earned a spot in the conference playoffs and faced the Dayton London Bobby Pros in a best-of-three series to determine the western division title. They split the first two games to set up a final confrontation in Fort Wayne. At 4 P.M. on game day, Dayton manager Bill Hosket wired Fort Wayne manager Ray Lindemuth to say that the team was on the way to Fort Wayne. Hundreds of fans began to line up outside the gates of the GE gymnasium in eager anticipation of the final showdown. At 7 P.M., Lindemuth got a phone call in his office. It was Bill Hosket. His message was blunt: "The London Bobbys will be unable to attend the basketball game in Fort Wayne tonight." When Lindemuth demanded an explanation, Hosket simply stated, "The team will not be there tonight," then abruptly hung up.

While it seemed strange that the Dayton team refused to play, another aspect of the mystery was even stranger. Though Hosket notified the Fort Wayne management that the team would not appear, he apparently failed to inform all of his players of the cancellation. An hour or so before the game was scheduled to begin, Dayton center Norman Wagner arrived at the gym, having driven more than 120 miles, to discover that his teammates and his coach were back home in Dayton. The *Fort Wayne Journal Gazette* speculated that the cancellation was due to "a dissatisfaction between the players and the management, making it impossible to assemble a team of eligible players."

Midwest Conference commissioner Hubert Johnson was there that night. After several failed attempts to reach the Dayton management, Johnson declared the final game a forfeit. By default, Fort Wayne became the western division champions of the Midwest Conference and would meet the Akron Goodyear Wingfoots, eastern champs, in a three-game series to determine the national championship.

Unlike Dayton the previous week, the Goodyear team showed up along with a large delegation of Ohio fans clamoring on the sidelines. Fort Wayne fought valiantly throughout the series, but Akron completely outclassed the Hoosier club, capturing two straight wins and the league championship. The *Journal Gazette* called Fort Wayne's tournament loss "heartbreaking." But the efforts of this first-year franchise impressed Commissioner Johnson, who sent Coach Lindemuth a wire congratulating his team for an excellent season. Johnson pointed out that his words echoed the sentiments of all league officials.

The Hoosier state ushered another entry into the world of semiprofessional basketball during the 1936–37 season: the Ciesar Chrysler-Plymouth All-Americans from Whiting. This northern Indiana town sits in the heart of the Calumet Region, a 16-mile stretch of cities that girdle the eastern banks of Lake Michigan and stand in the long shadow of Chicago. Massive iron girders and smokestacks tower above the steel mills and oil refineries along the shoreline. For years the sight of smoke chugging and the smell of crude burning were signs of progress and prosperity for townsfolk in the Region.

During the 1930s the game of basketball had grown very popular among sports fans in the Region. Rex Williams, owner of the Hoosier Theater in downtown Whiting, often booked traveling basketball acts as preshow entertainment before movie premieres. One theater ad in the *Whiting Times* read: "See the 'Ball Tossers,' featuring the Oklahoma Oilers world champion professional exhibition of fast and furious playing that will put you on the edge of your seat breathless with excitement. Their entire bag of trick plays, lightning speed and dazzling brilliance is shown in a style that emphasizes the stellar caliber of this champion team. Whether you are a dyed-in-the-wool basketball enthusiast or not, you will get a slant on this popular sport that will surprise you."

One northern Indiana basketball enthusiast was Ed Ciesar, a dapper young automobile dealer in Whiting. Ciesar sold Chryslers and Plymouths and ran an auto repair shop on Indianapolis Boulevard in the heart of downtown. He had a reputation as a flamboyant promoter. Several advertisements in the *Whiting Times* featured Eddie's new line for 1936—a Chrysler Airflow Imperial Sedan, with a sticker price of $1,475.

"Eddie Ciesar and his brother sold a lot of cars in those days," Ciesar's longtime friend Joe Sotak recalled. "They had one of the biggest Chrysler dealerships in the state. They had all these citations on the walls for record sales, 300 to 400 cars a year—and this was during the Great Depression! You could walk around Gary, Whiting, Hammond, East Chicago, anywhere in northwestern Indiana, and it seemed like every car had a 'Ciesar' name on the back of it."

Like many Hoosiers, Ciesar was fascinated by basketball. And always the business opportunist, he capitalized on the widespread interest. The Chrysler-Plymouth All-Americans, the basketball team Eddie sponsored in the Whiting industrial league, generated even more excitement than his auto ads.

Sotak recalled: "I used to hang around with Ed after the showroom closed. We'd just sit around and 'jabber-jab.' Once he mentioned to me that he would like to sponsor a basketball team. At the time I was playing with a group of guys at the Whiting Community Center. The place was a real hangout for the top players in the Region. Mike 'Whitey' Wickhorst was the athletic director there, and he opened up the gymnasium for several of us to play every evening after work. So I suggested that Eddie talk to Whitey. Whitey was a real motivator in getting Ed to commit to sponsoring a team."

The All-American squad was Ciesar's biggest promotional tool. At the start of the 1936–37 season, he entered his club as a franchise in the Midwestern Basketball Conference. That season he recruited two top talents for his squad, Bill Haarlow and Joe Rieff. Haarlow was a recent graduate of the University of Chicago and a two-time All-American forward. Rieff was a former luminary from Northwestern University who had set the Big Ten single-season scoring record. The *Hammond Times* dubbed Haarlow and Rieff "the field goal twins."

Another Chicago product, Vince McGowan, played center for the Ciesars. McGowan, who stood 6'6", had seldom lost the center tip during his playing days at the University of Loyola. Stocky Joe Stack started at one of the guard positions. Stack was a veteran of the semipro game, having played with the Chicago Bruins in the old ABL days. The *Hammond Times* once noted that Stack was "one of the niftiest guards ever developed in the region."

Sotak played the other starting guard on the club. He recalled: "They paid me $50 a game, and I loved it. I might have been the lowest-paid player on the team, but I didn't care. I did it for the love of the game. You have to understand that literally every night I would come home from my job at the oil refinery, eat a quick supper, and then run down to the community center a block away to play basketball. Ol' Whitey would let me in early, and I'd play with the other guys until about nine o'clock every night. That's what I did for entertainment. It was such a big part of my life. And now Eddie was offering to pay me to play and travel with the team. It was great."

The Whiting Ciesars got an early test on their new semipro tour when the barnstorming House of David club paid a visit to the frozen regions of northern Indiana. The House of David was a religious colony in Benton Harbor, Michigan, that featured an expansive campus, an impressive three-story resort hotel, daily performances by brass bands, and miniature train rides. Every member of the House of David squad sported long hair, often to their waists, and many had thick, bushy beards. The club often ran trick plays and entertained crowds with dazzling passing and shooting exhibitions before the contest.

House of David featured Gilbert "Tiny" Reichert, the tall-est man in basketball. Reichert stood eight feet tall, weighed 315 pounds, and wore a size-23 shoe. Many of the House of David's comic routines paired Reichert with his diminutive teammate, 5′8″ Bill Steinecke, a two-sport sensation who played with the Philadelphia Athletics professional baseball team during the summer. "They were circus clowns," Joe Sotak laughed. "They were all good ball handlers. They had many trick shots and fancy plays. House of David was always very popular with the fans. They were a real show, just like the Globetrotters became in later years."

Before an overflow crowd at the Whiting Community Center, the Ciesars squared off against their northern foes in Whiting's first pro game. The pace was intense. The *Hammond Times* noted: "There will be more basketball thrillers in the future, but none more thrilling than that played yesterday." Referee Ray Gallivan told reporters after the contest that it was the hardest game he ever officiated. In the game's final minutes Bill Haarlow came alive. The Whiting forward pumped in two consecutive hook shots in a little more than two minutes to bring the Ciesars within a point. As the clock wound down the two teams fought to a defensive standstill. The *Hammond Times* called the final quarter "the wildest, roughest, give-and-take period seen in the Region in many a day." With only seconds left, Whiting regained possession and tossed the ball the length of the floor. Haarlow dashed to the other end and caught the pass. He only had time to toss a desperation hook shot at the basket. The final gun sounded as the ball left Haarlow's hand. The shot banked off the backboard and ripped cleanly through the net. Whiting won 38–37.

The win was huge for Ciesar and his new club. The players rode their momentum through the remainder of their preseason schedule. They built an impressive record of six wins and only one defeat. Their victories included an impressive outing with the Harlem Globetrotters in Chicago, witnessed by more than 3,500 fans, as well as a 48–27 blowout of another strong eastern touring club, the Boston Majors, before a sellout crowd in Kankakee, Illinois.

"Ed used to take us around to all these games in a chauffeur-driven limo," Sotak recalled. "The limo driver, Fred, was one of Ed's mechanics at the garage. Whenever we had car problems on the road, Fred was on hand to take care of the problem. On the side of the limo, Ed had a sign that said 'Whiting Ciesars Professional Basketball.' I remember going to Akron, Ohio, Fon du Lac and Oshkosh, Wisconsin, several times. Those were long trips. We had to travel to the game and get back home the same night. We all had jobs to get to the next day, and we often wouldn't get back to Whiting until two or three in the morning. It was tough."

After several strong victories in league play, Whiting hit a downward skid toward the end of the season and finished third in the western division behind Fort Wayne and Dayton. Whiting narrowly missed the conference playoffs. But before Ciesar closed out his team's season, he booked the club for an engagement with the mighty New York Celtics, appropriately scheduled on St. Patrick's Day. The promoter invited many high school coaches and players from the Region to attend the contest in Whiting. A pre-game clinic by the Celtics featured proper offensive and defensive techniques for students of the game. Apparently the Ciesars needed a few pointers from the demonstration. In the main feature the Celtics put on a stunning basketball exhibition before the sellout crowd. New York guard Nat Hickey scored 23 points on many long-range bombs, and Davey Banks added 18 from the field. The *Hammond Times* lamented: "The old New York Celtics now have small wrinkles in their brows and very big wrinkles in their tummies, but they can still dish out lessons in the art of basketball to collections of former collegiate players."

John Wooden, whom Ciesar had enticed to play in the exhibition, tallied 15 points, but it was scarcely enough. The Irish pummeled the Ciesars 62–42. The *Hammond Times* announced that following the game Ciesar had signed Wooden to a one-year contract. The *Times* dared to predict that the Ciesars "will be back stronger than ever next year."

By the 1937–38 season the Midwest Basketball Conference had changed its appearance again. The league had added two new clubs, the Richmond, Indiana, King Clothiers and the Kankakee, Illinois, Gallagher Trojans. Clothing store owner Bob McConas teamed with Dayton promoter Jack Werst to sponsor the Richmond club. But just three games into the season, the time and money spent on the team became too great a burden for McConas. The franchise soon transferred to Cincinnati and became the Cincinnati Comellos.

The conference also changed names. Kautsky, Sheeks, and other pro team owners held an annual meeting to discuss the upcoming season's schedule. Kautsky proposed to the group that the conference change its name to the National Basketball League. No doubt Kautsky reasoned that the new name would lend a certain grandeur and importance to the world of professional basketball. The group enthusiastically embraced the new moniker. The first week of December, the newly christened league opened its 1937–38 season.

Kautsky was a major cog in this new organization. He became one of the league's top promoters. Besides owning and operating a successful league franchise, he organized special one-night roundball events with some of the best names in the game. And he staged an annual battle for "the world's professional basketball championship" between the New York Celtics and the New York Renaissance at Butler Fieldhouse. His promotional scheme attracted more than 10,000 fans who thrilled to the athletic artistry of these two powerhouse clubs. The Celts-Rens tilt was the main attraction in a twin bill, with Kautsky's club and a top National League foe featured in the preliminary contest.

Kautsky used the Celtics/Rens event as a promotional tool not only for fans but also for other professional team owners. He scheduled the event to coincide with the National League's annual meeting. Each spring the Indianapolis grocer was a gracious and enthusiastic host to professional basketball's top executives who traveled to Indianapolis to enjoy the exhibition and discuss league business. Through his promotional efforts Kautsky positioned Indianapolis and the entire state of Indiana as an important hub for professional basketball.

On the college hardwood, Coach Ward Lambert did it again. The skipper of the Purdue Boilermakers guided his club to the 1938 Big Ten basketball championship, led by a trio of stars, Jewell Young, Johnny Sines, and Pat Malaska. And the day after their final college game, Malaska and Young turned pro, traveling immediately to Whiting to play for Eddie Ciesar and the Chrysler-Plymouth All-Americans. Malaska recalled: "It certainly was a big change. In college we played against maybe two or three [good players]. But when we got to the pros, they were *all* good. They even had good players coming off the bench. We were amazed at how talented they all were."

Malaska also recalled that Ciesar paid well: "Jewell and I got $50 a game, which was good money back in '38. But I remember it was very difficult for Jewell and I, because Ciesar tried to schedule as many games as he could. Sometimes we played three games a week. You have to remember that Jewell and I were still in school at the time. We always traveled by car. So it was tough to play all those games on the road and get back to class on time."

Ciesar added yet another impressive name to his roster that season—John Wooden. "It was big news when Wooden signed," Sotak recalled. "I remember the newspapers making a big splash of it. Attendance at our games went up, because Johnny was playing. When we'd go out of town, people made a big deal about our coming. I mean, we had Bill Haarlow, Bunny Levitt, who held the record of more than 490 consecutive free throws at the time, and now John Wooden. He was one of our biggest drawing cards. Ed put together a large number of 'celebrity-type' players on his teams. . . . Investment-wise, he really went into this business venture in earnest. He could have just as easily put together a bunch of local guys nobody'd ever heard of and hit the road, and no one would give a damn about them. But Eddie knew how to bring in these big names to attract the fans. That's why [the investment] was so successful for him."

In February 1938, Hammond, a city located, like Whiting, in the Region, celebrated the opening of its newest attraction, a 6,000-seat, $600,000 civic center. The facility featured a spacious balcony that encompassed a shiny basketball floor. One day after the opening ceremonies, Hammond city officials approached Ciesar, who by then had one of the hottest acts in the Region. They asked him to bring the All-Americans to Hammond to play out the rest of their schedule. With the possibility of doubling gate receipts, Ciesar readily accepted.

The timing could not have been better for civic center promoters. The Ciesars' next contest was against league-leading Oshkosh. The All-Stars brought a 10-2 record into Hammond, fueled by the awesome firepower of "Cowboy" Edwards, the league's leading scorer. Edwards and the All-Stars faced a Ciesars team that held a seven-game winning streak, led by the league's second-leading scorer, Wooden. The *Hammond Times* billed the game as "a high-powered professional affair." The capacity crowd was not disappointed.

The two teams battled back and forth, with no more than three points separating them throughout the game. In the waning seconds of the contest, the Ciesars fell behind by two points. In storybook fashion Whiting team members handed the ball to Wooden for some last-second heroics. The All-American guard drove down the middle and banked in a perfect shot to tie the game at 35 apiece as the buzzer sounded.

The two weary teams squared off in overtime. This time it was Edwards's opportunity to be the hero. With the Ciesars leading 37-36, the big Oshkosh center stepped to the free-throw line for two shots and no time left on the clock. The crowd yelled wildly as the league's leading scorer stood alone on the court. The first shot smacked hard off the rim and ricocheted back to the dejected Edwards. The partisan fans screamed in ecstacy. The red, white, and blue banners that hung from the balcony of the Hammond Civic Center shook frantically as the crowd stomped with glee. But on the second toss Edwards proved why he was considered the pro game's top talent. Without hesitation, the Indianapolis native sank his final free throw to tie the game for Oshkosh. Bloody and exhausted, the two teams geared up for a second overtime period.

One minute into the second overtime, Edwards tossed in an outside set shot to give Oshkosh a 39-37 lead. Ed Campion answered for the Ciesars with a half-court bomb that tied the score again. After an Oshkosh miss, Vince McGowan drove the ball down the left side of the court and dramatically backhanded the ball into the basket for a two-point Ciesars lead. With time running out, Oshkosh looked to the mighty Edwards again. But this time Wooden anticipated the pass, stepped in front of his giant rival, and stole the ball. Edwards quickly fouled Wooden to stop the clock. But the former Purdue great was not fazed by the pressure situation. Wooden's free throw tore through the net and put the game out of reach. Wooden had outdueled Edwards in the individual scoring column, 17–13. And the Ciesars defeated Oshkosh by a final score of 42–39.

The high-profile talents of Wooden, Edwards, and others now drew greater national interest from sportswriters and fans. Just before the 1938 National Basketball League championship tournament in February 1938, *Country Gentleman* magazine reported that basketball was drawing more than 80 million cash customers per year. That figure surpassed major league baseball's draw by nearly 30 million fans. While professional baseball still received more attention from the press, Naismith's game was rapidly gaining support. *Country Gentleman* went on to point out that basketball ranked with such recent inventions as McCormick's reaper and the automobile as a boon to those who lived in rural districts.

During the season team members often paired up to ride in cars to out-of-town contests. Malaska recalled one such trip he and his two fellow Boilermaker alumni made to Oshkosh during his rookie year with the Ciesars: "Jewell [Young] and I were still in school, and John Wooden coached at South Bend Central High School. So Jewell and I took a train from where we lived in Lafayette to South Bend to meet up with John. Then John drove us to Oshkosh for the game. On our way back, we were running late, and Jewell and I had to get back in time to catch our train [back to school]. And John was driving pretty slow. So we told him to speed it up. We were in a hurry, you know. Well, to make a long story short, the police picked him up and fined him $13 for speeding. For years afterward, whenever we talked to John, he told us that we still owed him $13."

Young and Malaska also formed their own barnstorming club in the off-season with their former Purdue teammate Johnny Sines. Calling themselves Jewell Young's All-Americans, they sported gold-and-black uniforms similar to those of their alma mater. For one hectic month in the spring of 1938, the former collegiate all-stars traveled to dozens of cities throughout the Midwest. They played local church league and industrial clubs and even booked a few engagements with the New York Celtics and the New York Rens. They faced Frank Kautsky's squad near the end of its 1937–38 campaign in an exhibition in Crawfordsville, Malaska's hometown, soundly defeating the pro leaguers, 44–27.

The Purdue graduates impressed Kautsky. After the contest, the Indianapolis grocer met with Young, Sines, and Malaska to talk about their future in semiprofessional basketball. By the beginning of the 1938–39 season, Sines and Young had signed NBL contracts with the Kautskys. The following year, Malaska followed suit, and the three were together again. Young's and Malaska's move to Indianapolis was a huge victory for Kautsky and a giant loss for Ciesar and the All-Americans. Joe Sotak explained: "Frank Kautsky and Eddie always argued over ball players, particularly the ones coming out of the big colleges, like Indiana University and Purdue University. Kautsky would always try to outbid Eddie for the top players in the state. I think Kautsky might have offered them a little bit more money than Eddie. So it was hard for Ed to keep some top players."

To offset his losses, Ciesar secured the services of former University of Illinois standout and baseball great Lou Boudreau early in the 1938–39 season. As the season began, the future looked bright for Ciesar in Hammond. But things only got worse. Five games into the league schedule, the Ciesars' top assist man, Johnny Townsend, announced his early retirement from the semi-pro game. Townsend was the assistant basketball coach for his alma mater, the University of Michigan, and conference and university officials frowned on Townsend's moonlighting. That was a tough blow for Eddie. The knockout punch came less than a week later: Johnny Wooden quit the team.

Ciesar typically offered contracts that promised each player $50 a game. But his contracts were often confusing. One player, Chuck Chuckovits, recalled that Ciesar withheld $5 a game from each player's paycheck in case one of them decided to skip the club.[4] It was this type of business practice that caused Ciesar to lose his biggest drawing card.

Wooden enjoyed the camaraderie of his teammates as they traveled down the back roads on their NBL tour. But life on the road had a way of taking its toll on players. In fact, it was a harrowing winter road trip that led Wooden to end his tenure with the Ciesar All-Americans. Earlier in this chapter Wooden shared his memories of the road trip he and Bill Perigo took to play the NBL's Pittsburgh Pirates in late December 1938. Here is the rest of Wooden's story:

"The weather was so bad, we would hit slick spots and our car spun completely around. It was very dangerous. We got stuck out on the roads for a while and didn't make it to the game until the end of the first half. Well, we got dressed and came out and played the second half. We actually had an exceptionally good game. In fact, we came back and won it. After the game, we were in the locker room and Ciesar handed out the checks. My check was for only half of what I was supposed to get. Bill's was the same way. I said, 'What's the idea here?' And he told me that I only played half the game, so that's all I was going to get. And I said, 'But we risked our lives just to get here.' And he said, 'Sorry, you only played half the game.' So I said, 'Fine. We're heading back home.'

"You see, we were supposed to finish that game, then travel to another city for an afternoon game the next day. When I told him we were heading home, he was very upset. He told us that we couldn't just go home. We had another game to play. I protested that if he was going to treat us this way, we were leaving. He eventually gave us our money, but he raised an awful fuss. Bill and I agreed to play the next game, but we quit right after that. We decided that we'd rather go back down to Indianapolis and finish out the season for Frank Kautsky."

News of Wooden's departure all but crushed the Whiting Ciesars. Ironically, their next league contest was against Kautsky's squad. Ciesars player-coach Mike "Whitey" Wickhorst could not regroup his remaining troops in time for the game. Kautsky granted Ciesar a reprieve by postponing the contest to a later date.

In place of the scheduled game against Whiting, Kautsky booked the Butler Fieldhouse for an engagement with the New York Celtics. It was the perfect occasion for him to show off the new talents on his squad. The Celtics rode a 32-game winning streak into Indianapolis. Now the New Yorkers faced a team that featured Wooden and several other former college All-Americans.

Wooden, Young, Sines, and the rest were too much for the road-weary Celtics. The *Indianapolis News* reported the following day: "The Original New York Celtics were on their way to Detroit today smarting under a 68 to 48 shellacking given them by Kautsky's All-Americans of Indianapolis last night at Butler Fieldhouse before 4,500 happy fans. Delayed on their trip here by bad weather and an accident involving one of their cars, the slickers from the big city, who claim the world's professional basketball championship, kept the crowd waiting a half-hour before they listlessly demonstrated a couple of their twenty-five-year-old plays in an exhibition prior to the game. . . . Despite the efforts of the Celtics to slow things up by strengthening their defense, Young, Sines, and the others hit so often the Kautskys made it a rout against the tired old-timers."

Probably one of the most influential rule changes in the semi-professional game came in 1938 with the abandonment of the center jump following each successful basket. Under the old rules, play stopped after each basket. The two teams then strolled back to midcourt for a new jump ball. Under the new rule, after each successful basket the opposing club simply took the ball out of bounds, tossed it back onto the court, and play resumed.

This change had a dramatic impact on the pace of the game as well as the score. It perfectly suited Wooden. "I've always thought that it would have been great to have played my entire career under those new rules," Wooden commented in his book *They Call Me Coach*. "The year after the center jump was eliminated I scored twice as much as I had ever scored before, even though I had slipped some because of a leg injury. The game without the center jump was right up my alley." Other outside shooters such as Young and Malaska also boosted their scoring averages. As a result, professional basketball became a full-court game. Speed was now as essential as size to team owners and coaches. This new pace created more exciting exhibitions for a growing legion of spectators.

The game's popularity was on the rise, and in the semiprofessional game was partially attributed to the team owners. Kautsky, Sheeks, and other managers were able to keep admission prices low and spectator interest high with top-name recruits, and team owners held special benefit nights to aid local organizations and charities. Kautsky often invited children from the Indianapolis Orphans Home or newspaper carriers from the *Indianapolis News* as his special guests to enjoy the game for free. His philanthropy endeared Kautsky to the city as more and more fans came out to support his basketball club.

On November 28, 1939, the National Basketball League season was under way when word came that James Naismith, the father of basketball, had died at age 77. Naismith lived to see his game grow from a mere recreational activity to a popular national and international sport. In what he called his greatest moment, Naismith attended the first gold-medal basketball exhibition at the 1936 Olympic Games in Berlin. Editor William Allen White of the *Emporia Gazette* wrote of Naismith's passing: "The death of Dr. Naismith at the state university closes the life of a notable man who gave something to his generation. It was a game—the game of basketball. . . . Here is a man who has done a real service to humanity."[5]

Across the Atlantic, tensions mounted and terror reigned. By October 1940, Nazi bombs were rocking London as Hitler's army raged through Europe. Professional athletes from throughout the United States were abandoning their uniforms to sport new togs for Uncle Sam's team.

In an election year in which Franklin Roosevelt captured an unprecedented third term as president, the city of Indianapolis saw one of the closest mayoral elections in many years. In the final outcome, Marion County Sheriff and former Indianapolis Em-Roes basketball star Al Feeney performed the same magic in the political arena that he had in the basketball arena. Through hard work and determination, the former semiprofessional basketball player persevered and nosed out a victory. And in northern Indiana, another former semiprofessional star, Homer Stonebraker, decided to throw his hat in the ring and run for United States Congress to represent Indiana's second district. Upon his retirement from basketball, the former Em-Roes and Fort Wayne Hoosiers star served two terms as sheriff of Cass County and was also the head of the state excise police force. In the May 1938 primaries, Stonebraker captured the Democratic nomination. But unlike Feeney, Stonebraker fell a few hundred votes shy of his Republican counterpart in the November elections.

John Wooden retired forever from professional basketball in 1939, and for two seasons Kautsky searched to fill the huge void left by the former All-American. By 1941 the grocer had found his answer in two Midwestern college standouts: Robert Dietz and Paul "Curly" Armstrong.

Indianapolis News sportswriter Angelo Angelopolous once said of Bob Dietz: "He's the kid who's perfection on the field, a gentleman off of it, and a scholar away from it. He's the natural whose sports deeds become the alma mater's myths. Like opportunity, he'll probably come only once in a coach's life." Dietz was the captain of the Butler Bulldogs. He held the school's three-year scoring mark with more than 500 career points. In the final game of his senior year, he set Butler's single-season scoring record by surpassing the old count of 208 points. He was a lanky, tough-nosed guard who played tenacious defense and banged inside for rebounds against much taller and stronger foes. One college referee, Larry Goetz, commented that Dietz was the finest conditioned athlete he had ever seen.

After graduation Dietz took a coaching position at Brownsburg High School, just northwest of Indianapolis. Shortly after he began his high school coaching career, he received a call from Indianapolis Kautskys' team manager Abe Goldsmith. "We didn't deal with contracts back then," Dietz recalled: "I don't think any of us had a permanent contract. It was just a handshake between Frank and me. We got paid by the game, and there certainly wasn't any livelihood in the game at that time. The money was nice, but the truth is, I would have played for nothing. I just really enjoyed the game."

Dietz recalled one of his first professional games in Wisconsin: "The gym in Sheboygan had a stage on one end. People sat on the stage and jumped up and down. Well, the supports for the goal were on the stage, so when they jumped, the goal swayed. So you not only had to play against your opponents. You had to play against the crowd, as well."

Armstrong, Kautsky's other new recruit, was once referred to as "a ball player's ball player" by the *Indianapolis Star*. Midway through his senior season at Indiana University, Armstrong led the Hurryin' Hoosiers in scoring with more than 375 total points. He was the senior captain of Coach Branch McCracken's squad and well on his way to earning All-Conference honors for the second straight year. But in his final season in 1941, a failing grade in his Roman History class kept Armstrong from finishing his impressive collegiate basketball career. That February, McCracken was informed that his star forward was academically ineligible to play for the remainder of the season.

Armstrong's basketball career was over, but for only one week. Seven days after Armstrong's dismissal, Kautsky approached him with an opportunity to display his hardwood skills with the Kautskys in the ranks of the National Basketball League. "Curly Here Monday Night," screamed advertisements in the *Indianapolis News*. "Paul 'Curly' Armstrong, recently declared ineligible at Indiana University, will be in the lineup of Indianapolis Kautskys professional basketball team, which engages the New York Rens, one of the top pro outfits."

Without the leadership of Wooden for two seasons, Kautsky had enjoyed only moderate success in the National Basketball League. But in 1941, with Dietz and Armstrong on board, Kautsky once again built a winner. Kautsky's two league rookies joined the seasoned talents of Young, Malaska, Townsend (recently cleared by the Big Ten Conference to play pro ball), and Baird—each an All-Conference or All-American selection in college.

The Indianapolis Kautskys stormed past the New York Rens in a preseason contest, 36–27. Then on a four-game Midwestern tour with the Harlem Globetrotters, Indianapolis swept the series to run their record to 5–0. It seemed as though Frank Kautsky's club was rolling into the start of the 1941–42 season with a full head of steam.

Five victories over some of the nation's top talent gave Kautsky's team added momentum as league play began. The *India-*

napolis News reported on the Kautskys' first league tilt in Ohio: "The best-looking representative this capital of the hotbed of hardwood ever has had in professional circles began its loop competition with an impressive 51–37 victory over the Toledo Jim White Chevies yesterday. . . . John Townsend's magic passes have coordinated their offense, while Bob Dietz made the step from the Collegiate All-Stars to the bread-and-butter league in double-loaf fashion, scoring six field goals, the most of anyone on the floor. . . . Armstrong added ten points, as well as applying the brakes to the Chevies' high speed."

Through the years Kautsky had built strong, competitive ball clubs. Several times his teams had earned a spot in the playoffs. Yet the Indianapolis grocer had never won a league crown. But now Kautsky was fielding his best team ever, having melded a group of young talent into a well-oiled scoring machine.

In early December, the Kautskys were undefeated, with five pre-season victories and two league wins. On December 6 the Kautskys boarded the bus for a weekend road trip to Ohio, where they were to face the Akron Goodyears in a Saturday night contest, then head to Toledo for a rematch with the Jim White Chevies. The *Indianapolis News* touted: "The Indianapolis Kautsky club appears ready to ask the rest of the National Basketball League a lot of questions with some home-grown products who know all the answers." Frank Kautsky must have looked forward to the season with great hope and confidence. His team was a powerful force in a growing league that he had helped create.

It took basketball owners with a great deal of business savvy and the sheer will of their own personality to manage to make enough money to make the payroll. They simply did what had to be done to move professional basketball into the zenith it is today. And that's what Fred Zollner did for the Fort Wayne Pistons."

—Dick Rosenthal, Fort Wayne Pistons, 1954–57

6. Major League

On December 7, 1941, the Indianapolis Kautskys marched onto the floor for the second half of a contest in Toledo against the National Basketball League's Jim White Chevies. As the two clubs completed their warm-up drills, an announcement blared over the public address system.

Frank Baird recalled: "Suddenly the announcer said, 'We have an important announcement. Japan has bombed Pearl Harbor.' We stopped warm-ups and started talking with each other at midcourt. I remember so well that when we got together, we got into a bit of an argument, so to speak. We didn't know whether Pearl Harbor was in the Philippines or in Hawaii. Just goes to show how few of us had even heard of Pearl Harbor to that point. Most of us thought that Pearl Harbor *had* to be in the Philippines, because we thought there was surely no way the Japanese could come all the way over to bomb Hawaii. Well, of course we were wrong, unfortunately." Bob Dietz added: "At halftime they didn't know whether to continue with the game or not. But they did decide to finish. I honestly can't tell you whether we won or lost that day. All the way back we had the radio on with all the news about what happened. It got progressively worse the more we listened."

The events in Hawaii had a tremendous impact on Dietz's life: "I had already been sworn into the Navy. I knew my date to report was January 29. I was coaching at Brownsburg High School at the time, and the school board kept saying, 'We'll get you a deferment. Don't worry about a thing.' Well, after I heard that [announcement], I knew that deferment was long gone. We knew that once war was declared, we were on our way."

Dietz played 15 league games for the Kautskys that season. Three days before he reported for duty, the former Butler University luminary led the Kautskys to a 36–31 victory over Sheboygan at the Southport High School gymnasium. Dietz and his teammates agreed to donate the proceeds of the game to the American Red Cross for war relief funds. At the conclusion of the contest, Dietz bade his teammates farewell, then proceeded to the Navy Airs Corps training center in Greenview, Illinois.

Joining Dietz was Angelo Angelopolous, sports reporter for the *Indianapolis News*. Angelopolous had followed Dietz's college career by covering Butler basketball games. Now he enlisted with Dietz. As the two men boarded a train at Union Station in Indianapolis, a group of loyal Butler and Indianapolis Kautskys fans, including Indiana Governor Henry F. Schricker, cheered and cried. The *Indianapolis News* ran a photo of the ceremony the following day. As Dietz and Angelopolous mugged for the camera, a poster waved in the background behind them: "Remember Pearl Harbor."

The draft also claimed Ernie Andres, another member of Kautsky's club. Andres, a ball-handling wizard from Indiana University, had signed in the preseason. But before he had the opportunity to don a uniform for the Kautskys, the Navy issued him another set of togs. By mid-December 1941, Andres was on the court again, this time with the Great Lakes Naval Station basketball team.

Without two of its top stars, the Kautskys limped through a lackluster season. They managed to earn a spot in the league tournament by finishing fourth in the standings. But in the first round of the playoffs, the Oshkosh All-Stars quickly eliminated them. Baird recalled: "After the playoffs many of the fellas on the ball club enlisted or were drafted. There was a real shortage of players. And Frank Kautsky thought that this just wasn't the time to keep an NBL franchise going."

At the end of the season Kautsky announced that his club would cease operations for the duration of the war. "I felt as though I'd be doing something wrong," he told an *Indianapolis Star* reporter. For the past four years the National Basketball League had struggled to gain financial momentum and popular support. Now, as many of the league's top players abandoned the world of professional basketball to join the Allied forces overseas, the talent pool dwindled quickly. The league continued, but the caliber of play was much weaker. Akron businessman Paul Sheeks followed Kautsky's lead and pulled his club from league play for the duration of the war. By the beginning of the 1942–43 season only five teams were left in the NBL.

The war might have caused the entire league to collapse. But instead it gave rise to a new leader with a new vision—a leader who sought to marry the needs of the country with the needs of the league. What the NBL needed was a maverick with corporate moxie and financial prowess to take a foundering business and turn it into a thriving institution. Fortunately for the league, there was Fred Zollner of Fort Wayne.

Zollner and his father, Theodore (called "Teddy"), ran the multimillion-dollar Zollner Machine Works on Bueter Road in the Fort Wayne business district, having moved the firm's operations from Duluth, Minnesota, in 1931. During the 1930s, the piston plant had doubled in size, aided by hefty government military contracts. War preparations had sparked a boom in piston production, and soon after the United States entered the war, Fred activated the Wright Aeronautical production line. With thousands upon thousands of critical components for U.S. bomber and fighter planes rolling off the Wright line, employment at Zollner soared to 1,800.

In a 1967 profile in *Sports Illustrated*, Detroit columnist Myron Cope noted of Zollner: "He is short and stocky, a dapper man sporting peak lapels, a silk shirt, a constant tan, and an unruly coiffure that suggests he is about to mount a podium and conduct Beethoven's Ninth. . . . He is the sort who would not harm a fly. Rather than swat one, he would catch a cold holding the door open until the fly got ready to leave." *Holiday* magazine also profiled him in a story on Fort Wayne entitled "Hoop Happy Town." "Zollner," the article read, "is a soft-voiced, curly-headed manufacturer, a friendly man with a taste for expensive, striped suits, and the engaging knack of making them look as if he'd worn them to bed."

Both Fred and his father were sports enthusiasts. Ted had always been a crack-shot hunter and a good fisherman. He even built his own two-lane alley to feed his passion for bowling. Fred, less of an athlete, thrived on the thrills of athletic competition. In 1938 he had formed a company softball team that competed in the Fort Wayne industrial league. Normally a reserved, distinguished businessman, Fred paced the dugout at every contest. He ranted and raved at missed plays and vociferously encouraged his teams to victory. He chose his players wisely, recruiting only those whose ability matched his own ambition.

In the fall of 1939, several of the men in Zollner's shop had convinced Fred to sponsor a company basketball team. Plant worker Jim Hilgeman, a seasoned talent who had broken into the professional ranks with the Fort Wayne General Electrics in 1936, volunteered to organize and coach the squad. He recruited former high school and college basketball standouts to work for the company during the day and play ball for the company's YMCA industrial league team at night. Zollner once recalled: "We rarely lost. And since we were playing neighboring industries, we were making enemies instead of friends."[1]

When the big YMCA tournament rolled around, Hilgeman asked Zollner if the players could get out of work at noon to rest for the big game. At the time, the plant employed only about 35 workers, and granting Hilgeman's request would mean sending nearly a third of the workforce home early. Zollner refused and suggested to Hilgeman that the players' first responsibility was to the plant, then to the court. The owner's decision enraged Hilgeman; the fiery-tempered coach resigned his post on the spot and stormed out of Zollner's office.

Fred had to act quickly to find a new coach for the ball game later that evening. He approached mild-mannered Carl Bennett, a top-notch first baseman in the Fort Wayne industrial softball league. Just hours before the Zollners tipped off in the finals of the YMCA basketball tournament, Bennett took over the reins as coach. Bennett recalled the day well: "I guess Jim Hilgeman was just a little too feisty and told Fred that he didn't want to run the team any more. About five minutes later, Fred called me in and asked me if I wanted to run the basketball team. I wasn't much on basketball strategy, but I said yes, I would. So I took over, and the team went on to win the championship of the YMCA playoffs. Of course, I didn't have anything to do with winning the trophy. The players did it. I just went along. But we won the championship, and I became the winning coach."

In their second year, the Zollner Pistons dominated the industrial league. They were undefeated during both halves of the season and competed against their cross-street rivals, International Harvester, for the city championship. The game held greater consequences than mere bragging rights within the city. Two years earlier, Leo Fischer, sports editor for the *Chicago Herald-American,* had organized the Chicago World Tournament, the nation's largest invitational championship for professional basketball teams, and in 1941 Fischer offered the city of Fort Wayne a place in the 16-team field. The winner of the Zollner-Harvester game would earn a spot among the best professional teams in the nation and play before 20,000 spectators at Chicago Stadium.

On February 26, with 2,000 spectators out to watch the game as part of a basketball triple-header at the GE Club in Fort Wayne, Zollner's factory team, a conglomeration of former high school cage stars and semipro veterans, struggled against the more experienced Harvester squad. The Pistons trailed 13–9 at halftime and 27–17 at the end of the third period. But a last-minute rally brought the two teams even at 31 and the game went into overtime. The Pistons prevailed in the extra session, 37–35, to slide into a spot in the Chicago World Tournament.

The championship was a single elimination affair, with games played every hour on the hour. Unfortunately for the Pistons, their draw pitted them against Lon Darling's Oshkosh All-Stars, who had won the National Basketball League championship just two weeks earlier. The inexperienced Pistons stood little chance against "Cowboy" Edwards, Charlie Shipp, and the rest of the powerful Oshkosh machine. But Zollner's plant workers gave the Wisconsin men a challenge before bowing out, 47–41. Oshkosh went on to reach the finals of the World Tournament before losing to the Detroit Eagles in the championship game.

His team's strong showing in the World Tournament encouraged Zollner. The narrow loss proved that his industrial team was able to compete with the best professional basketball teams in the country. Carl Bennett recalled: "After the championship, Fred asked me, 'What do we do about getting some better basketball teams to play exhibitions against?' So I went to talk to Leo Fischer in Chicago. Leo was not only the head of the Chicago World Tournament, but he was also the president of the National Basketball League at the time. I told Leo that we were interested in scheduling Oshkosh, Sheboygan, and some of the others for preseason exhibitions. He said, 'Instead of exhibitions, why don't you guys join the league?' So I posed the question to Fred. He liked the idea and told me to handle the details. In no time we became the NBL's newest franchise. Fred appointed me the coach, manager, recruiter, scorekeeper, equipment manager, and the head of ticket sales. I did it all."

In 1941 Bennett, now manager of the Pistons, landed two ringers for Zollner's team. Fort Wayne natives Herm Schaefer and Paul "Curly" Armstrong had just led Indiana University to the national collegiate championship under Coach Branch McCracken, and Bennett convinced both stars to return to Fort Wayne and join Zollner Machine Works. Schaefer had starred as a guard for Fort Wayne Central High School. Armstrong, a forward, had been Schaefer's teammate. Earlier that year, Frank Kautsky had lured Armstrong to Indianapolis for a series of professional exhibitions, and he offered the Hoosier forward an opportunity to play again in Indianapolis during the 1941–42 campaign. But the Fort Wayne native opted instead to join Schaefer on Zollner's squad. Both stars were extremely popular in the Fort Wayne area. Schaefer became the team's coach as well as a player.

The club also featured 6′5″ Carlisle "Blackie" Towery, a former All-American from Western Kentucky. His college coach, Ed Diddle, proclaimed him "the greatest player in Western Kentucky history." The *Fort Wayne Journal Gazette* once noted of Towery: "The big man of the Pistons comes through with pivot plays and scoring that always is a big factor in overcoming flashy opponents. . . . [He] is always popping up just in the right spot with his speed and ball-handling ability."

Towery's interest in basketball came when he was a youngster down on his father's farm in Marion, Kentucky. "We never had an indoor gymnasium until my senior year in high school," Towery recalled. "I remember during the high school season we'd play all our home games on an outdoor court—that is, until the court froze over or got too muddy. Heck, there were only two indoor gyms in the entire county. When it got too cold, we'd try to schedule most of our games away from home, especially if our opponents had an indoor gym. But we had no set schedule at the time. We just played games whenever we could."

After he graduated from Western Kentucky, Towery got a call from Schaefer, who invited him to visit the Summit City and discuss employment opportunities with Fred Zollner. "At the time, I had offers from Firestone, Goodyear, and Phillips 66 to play ball and work in the plant," Towery recalled. "Those firms offered me a good job in the plant but only promised that I could play just two years of basketball. I really wanted to play more than that. So when Herm and I went to Fort Wayne, Fred offered me more [playing time]. Just sitting down and talking with Fred was like talking to one of your old school buddies. We really hit it off. I realized then and there that Fort Wayne was where I wanted to be."

More than 2,500 fans crowded into the Fort Wayne North Side High School gymnasium for the first outing of the new pro team, the Fort Wayne Zollner Pistons. What the crowd saw was a good sign of things to come. With five minutes to play in their first game against the Chicago Bruins, the Pistons bolted to a seven-point lead. A heroic effort by Chicago center Mike Novak in the final minutes brought the Bruins back to within a point. But a last-minute free throw by Armstrong sealed a narrow victory over the Windy City team, 48–46. The *Journal Gazette* lauded the team's effort: "The Pistons looked good in downing the Bruins . . . and made an immediate hit with the near capacity crowd. . . . Practically all the boys gave a good account of themselves. The old Armstrong-Schaefer combination frequently proved effective."

A few days later in his weekly column "The Sports Roundup," *Journal Gazette* columnist Robert A. Reed predicted: "The National League team should do well for several reasons. In the first place the town was ready for some kind of league basketball. Competition that involves standings and championships, beating rival cities that are as large or larger than your own, always helps to stimulate interest. And in the second place, the Pistons, being built largely around six former local high school stars, have the drawing power that naturally would follow these boys from their high school and later college performances. . . . The Pistons two-point victory [over Chicago] indicates that competition will be keen all along the line."

Schaefer was on his way to earning a spot among the league's top scorers, while Armstrong was proving to be a scoring threat from long range. And the addition of a New York Celtics super-star brought national attention to Zollner's young club. "Bobby McDermott, Celtics Star, Joins Local League Club," proclaimed the *Journal Gazette* on December 14. "McDermott, late star of the New York Celtics and often referred to as the greatest player in the country today, was signed by the Pistons yesterday and worked out with the club last night for the first time. It was possible to secure McDermott because of the fact that the team was able to offer him regular employment in the Zollner plant in addition to his playing and will be on the same basis as the rest of the squad in that respect. While Herman Schaefer will remain player/coach, McDermott's long experience in the professional game will be utilized to the greatest possible extent in an advisory capacity in matters of strategy. McDermott will move his wife and two children here within a few weeks and plans to make Fort Wayne his permanent home." Bennett, the Pistons' manager, said

"Bob McDermott was our biggest coup. I watched him play in exhibition games, and he was amazing. He was making shots from at least 40–45 feet away from the basket. It was incredible. It certainly didn't take us long to realize what a talent he was. It really wasn't very difficult to convince him to come to Fort Wayne, because all of Fred's basketball players worked in the plant. So we guaranteed him a job during the week and plenty of basketball games on the weekend. When you have a family and you're looking for a good-paying job, it's not hard to convince someone like McDermott that Fort Wayne was the place to be."

At 5′11″ and 170 pounds, McDermott was one of the smallest members of the squad. But he had the speed and mental toughness to excel against much larger men. He had learned his gritty, in-your-face style of play on the sandlots of New York and had starred at Flushing High School, where he worked on a full arsenal of trick shots, including long-range set shots from well beyond half-court (nearly 45 feet). Even at the end of a game, with legs tired and muscles sore, McDermott could stand at center court and hit eight out of ten set shots.

McDermott began his professional basketball career at age 17. He joined the Brooklyn Visitations of the American Basketball League in 1932. Over the next four seasons, he dominated the league and earned the ABL scoring title twice. He quickly drew the interest of the Celtics, who offered him a contract in 1936. With the Celtics, he played more than 120 games a season in small towns throughout the country. He quickly gained a national reputation for his incredible shooting skills. In one contest he connected on all 11 attempts. In another game in Atlanta, he tallied 56 points, to that time the most points ever scored by any professional player.

"He was the greatest two-hand set-shooter I ever saw," Fort Wayne sports broadcaster Hilliard Gates remarked. "Bobby had the greatest competitive spirit of them all. He was too aggressive. He was too excitable. But, I tell you, he had the talent to go with it. What made him so spectacular was that his shots, most of the time, were *way* out on the floor. Frequently in the North Side gym he would stand in the center of the floor and hit a shot—and at crucial times of the game! He had so much arch on his shots that the ball would seem to scrape the top of the ceiling of the North Side gym."

"Mac was just plain ornery," Ed Stanczak, a former professional star at Fort Wayne and Anderson, recalled. "He'd get up close to you, spit in your face, then go around you. Players would be left there wiping their faces, and Mac was around them scoring another basket. . . . That's the way Mac played basketball."

Zollner's club started the 1941–42 season with two wins and two losses. Then over the next twelve games, with McDermott in the lineup, the Pistons won eight and lost four. Three of the four losses came when Schaefer injured his leg and was forced to sit out for a number of games.

As Fort Wayne prepared for their final drive to the playoffs that year, Zollner registered another off-court victory, strengthening the ranks of his team by securing the services of another Celtics star, Paul Birch. The Celtics were on a tour of the South when Carl Bennett visited Birch in Birmingham. The *Journal Gazette* termed the deal "a master stroke for the Pistons management, with McDermott playing a big part in securing the second star from the famous Celtics combination." Birch was an all-American forward from Duquesne University. He stood 6′1″ and weighed nearly 200 pounds, stockier than McDermott but with a similar aggressive style of play and stellar defensive skills. He was a true student of the game as well as a teacher. During his tenure with the Celtics, he had also coached high school basketball in Homestead, Pennsylvania. He was 31 years old when he joined the Pistons, and he brought maturity and court savvy to the young franchise. Blackie Towery recalled: "McDermott and Birch played so well together. Paul could really read the defense and set Bobby up like nobody's business. Birch would set picks for him, dish off the ball, then Mac could get off one of those long, two-hand set shots. They were really a tough two-man team."

With Armstrong, Schaefer, McDermott, and now Birch, the Pistons were tough to beat. One week after Birch signed, Fort Wayne scored an impressive 13-point win against the league-leading Oshkosh All-Stars. The following week, in a nonleague tilt, the Pistons defeated the New York Rens before a packed house at the North Side gym. By the end of the season, the Pistons had placed three men on the top ten scoring list: McDermott (second), Schaefer (sixth), and Armstrong (ninth). The Pistons won six of their final eight games and were on a roll heading into the playoffs. In one short season, Zollner had built one of the most powerful clubs in the National Basketball League. The Pistons ended the season second in the league standings with a 15–9 record.

The Pistons faced the Akron Goodyears in the opening round of the NBL playoffs. The Goodyears featured big George Glamack, a power forward from North Carolina. Glamack was known as the "Blind Bomber" because he could barely see beyond the foul line. He still managed to win All-American honors in college and led the Goodyears in scoring at nearly 11 points per game. This was the Pistons' first pro tournament. The Akron players, on the other hand, had five years of professional tournament experience behind them. But the Pistons proved to be a formidable foe, sweeping the Goodyears in two straight games. In only their first year of league competition, the Pistons headed to the NBL championship round against the Oshkosh All-Stars.

Lon Darling, the Wisconsin promoter and businessman who managed the All-Stars, had a unique approach to marketing and managing his ball club. Unlike the Fort Wayne Pistons, Akron Goodyears, and Toledo Chevies, all of which had corporate sponsors, the All-Stars were owned by the city of Oshkosh. The success of Wisconsin's other city-owned sports attraction, pro football's Green Bay Packers, had inspired Darling to sell stock in his club, and more than 100 businessmen, industrialists, and fans had purchased shares in the franchise, guaranteeing good salaries for the players and bolstering community support for the team.

Oshkosh had dominated the regular season. Its 20–4 record was five games better than Fort Wayne's 15–9. But in the first game of the championship series in Fort Wayne, the Pistons played inspiring basketball. With the look of champions, the team thumped the heavily favored All-Stars, 61–43. "The Pistons were the hottest thing that has been seen on a local court for many a moon," the *Journal Gazette* proudly proclaimed. "They simply outclassed the mighty men from the north. . . . The Pistons flashed a brilliant brand of basketball, both individually and as a team. Everything they tried clicked beautifully. . . .

Every man who was in there worked his head off and contributed to the victory."

The two teams traveled to Wisconsin to continue the series. There the All-Stars showed their championship form by staving off the pesky Pistons in two hard-fought contests, the final a narrow 52–46 win for the NBL title. Although Oshkosh captured the championship, the young opponents raised many eyebrows among professional basketball fans.

When the United States entered the war, several of the NBL's top teams lost their best players to the military draft. Two teams, the Indianapolis Kautskys and the Akron Firestones, ceased operation at the conclusion of the 1941–42 season as the nation's young men marched off to war. But World War II had just the opposite effect on Zollner and his Pistons. Because he offered draft-deferred jobs in a company that served the military industry, he had a vast pool of basketball talent eager to work for his Fort Wayne corporation.

George Yardley, an all-American forward from Stanford University who went to the Pistons in the early 1950s, recalled Zollner's stature and importance in the young professional basketball industry: "He was, by far, the best owner to play for. His company was so successful, and that company was the financial backbone for our team. Therefore his team was the most stable in the league, and Fred paid the highest salaries in the league. So from a financial point of view, there was nobody better to play for." Dick Rosenthal, another former Piston standout in the 1950s, said: "I think Fred Zollner was the consummate professional team owner. He was a genuine fan of his basketball team. He had a very significant, important, and large piston manufacturing business that demanded most of his time and attention. Yet in the span I played with the club I can't remember Fred *not* attending the games. He was never too busy for his team. He was always there."

Hilliard Gates, who since 1935 had covered nearly 120 basketball games a season for radio station WOWO on both high school and collegiate levels, was a natural choice to cover the action for Fort Wayne's newest professional franchise. The *Journal Gazette* noted that Gates's "clear, accurate delivery has distinguished him among sports commentators" and promised that "WOWO listeners will be assured of complete game coverage." After the Pistons' inaugural season, Gates left the microphone to serve a 22-month stint in the Army. Upon his return in October 1944, he hooked up again with Zollner's club, and sportswriters from the *Journal Gazette* heralded the return of Fort Wayne's "glib-tongued, quick-eyed sports commentator."

Gates earned a reputation as "the Voice of the Pistons," building a strong friendship with Zollner. "I think Fred was a remarkable man," Gates said. "I liked him. He was always poised on winning. He wanted the best. Everything associated with his team had to be 'major league.'" Zollner designed the Pistons' logo himself. The big red, white, and blue "Z" was one of the most distinguishable monograms in the league. Inscribed within the bold "Z" were the words "Major League." It was more than a slogan. For Zollner, it was an attitude, a way of life.

Zollner bought a plane, dubbed "the Flying Z," and used it to transport the team. That was just one of the ways he set new standards for the professional game. Manager Bennett chuckled when he recalled the story: "The funny thing about the plane was that Fred was not a flyer. I mean, he was a real 'white-knuckler' when it came to flying. Early in 1952 we had a game in Rochester, New York, one night, then another game scheduled back in Fort Wayne right after that. So I asked Fred if we could charter a plane to get the team back quickly to rest for their second game. Fred said, 'Well, if that's what's best, let's do that.' Well, when Fred gets an idea in his mind, he wants to do it and do it *now*. So he called me into his office the next day and said, 'If we're going to fly in an airplane, we ought to fly our own. Where do you buy an airplane?' Can you believe it—just like that! 'Where do you buy an airplane?' . . . Well, the next thing I knew, Fred was on the phone with a guy on the West Coast and asked him how long it would take to get the plane. He told him, 'About ten days or so.' Fred said, 'We'll take it.' The guy must have fallen out of his chair. He said, 'Well, Mr. Zollner, wouldn't you like to at least come out and see the plane?' 'I don't know anything about planes,' Fred told him. 'You said it was good, didn't you? Well, that's good enough for me.'"

Zollner later had the DC-3 remodeled for the comfort of

his team. Improvements included such amenities as reclining easy chairs, a sofa, a bar, an expansive "picture window," and booster rockets to help lift the plane out of tiny airstrips. The sight of the "Flying Z" in visiting cities often filled the management of opposing clubs with anger and envy. Season after season, despite Zollner's generous nature with other teams, the league consistently arranged the worst schedules for the Pistons. League officials reasoned that the Pistons gained an unfair advantage on road trips, since their players were more rested. Zollner never complained.

Within his own organization, Zollner happily rewarded his players with the highest salaries in the league. Not only did he pay them good daily wages for work in the plant; he also collected profits from game receipts into one large kitty, and, at the end of the season, divided it equally among his players. Carl Bennett explained: "The rent for North Side gym was $175 a night. After that and other expenses were paid, the rest went into the kitty. I remember the first year, when we divided the kitty up, we gave each person $2,500, which was a pretty good chunk of change in those days. I think the players probably would have played for nothing. But the kitty was nice. And when we started winning, the kitty just got bigger and bigger."

Zollner's aspirations for a major-league business venture extended beyond his own Pistons franchise. As the National Basketball League struggled to survive during the war, professional team owners often could not afford to pay their league dues. To compensate for his fellow owners' shortcomings, Zollner contributed thousands of dollars to the NBL to keep the league alive. "He never wanted anyone to know how he helped keep the basketball league going," Carl Bennett stated. "He might help a particular team stay afloat for a period of time. Maybe he'd buy a player's contract for a large sum of money to help the other team meet its payroll. Or maybe he used his airplane to help transport *other* teams to games and cut down on their transportation costs. All this to say nothing of what he did for the community in Fort Wayne with his charity fund raisers and youth organizations."

Were it not for Zollner's deep and generous pockets, the entire professional basketball industry might have crumbled during the early 1940s. Zollner's investments in the league were heavy.

The dividend he reaped was owning a team that soon became the most dominant professional basketball club of the decade.

By the start of the 1942–43 season, the military draft had taken its toll on professional basketball. Indianapolis and Akron no longer fielded teams in the league. The Detroit Eagles franchise, managed by legendary New York Celtics star Dutch Dehnert, folded early in the season when every player on the roster was drafted. Overall, more than 50 percent of the players in the National Basketball League now served in the military. Once again, the league and the game were in jeopardy.

Sid Goldberg, manager of the Toledo Jim White Chevies, and Johnny Jordan, coach of the newly formed Chicago Studebakers franchise, independently came up with the same solution. Both decided to tap into the pool of available black players, and for the first time, appreciable numbers of African Americans joined the white professional league. Four years before Jackie Robinson signed with the Brooklyn Dodgers, the National Basketball League brought racial integration to the world of professional sports with no fuss and no fanfare. Racial integration was born out of simple necessity.

Goldberg welcomed four local African American stars to his Toledo franchise. Shannie Barnett, Al Price, Casey Jones, and Zane West beefed up Toledo's numbers on the bench. But even with the talented newcomers, Goldberg struggled to keep his troupe together as the draft continued to bleed his club of top talent. Scoring stars Chuck Chuckovits and Bob Gerber both left for military duty, as did reserves Jack Ozburn and Benny Schall. Many personnel changes in the early part of the season discombobulated the squad, and fan interest quickly dwindled. After losing the first four league contests, Goldberg disbanded his club.

The Chicago Studebakers, on the other hand, found tremendous success with integration. Coach Johnny Jordan recruited top players from both the Harlem Globetrotters and the New York Rens, including high-scoring Sonny Boswell and "Babe" Pressley, known as the "Cleveland Comet." Other talented African Americans, such as Duke Cumberland, Ted Strong, Roosevelt "Roosie" Hudson, Bernie Price, and Hillery Brown, also joined Chicago's National Basketball League franchise in 1942.

Chicago opened the 1942–43 season at Fort Wayne against the Pistons. The *Journal Gazette* noted that the visitors were "probably the most unusual team in pro or semipro basketball, being partly composed of colored and partly of white players. . . . The semi-dusky club from the Windy City is one of the fastest, best-conditioned and most-accurate shooting clubs in the country today." Before 3,500 fans at North Side gymnasium, the Studebakers put on an impressive display of teamwork and fancy ball handling to stun the locals by a final tally of 54–47. The *Journal Gazette* reported: "The little, speedy colored boys on the Chicago club seemed to be in great shape, and their tireless play and accurate shooting were the big factors in the Pistons' downfall, although the entire Chicago club looked good."

The loss to Chicago was one of the few defeats the Pistons suffered all year long. After a lackluster start of five wins and four losses, they exploded to win 12 of their last 14 league contests. The streak rocketed them to the top of the NBL standings at play-off time. Leading the Pistons to the regular-season crown was McDermott, who topped the league in scoring at 13.7 points per game.

The 1943 NBL tournament promised to be an intense competition. While Oshkosh battled Sheboygan in one first-round series, the Pistons and the Chicago Studebakers met at the North Side gym for the first game of their best-of-three match. Fort Wayne found its opponents still pesky and stubborn. It struggled to capture the first game of the series, but Chicago fought hard to win game two.

Early in the final contest, played at North Side, Fort Wayne fans had cause for concern when a Chicago player slammed into the Pistons' Herm Schaefer. The collision sent the Hoosier through the air and out of bounds. Unfortunately for Schaefer, additional seats had been placed near the floor to accommodate the overflow crowd, and his unexpected flight sent spectators sprawling as he smashed into the temporary seats. With blood streaming down his face, he boarded a police ambulance that rushed him to St. Joseph's Hospital for treatment.

Fans watched anxiously as the Pistons' lead shrank from 12 to six points in the final quarter. With only minutes remaining in the game a sudden cheer went up. Both teams looked up to see

Schaefer returning to the court. With a black eye that was nearly swollen shut and stitches above his left brow, the former Fort Wayne high school star showed his courage and thrilled the hometown crowd. He also gave the Pistons' attack added momentum. In the last four minutes of the game, Fort Wayne built its lead back to 12 points and coasted past Chicago, 44–32.

With the victory over Chicago, Zollner's players found themselves in the NBL finals for the second straight year. This time they faced the Sheboygan Redskins, a team that had accounted for four of the Pistons' six regular-season losses. The Redskins centered their game on a late-season acquisition, Harold "Buddy" Jeannette. Before the opening game, the *Journal Gazette* predicted that Jeannette would be "one of the Pistons' greatest worries in the playoffs." The paper's prediction proved to be true, as Jeannette and company overcame an early six-point deficit to defeat the hometown Pistons, 55–50. The *Journal Gazette* termed game two "a dogfight." The two squads battled to a 44-all tie at the end of regulation time. In the overtime session McDermott found the mark from long range to lead the Pistons to a thrilling 50–45 victory.

Ticket demand for the final game in Fort Wayne was so high that North Side officials deemed that all tickets, even the general admission seats in the balcony, must be sold at the reserved seat price. Surrounded by what the *Journal Gazette* called "3,500 slightly hysterical fans," the Pistons took the floor for the deciding game.

No more than four points separated Sheboygan and Fort Wayne during the contest. The *Journal Gazette* reported that the fourth quarter was "a hair-raising battle. Bobby McDermott began to find his range after three periods with only one field goal. His sniping from long range looked as if it would pull the game out of the fire. He tied the game at 23 and again at 28." In the final minute of play, "Curly" Armstrong stepped up to the free-throw line with the score tied at 28 and the fans in high excitement. Cool and emotionless, the Fort Wayne forward sank the free toss to give Zollner's club a one-point lead.

The scoreboard read Fort Wayne 29, Sheboygan 28, with ten seconds remaining on the clock. The Redskins had time for one last play. Their target was 6'7" center Ed Dancker. A half-court heave found Dancker open in the corner of the court. The big Sheboygan center let loose a sweeping, one-hand toss over his head. The ball banked off the backboard and through the net for the go-ahead basket. The ball hit the floor with a resounding thump. The final gun sounded. The scoreboard now read Sheboygan 30, Fort Wayne 29. Manager Carl Bennett called it "the most heartbreaking moment in my career with the Pistons."

One week after their devastating loss in the NBL championship, the Pistons entered the Chicago World Tournament and reached the semi-finals before losing to Oshkosh by one point. In the consolation game, Armstrong tallied nine points and earned most valuable player honors as the Pistons surged past Dayton for a 58–52 win and a third-place finish.

Over its first two seasons Fort Wayne had won more league games than any other professional team. But the Pistons had yet to win a national championship. Zollner proclaimed that he would do whatever it took to bring a professional basketball championship home to Fort Wayne, and he was true to his word. The following season, Zollner's team embarked on one of the most successful runs in professional basketball history.

As the United States entered its second full year of World War II, the entire professional sports industry nearly collapsed under military and political pressures. In February 1943, professional athletics fell under the scrutiny of the War Manpower Commission, a government body that determined whether certain occupations were essential to the war effort. If a job was deemed "nonessential," those workers were subject to the military draft. One year earlier President Roosevelt had stated that professional athletics, particularly professional baseball, was necessary for civilian morale. But in 1943 the WMC announced that while the game itself may be essential for morale, no single player could be deemed "essential." Professional baseball and football continued with plans for their upcoming seasons, even if many of the top players from each sport would not be in the starting lineup.

For Fred Zollner 1943 marked the beginning of a wartime dynasty for his Pistons franchise. But the team's explosive run started with more of a fizzle than a bang. After an opening victory against the East Coast champion Philadelphia SPHAs, the Pistons dropped four straight exhibition matches to the Washington, D.C., Bears, an aggregate of African American all-stars from the old New York Renaissance club. During the string of losses, Zollner was hit with more bad news. Paul "Curly" Armstrong and Herman Schaefer, two vital cogs in the Pistons scoring machine, received their draft notices and left for the Great Lakes Naval Station in Michigan. Gus Doerner, a promising 6'2" recruit from the University of Evansville, also received his orders from Uncle Sam. Zollner had to act quickly to find replacements.

With the help of floor guard McDermott, Zollner secured the services of two East Coast standouts, Chick Reiser and Buddy Jeannette. Reiser was a product of New York University. The *Journal Gazette* described him as "a small, driving player with plenty of hustle and one who should be popular with the fans." He had starred at point guard for Kate Smith's New York Celtics, a barnstorming group financed by the popular singer. He also had played with the Wilmington Bombers in an independent eastern defense plant league. Jeannette was considered by sportswriters to be Zollner's biggest coup since signing McDermott. Jeannette was a 5'11" point guard who had often burned the Pistons with impressive shooting displays when he played for the Sheboygan Redskins. The *Associated Press* called him "a catlike star, and, undoubtedly, one of the fastest players in the game." Jeannette and McDermott, now together in Fort Wayne, made the most formidable guard combination in the professional ranks.

With their newest recruits aboard, the Pistons marched on through a high-scoring assault of the National Basketball League. Jeannette finished sixth in the national scoring race with an 8.4 average. McDermott ended the season four spots above Jeannette. His 13.9 point average was second only to Mel Riebe of Cleveland. The fact that McDermott was even close to the scoring title was an astonishing fact, considering that he played most of the season in poor health. In January, X rays revealed that McDermott's appendix was dangerously close to rupturing. Physicians recommended surgery, complete with a lengthy recovery period. McDermott refused. He vowed to finish out the long season first. With a monitored diet and the supervision of trained team physicians, the Pistons' leader played through the pain to lead his team in scoring during the 1943–44 season.

McDermott and Company rolled into the 1944 NBL playoffs at the peak of their game. Interest in the playoffs was so high that the Office of War Information in Washington requested scores and statistics for weekly shortwave radio reports to U.S. soldiers overseas. The Pistons crushed their first-round opponents, the Cleveland Chase Brassmen, in two straight games by an average margin of 18 points. In the finals against their old rivals, the Sheboygan Redskins, the Pistons ripped the Wisconsin club in three straight contests to take the crown.

Zollner finally enjoyed his first national championship. McDermott and Jeannette earned first-team all-star honors. The Pistons' dominance in five straight tournament games inspired the *Philadelphia Inquirer* to write: "When it comes to long-distance shooting, Bobby McDermott is right in the limelight, with the rest [of the team] demonstrating clever passing and cutting. . . . Not since the days of the famous Celtics has a better team taken the floor than the Fort Wayne Pistons."

One week after earning the James Naismith Memorial trophy as champions of the NBL, the Pistons rolled into Chicago for the 1944 World Tournament. Before more than 14,000 fans, Zollner's club demonstrated its winning form by rolling over the Dayton Acme Aviators in the quarter-finals and the New York Rens in the semi-finals. In the final contest against the Brooklyn Eagles, Pistons center John Pelkington scored 19 points and McDermott totalled 14 as Fort Wayne coasted to its second straight postseason championship, 50–32. During the third quarter of the contest, referees stopped the game to announce that arena officials had voted McDermott the most valuable player of the tournament.

One week later the Pistons put the wraps on pro basketball's triple crown by winning a final exhibition over a team of NBL All-Stars, 45–39. NBL president Leo Fischer was on hand in Fort Wayne that night to congratulate the victors and present the championship trophy. Fort Wayne mayor Harry Baals gave a short speech at halftime that lauded the Pistons for their winning efforts. The *Journal Gazette* also sang their praises: "The Zollner club gave a dazzling exhibition of passing, play-making, and shooting, sweeping teams off their feet. . . . The local cagers demonstrated that they were the class of the league." Fred Zollner had achieved in basketball what he had achieved in business; both of his organizations were truly major league.

I just want to have fun. I don't need a job, but I need something to do to keep me out of trouble. I'm the luckiest man on earth, because I'm doing just what I really want to do.

—Ike Duffey, owner of the
Anderson Duffey Packers, in
Indianapolis Star, 1947

7. Wheeler-Dealer

With World War II raging on, six National Basketball League teams embarked on modest schedules as the 1944–45 season opened. For the Fort Wayne Pistons, the new season brought new challenges. By autumn 1944 Carlisle Towery and Dale Hamilton had joined other former Piston players in the lineup for the Allied forces. Pistons manager Carl Bennett had only eight players on his roster at the start of the season. And aging player-coach Paul Birch was doing much more coaching than playing. But even with limited numbers, the Pistons still played the best ball in the league.

On a five-game preseason eastern road trip, the Pistons faced some top squads, including the Wilmington Bombers, the American League champs, and the Philadelphia SPHAs. The Pistons went undefeated, led by their long-range scoring machine, Bobby McDermott, and backed by the steady floor leadership of Buddy

Jeannette, and the strong inside play of center John Pelkington. The *New York Journal*'s sports editor, Garry Schumacher, lauded the visitors: "Bold lettering on their dress uniforms proclaimed them champions of the world. Fans here found no reason to dispute the claim. . . . The addicts were deeply impressed with the evidence of the Fort Wayne team's class. The Hoosiers were compelling, as individuals and as a smoothly-functioning team. . . . What impressed the older pro observers about the Fort Wayne players was their grasp of defense tactics. That is what the coaches and the basketball purists look for, and what so few teams can show them. Fort Wayne met all the requirements, however."

The season brought two new franchises into the NBL fold: the Pittsburgh Raiders, sponsored by R. J. Corbett, sheriff of Allegheny County, as a promotional tool for his political campaign, and a Chicago team, sponsored by the American Gear Corporation. But the new franchises were no match for the mighty Pistons' scoring machine. In one early-season contest in Chicago, Fort Wayne defeated the American Gears, 73–64. The 137-point total was the highest to that date in a professional basketball contest. The loss left Chicago Coach Jack Tierney shaking his head in disbelief: "As a player and coach I never thought I'd see the day when a team could score 64 points and lose a ball game such as we did against the Pistons."

After an early loss to Oshkosh, Fred Zollner's Pistons ran off 14 straight victories to rocket to the top of the NBL standings. That streak was all Fort Wayne needed to secure its second straight regular-season title. It was the only team to finish the season above .500. Its 11–4 league record (20–4 overall) was four games better than second-place Sheboygan.

The Pistons reached the NBL finals for the third straight year. There they faced their old nemesis, the Sheboygan Redskins. The previous year Fort Wayne had manhandled Sheboygan in three consecutive games. But this time, the Pistons found the road to victory much rougher than before. Before two sellout crowds in Sheboygan, the Redskins handed Zollner's gang two straight defeats. After the second contest, manager Bennett told the *Fort Wayne Journal Gazette* that the improved play of the Redskins surprised him, but he noted that the Pistons were far from ready to concede the title. Within the friendly confines of the North Side gym, Fort Wayne bounced back into its championship form. Four Pistons players scored in double figures while holding Sheboygan's high-scoring big men, Mike Novak and Ed Dancker, to six and eight points respectively. The Pistons took game three, 58–47, then evened the series the following night, 58–41.

"The chips are on the line tonight at the North Side gym for both the Zollner Pistons and the Sheboygan Redskins," the *Journal Gazette* declared before game five. "Past games don't mean anything, except to leave them all even, just where they started. Only one game counts, and that is tonight's, when the National Basketball League playoff title will be decided." Despite a driving thunderstorm, fans flooded the gates of North Side gym to watch Bob McDermott and Buddy Jeannette rain baskets all over the Redskins. McDermott ended with 19 points and Jeannette added 10 more as the Pistons captured their second consecutive NBL crown, 59–49. The *Journal Gazette* reported: "The Pistons again showed their superiority over the Redskins in a game that followed pretty closely the pattern of the first two played on the local floor. They jumped away to an early lead, were threatened a couple of times along the way, and then finished breezing with plenty to spare." To add to the victory celebration, the NBL announced that Jeannette and McDermott had earned spots on the 1945 All-Pro team.

The victory was all the momentum the Pistons needed as they headed to the Chicago World Tournament the following week. After an opening round bye, Fort Wayne defeated Oshkosh by eleven points, then ripped the New York Rens, 68–45, to meet the Dayton Acme Aviators in the final game. The Pistons took charge early and never looked back. Jeannette, McDermott, John Pelkington, and Chick Reiser completely outclassed their opponents on both ends of the court. Fort Wayne walked off the floor with a decisive 78–52 victory and its second straight World Tournament title. Two days later the Pistons completed pro basketball's triple crown by downing an aggregate of NBL All-Stars for the second straight year, 59–47.

Over two seasons, Zollner's club had built a 43–9 record in league play, a 10–2 record in the NBL finals, a 6–0 record at the prestigious Chicago World's Tournament, and two straight wins over the NBL All-Stars. Carl Bennett recalled the mood of celebration in Fort Wayne: "When we got home from the Chicago World Tournament, the mayor proclaimed 'Zollner Piston Day.' There was a big city celebration where they introduced the players to the fans, and that sort of thing. They were heroes. Bob McDermott was as big in Fort Wayne in his day as Michael Jordan is today. It was that kind of an atmosphere and that kind of a time for sports in the city. It was a special way of life in Fort Wayne."

On September 1, 1945, at 7:00 P.M. Indiana time, Japan signed its formal surrender aboard the USS Missouri. The war was over. Soldiers came home to take their places again among the U.S. workforce. Athletes who were once members of the Allied forces returned to the ball fields, tracks, rings, and courts. As a result, the nation witnessed its largest sports boom since the 1920s.

The NBL immediately expanded from six to eight clubs for the 1945–46 season. One new entry was the Rochester Royals, owned and coached by Les Harrison. The previous year Rochester had been a strong independent barnstorming team. It featured top-shelf talent, including "the Blind Bomber" George Glamack, Bob Davies, an All-American guard from Seton Hall, Red Holzman, a long-range shooter from Community College of New York, and the multitalented Otto Graham, whose football exploits at Northwestern University overshadowed his extraordinary basketball skills. From their initial year in the league, the Royals were among the league's predominant competitors.

The 1945–46 season also marked the return of the Indianapolis Kautskys to big league basketball. Early in the season, owner Frank Kautsky and general manager Abe Goldsmith signed the old Celtics pro, Nat Hickey, to coach the club. In November, the *Indianapolis News* announced that Hickey was "counting on a shooting average of .300 and a tight man-for-man defense to keep the team in the thick of the National Professional Basketball League race this season. The Kautskys are practicing daily in preparation for the start of the season this week."

The postwar Kautskys were basically a loose aggregate of former high school talents from the Indianapolis area. The club offered some excellent players, most notably Jerry Steiner, a high-scoring guard from Butler University. But the rest of Kautsky's squad had difficulties competing in the pro circles. Indianapolis dropped nine of its first ten league games and settled into last place in the NBL standings. It did not take long for Hickey and Kautsky to realize they needed some major readjustments.

Luckily for Kautsky, the troops came marching home by mid-December. First to return to the court was Ernie Andres, the former Indiana University all-star who was home from his tour with the Navy. Ten days later, Bob Gerber, from Toledo University, traded his Navy blues for a Kautskys blue-and-white uniform. Hickey was still juggling lineups when Bob Dietz and Woody Norris, two Butler flashes, announced their return to the ball club. In short measure Kautsky, Goldsmith, and Hickey orchestrated a complete overhaul in personnel.

The grocer's biggest triumph of the new campaign came in January, when Kautsky inked a contract with former Ohio State University standout Arnie Risen. The 6'9" junior had been a dominant inside force in the Big Ten, and the 1945–46 season had promised to be his greatest. But poor grades prevented him from completing his third year with the Buckeyes. As soon as that became apparent, several professional coaches and team owners took great interest. Sheboygan coach Dutch Dehnert, a dominating center in his own right when he played for the Celtics, attempted to lure Risen to his Wisconsin club. But Kautsky and Goldsmith outbid him. Risen signed with the Kautskys.

Don Kautsky recalled: "My dad offered to pay Risen $75 a game. I thought to myself, 'My, goodness. Pop must have really lost his marbles. How's he going to pay someone that kind of money?' Reserve seats were only $1.50 in those days, balcony seats were 65 cents. We just didn't charge very much. I didn't know how we were going to afford to pay Arnie and keep the rest of the team on the payroll." But Risen's presence made an instant impact at the box office. At the time, the Kautskys sold game tickets over the counter at their grocery store. Seventeen-year-old Don, who ran the store while Frank managed the team, reported a $10,000 profit on Kautskys ticket sales after signing Risen.[1]

Risen's arrival came just in time for the Kautskys' heated rivalry with the current national champions and up-state rivals, the

Fort Wayne Pistons. But Fort Wayne's beefy front line of John Pelkington, Ed Sadowski, and Bob Kinney had a rude welcome in store for Kautsky's new recruit. The *Indianapolis News* described the rough style of play: "The application of the elbow and the knee . . . is done more precisely by the Zollners. This treatment proved disconcerting to Arnold Risen, six-foot-nine former Ohio State athlete, who was making his pro debut with Indianapolis. After the game, Risen wryly said he found pro players 'bigger and better and harder to move' than collegians."

Former Kautsky star Bob Dietz recalled: "Pelkington and Sadowski were about as tall as Risen, but they outweighed him by 100 pounds. By the second half, I think Arnie was running down the floor with his nose hanging about six inches above the ground. It wasn't pretty. Fort Wayne beat us, and Arnie learned quickly after that. He became a heckuva player for us." Risen managed only five points but still earned a tip of the hat from the league's leading scorer, McDermott. The fiery Fort Wayne guard noted that Risen "looked quite good for a pro rookie." Even though Indianapolis lost, Kautsky declared a victory at the gate. More than 4,000 spectators came to watch Risen's debut.

Coach Hickey continued to shuffle the lineup, looking for the right combination of players. The Kautskys were off to a dismal 3–15 start. But two upset wins in the latter part of the season gave Kautsky hope. The first was a four-point victory over the Pistons at an exhibition in Louisville. The second was a wild affair over the Rochester Royals, 47–36, a game in which an assistant manager for Rochester came to blows with the official timekeeper over a controversial call.

The Kautskys finished the season with a respectable 7–7 record to bring their season total to 10–22. Their late-season surge earned them an invitation to the Chicago World Tournament that March, but they dropped their first-round contest to a talented Michigan industrial league club, the Midland Dow Chemicals, 72–59.

Indianapolis News sports columnist Angelo Angelopolous saw great potential in the grocer's club and their new star. "The Indianapolis Kautsky basketball team," he penned, "apparently stood at the doorway to a brighter future. And one of the nicest things about the situation is having a fellow around who can look through the transom. The fellow is the aptly named Arnold Risen, who has risen until he's reached a height of five feet, twenty-one inches. . . . Risen, who left the Ohio State team recently because of ineligibility, has been learning while taking his lumps. There are happier assignments than for a young pivotman turning his back to wise old hands like Ed Dancker, Mike Novak, and Ed Sadowski."

In a postseason interview, Frank Kautsky gave a statement to the press that was part passion and part prophecy. "You can tell the fans this," he exclaimed to *Indianapolis Star* reporter Jack K. Overmyer. "Second place in the Western division isn't good enough. We're going to put back all the money we made, if not more, next season to get the players necessary to win the league championship and the world title." Overmyer continued the thought: "And judging from the boundless energy and enthusiasm with which [Kautsky] pursues that goal, you can be sure that he'll do everything possible to accomplish it."

In Fort Wayne the Zollner Pistons continued their winning ways. Big Ed Sadowski was with the club again after his debut during the playoffs the previous spring. Another big man, 6′6″ Bob Kinney, also joined the club for the 1945–46 campaign. When the two took the floor with big John Pelkington, the Pistons had one of the most formidable front lines in the league. Herm Schaefer, Paul "Curly" Armstrong, and Gus Doerner would soon be home from their military stints. And Buddy Jeannette and Bob McDermott led the offensive charge down court. As the season started, the Pistons were the preseason favorites to repeat again as National League champs.

A record crowd of 23,912 rolled into Chicago Stadium for the annual clash between the NBL's best and the College All-Stars. The Pistons seemed invincible after their recent string of victories. But a freak accident prior to the contest gave the team pause. En route by rail to Chicago, McDermott was walking from one car to the next when a breeze blew the door shut against his hand. The force pulled McDermott back through the window. Splintered glass gouged his arm. But the deep wounds had little effect on the Piston sharpshooter. He played as planned. With hand and arm heavily bandaged, McDermott poured in five baskets and three free throws to lead all scorers with 13 points, and the Pistons dismantled college basketball's best, 63–55.

As the season progressed, the nation's most successful pro franchise attracted plenty of attention from the fans. Carlisle Towery recalled: "The floor at the North Side gym was small, and I think the arena only held about 4,000 people. And it was full just about every ball game—exhibitions, as well as league games. People there really loved Armstrong and Schaefer, the two local boys. But especially after we got McDermott, that place would be packed full nearly every game. It was a great time to be in Fort Wayne."

On January 16, 1946, the Pistons achieved yet another milestone by defeating the Rochester Royals, 60–53, in a league tilt in Toronto. It was the first exhibition of professional basketball in Canada. For the first time more than 12,000 Canadians crowded Maple Leaf Gardens to watch an event other than a hockey match. "Most of them had never seen professional basketball before," manager Bennett chuckled. "They were all hockey fans. I'm not sure they knew exactly what they were watching. We'd make some spectacular plays, and they'd just sit there on their hands or clap politely. I've never heard 12,000 fans be so quiet before."

Two months later the Pistons faced Rochester in the semi-final round of the NBL playoffs. Fort Wayne was in familiar territory. But this time the league's newest franchise surprised the reigning NBL champs. The Royals rolled over the Pistons in two straight games. The final, a convincing 70–54 blowout, eliminated Fort Wayne from the playoffs. For the first time in three years, the Pistons did not compete in the NBL championship series.

For Zollner and crew, it was on to the Chicago World Tournament the following week. The previous season, the Pistons had become the first club ever to win back-to-back world championships. To win a third would solidify its place in professional basketball history. After the loss to Rochester, the Pistons were determined to have a strong showing in Chicago. Bennett, telling the *Fort Wayne Journal Gazette* that the team was exhausted after a long and arduous schedule and was not "at its top form" against Rochester, vowed that the team members would be back in full force by the time they reached the Windy City.

Bennett's comments were overshadowed by news coming out of Chicago that week. The American Gear Company, host of the tournament, announced just prior to the event that team president Maurice A. White had signed the college Player of the Year, 6'10" George Mikan from DePaul University in Chicago, to an unprecedented five-year, $60,000 contract. Mikan, who averaged 23 points a game in college, had never played a game in the pro ranks. Now he was the highest-paid player in all of professional basketball.

Mikan had been a hometown hit as the starting center for the Blue Demons, earning All-American honors three consecutive years. He led DePaul to the National Invitational Tournament championship in 1945 and had a tournament scoring average of 40 points a game. In one tournament game, Mikan racked up 53 points, a Madison Square Garden record.[2] By the time he finished his illustrious collegiate career, he was considered pro basketball's hottest recruit.

Naturally the hometown fans poured into Chicago Stadium in record numbers to catch a glimpse of Mikan and the Chicago Gears in action during the pro World Tournament. The lanky, bespectacled giant did not let them down. His deadly hook shot paced the team in scoring. He tallied 56 points in three games, more than 17 points per contest. Oshkosh finally squelched Chicago's momentum with a 72–66 victory in the tournament's semifinal round. But Mikan made an immediate and lasting impression on the world of professional basketball.

In the other half of the tournament bracket, Fort Wayne marched through familiar ground on its way to the championship game. Nearly 17,000 fans watched as the Pistons edged the Midland Dow Chemicals by three points in their first-round contest. Fort Wayne faced the Baltimore Bullets in the semi-final round. But before the two teams took the floor, attention turned to center court, where entertainer Martha Raye gave an impressive pregame performance. Then the Pistons put on a show of their own by knocking off the Bullets to reach the final round of the tournament.

Fort Wayne met Oshkosh in a best-of-three series to determine the world's champion. The Wisconsin team got the upper hand in game one with a narrow two-point victory, but the Zollners came back strong to take game two by nine points. The *Journal Gazette* critiqued: "The Pistons, after blowing the opener, came back fighting mad, mostly at themselves, because they will tell anyone they have the better ball club, although they have a deep respect for the other fellows. . . . The Pistons will probably have to do better work around the basket, both offensively and defensively, to win the third game and retain their title."

During game three Oshkosh's "Cowboy" Edwards, the Pistons' old nemesis, put on a remarkable 24-point shooting exhibition that kept the Fort Wayne defense on its heels. Fortunately for the Zollners, Bobby McDermott broke out of a late-season shooting slump to lead four Pistons players in double figures. Bob Reed, sports editor for the *Journal Gazette,* reported the final outcome: "For the third straight year, the Fort Wayne Zollner Pistons demonstrated that they were the world's best in professional basketball. They won the third and deciding game from the Oshkosh All-Stars, 73–57. With the chips on the line, the Fort Wayne ball club came through with the best game they have played all season. . . . From the spectator's viewpoint, it was undoubtedly the finest game of the tournament, with fine ball handling and shooting on the part of both clubs."

Tournament officials presented each Piston player with a gold watch. Fans from Fort Wayne who made the trip, more than 1,000 strong, cheered wildly and waved banners from the stands. As the exhausted but jovial squad posed for their championship photo, owner Fred Zollner crowded into the shot and smiled broadly. Bennett called it "Fred's finest moment with the Pistons."

In the fall of 1945 Howard S. "Gabby" Cronk, public relations director at the Anderson, Indiana, meat-processing plant owned by Isaac "Ike" Duffey, approached his boss with a promotional idea. He suggested that Duffey sponsor a semiprofessional basketball team in Anderson. The club would operate as a barnstorming unit and play other industrial teams in the state, as well as exhibitions against leading National Basketball League teams, such as the Indianapolis Kautskys and the Fort Wayne Pistons. Duffey agreed. In November 1945, the Anderson Chiefs took the floor as the city's first semiprofessional basketball team.

The new club owner was a big man. He stood 6′1″ and weighed 245 pounds. His personality matched his stature. His nephew Martin Duffey remembered the electric energy his uncle exuded: "Uncle Ike was always gregarious. He wasn't a family man per se. He had no children of his own. But he was a great uncle. He always had this big smile on his face. You could tell he really liked to be around people. He captured the activity of everything around him. Ike always had a head for business. He was a real salesman—a wheeler-dealer. He sure liked doing business."

As a young man Ike Duffey had helped his father, Isaiah, build a livestock business from scratch. Now at 38 years of age, Ike was a millionaire. He ran ten stockyards and owned two large meat-packing companies. In an *Indianapolis Star* profile, reporter Paul Janes quipped: "Hoosiers . . . like the type of blarney dished out by Duffey, and it's little wonder. He's a Hoosier himself, having been born and reared near Wabash, and he knows a thing or two about smooth salesmanship."

A member of Duffey's first squad was 6′3″ Ed Stanczak, a rough-and-tumble guard from Fort Wayne who had played with Zollner's amateur teams before World War II. He had honed his basketball skills at Fort Wayne Central Catholic High School, a two-time state and national champion, and built his strength at the Berghoff Brewery in Fort Wayne, where he hauled heavy oak-barrel kegs on the loading dock. He had also played on an independent basketball team in Marion, Indiana, sponsored by the Draper Brothers car dealership. "I got paid $25 a game," Stanczak recalled. "I thought that was big money back in those days. I only played there about a month when Gabby Cronk approached me. He told me that Mr. Ike Duffey was starting a team in Anderson. It impressed me because they were hoping to become a member of the NBL. And Duffey offered to pay me $100 a game. Well, that's all I needed to hear. I joined immediately."

Stanczak earned an early reputation as a bruiser on the court. He explained: "Some say I was overaggressive. I was just showing them that I wasn't going to be pushed around. There was even one time when a referee came over to me before the game started and blew the whistle at me. I said, 'What'd I do? I just walked onto the floor.' And he said, 'I just want to settle you down. I want you to know that I'm watching you.'"

The Anderson Chiefs were a competitive force on their midwestern barnstorming tour. Often they packed the 3,500-seat Anderson High School gymnasium, known to locals as "the Wigwam," the home of the Anderson Indians. Ike Duffey's nephew Martin recalled: "During the games, Uncle Ike would let me sit on the bench as the team's waterboy. I got to take the towels to the players, give them water, etc. The competition was always pretty fierce, especially when we'd play the Kautskys in Indianapolis or the Pistons in Fort Wayne. I remember that we sold out Butler Fieldhouse in Indianapolis when we'd play the Kautskys." Stanczak recalled: "That first year we played the Renaissance and the Globetrotters and other good touring teams. Ike would bring those clubs into the Wigwam, and the fans loved it. We routinely scored more than 100 points a game. Back then we were 'run-and-gun'—a real fast-break team. It was really something to see."

By the end of their inaugural season, the Chiefs had built an impressive 20–11 record against many top NBL squads. Their efforts earned them a spot at the Chicago World's Tournament. "We were a Cinderella team in the tournament," Stanczak said. "[The tournament] had all these big-name NBL teams and national touring teams. And we were this little team from Anderson, Indiana. Nobody'd ever heard of us."

In the first round of competition, Stanczak pummeled the NBL's Cleveland Allmen Transfers with 21 points as Duffey's team shocked the large Chicago crowd with a 59–46 victory. In the second round, the Chiefs were a decided underdog against a tough American League power, the Baltimore Bullets. More obstacles arose when a possible broken bone threatened to keep hot-shooting Stanczak on the sidelines. But Stanczak did manage to play. In fact, the gritty guard popped 11 points and dished out several assists to center Ed Lewinski, who scored 20 more for the Chiefs. With one minute to go, veteran Connie Mack Berry sank his first bucket of the night to bring the Chiefs within a single basket. But Baltimore's seasoned lineup successfully stalled out the remaining seconds to hold on for a 67–65 victory.

Through their strong performances in Chicago the underdog Chiefs proved to the basketball establishment and to Ike Duffey that a small-town team could compete on a national level.

Stanczak recalled: "I think after that tournament Mr. Duffey just wanted to keep getting better and better. So he started recruiting some big-name talent to come to Anderson to play. Basketball had become a very serious venture to him." That summer, at the NBL's annual organizational meeting in Chicago, Duffey bought the Pittsburgh Raiders franchise from R. J. Corbett. The wheeler-dealer from Indiana now owned the NBL's newest franchise—the Anderson Duffey Packers.

The 1946–47 season sparked a revolution in the world of professional basketball. The Midwest-based National Basketball League became a more stable business venture as the league expanded again. This time it welcomed new clubs from Toledo, Anderson, Syracuse, Detroit, and Buffalo. The Buffalo franchise relocated early in the season, when owner Leo Ferris reestablished his team in the Tri-Cities area that included three midwestern border towns: Rock Island and Moline, Illinois, and Waterloo, Iowa.

The league named a new commissioner in the summer of 1946: former Indianapolis Em-Roes star and Purdue University coach Ward "Piggy" Lambert. In 29 seasons with the Boilermakers, the fiery Lambert had led his troops to a record 11 Big Ten championships. A prepared statement by university president Frederick Hovde stated: "The administration has reluctantly agreed with [Lambert's] request to retire from an active and strenuous coaching duty, for his record stands next to none." At a Rotary Club luncheon in Fort Wayne shortly after he took office, Lambert outlined his plans for professional basketball's premier league: "My policy will be to insist on clean basketball, keeping unnecessary fouling to an absolute minimum, as I have instructed my officials to act accordingly. A majority of the players in the league are college-trained and know how to play the game with little fouling. . . . I believe that there are plenty of great [talents] out there and that professional basketball has a great future."

The NBL was going strong, and the nation's top attraction, George Mikan, was generating more spectator interest than ever in the game. But if Lambert sought to escape the "active and strenuous" environment he had known as a college coach, his move was a mistake. Shakeups began just after he took office.

That same summer several of the nation's top stadium owners convened out east. All were members of the Arena Managers Association of America. Most of these owners had major league hockey teams as their primary winter tenants. But there were many nights throughout the hockey season when their spacious arenas sat empty. For years Madison Square Garden in New York had enjoyed great success with college basketball double-headers. The games helped fill empty seats when no other major attractions were booked. Max Kase, sports editor for the *New York Journal-American,* along with Madison Square Garden owner Ned Irish and Walter Brown of Boston Garden, thought the time was right for a new professional basketball league.

The arena owners created a new organization, the Basketball Association of America, or BAA. Not since the initial days of the National League was there a more ambitious venture to establish a true nationwide professional circuit. Teams included the Washington Capitols, the Philadelphia Warriors, the New York Knickerbockers, the Toronto Huskies, the Boston Celtics, the Providence Steamrollers, the Chicago Stags, the St. Louis Bombers, the Cleveland Rebels, the Pittsburgh Ironmen, and the Detroit Falcons. The new league differed from the NBL in several of its rules. BAA teams played a 48-minute game of four 12-minute quarters, as opposed to the 40-minute game played in the NBL. The BAA also allowed players a sixth foul, one more than the NBL.

The owners chose as their president Maurice Podoloff, a 5′2″ fireball who was also president of the American Hockey League. The BAA absorbed many players from the East Coast–based American Basketball League, as well as military service teams and smaller eastern metropolitan leagues. The BAA's inaugural season tipped off that fall. But the real competition took place off court, where the NBL and the upstart BAA collided in an all-out player war.

At first, news of the new league did not alarm NBL officials. Fort Wayne Pistons manager Carl Bennett, in an interview with *Basketball Magazine,* stated: "We are not interested in a so-called war with the newly formed Basketball Association of America, and we are certain there are enough players to go around. We plan to operate together and in harmony, and perhaps even have a world basketball series between the two league champions, like they do in baseball." But already several NBL players had switched their alliance to the new BAA. Fort Wayne's Sadowski left Zollner's club to become player-coach of the Toronto Huskies. He brought with him Roy Hurley from the Indianapolis Kautskys. Oshkosh and Rochester also lost players to the new league. But the NBL still held the market on talent.

Lambert grew concerned over the unwieldy number of professional leagues that now existed. Just before the opening of the 1946–47 season, he invited each league president to join him in the formation of a new organization called the National Association of Professional Basketball Leagues. "Our aims are to promote and foster the introduction of professional league basketball throughout the United States and Canada," Lambert read from a prepared statement on October 21, 1946. "The organization will have a unified code of ethics, rules, eligibility requirements, protection of contractual rights of players and territorial limits." Joining Lambert were John O'Brien of the American League, Frank Basloe of the New York State League, Claude Davidson of the New England League, William Morgan of the Eastern League, and Robert Morris of the Pacific League. The new organization represented 52 teams in six leagues. Only one league president declined to participate—Maurice Podoloff of the BAA.

In the summer of 1946 Jackie Robinson broke the color barrier in baseball by signing with Branch Rickey's Brooklyn Dodgers club. Rickey, the innovator of the baseball farm system, sent Robinson to the Dodgers' farm club in Montreal for the 1946 season. One year later, Robinson was a member of the professional ranks. He took the field for the Dodgers on April 11, 1947. The news made national headlines.

Seven months before Robinson stepped to the plate for the Dodgers, Commissioner Lambert quietly ushered in a new era of racial integration in the National Basketball League when two African Americans debuted on the NBL hardwood in October 1946. The first was William "Dolly" King, an All-Scholastic honor student at Brooklyn's Alexander Hamilton High School, where he starred in baseball, football, and basketball. He had entered the semiprofessional basketball ranks as a forward for an eastern independent club, the Scranton Miners, then signed with

Lester Harrison and the NBL's Rochester Royals in the fall of 1946. The other was William "Pop" Gates, the New York Rens star. The same month King joined Rochester, Gates signed with Leo Ferris and the Tri-Cities Blackhawks.

"When Leo Ferris came to me, it was like a godsend," Gates said. "With the Rens I was playing one or two games a *night*. In the NBL, we only had to play one or two ball games a *week*, and I still got a nice paycheck. With Tri-Cities, the job was more stable, and there wasn't as much travel. So I was elated. Plus it was a real highlight in my career to be accepted by the NBL as one of only two blacks in the league. There really wasn't a big deal made about Dolly and me at the time. There really wasn't any of the publicity like when Jackie made the Dodgers. Baseball was just a much bigger sport at the time. Basketball was still up-and-coming. People had heard of us, but we didn't get the kind of ink in the press that Jackie got the following spring."

New challenges faced King and Gates as they embarked on their initial tour. Les Harrison recounted the difficulties King faced in his travels, particularly through the Hoosier state: "It was previously unheard of that a colored player be registered in a white hotel in Indianapolis, Fort Wayne, or Anderson. The only housing available for colored players at the time was at the colored YMCAs in those cities. The Claypool Hotel in Indianapolis would not serve Dolly King in the dining room, and the Royals showed true team camaraderie by also having room service for their meals."[3]

Gates recalled: "When I went to Tri-Cities I really didn't know what to expect. I had been prepared for resistance from my days with the Renaissance, but this was something different. . . . Fortunately I met very little resistance [on the floor]. I never received any resistance from our own ballplayers, and very little from other teams. I mean, there are always one or two guys out there who are going to object to what you are trying to do. But overall, most of the ballplayers we played against really respected us."

Racial integration may have been Lambert's greatest accomplishment in his tenure as NBL commissioner. Through the league's efforts and the initiative of owners like Leo Ferris and Les Harrison, professional basketball became a more representative American institution.

In Anderson, Ike Duffey geared up for his first season in the NBL. In August 1946, he appointed Murray Mendenhall to coach his squad. Mendenhall, the highly successful coach of Central High School in Fort Wayne, was widely respected around the state as "the dean of Hoosier high school basketball." He had graduated from DePauw University in Greencastle, Indiana, and played semiprofessional ball with a barnstorming troupe in Huntington, also in the Hoosier state. He was described in *Holiday* magazine as "a slim, jug-eared kid" who had a tremendous passion for the game.[4] "Mendy," as his friends called him, was a fast-breaking guard who was the nemesis of Homer Stonebraker and the great Fort Wayne Hoosiers during the 1920s. He coached Central High for 22 seasons and guided the Tigers to the state high school championship in 1943.

Although Mendenhall had never coached on the college or professional level, his appointment as head coach of the Packers was widely regarded as a grand coup for Duffey. The *Anderson Herald* commented in a banner article that the "signing of Coach Mendenhall as skipper of the Packers is received with wholehearted enthusiasm by local net followers and was another progressive step in Mr. Duffey's plan to give Anderson a contender for top honors in National pro circles."

One of Mendenhall's successful moves was signing two-sport sensation Howie Shultz. A graduate of Hamline University in Minnesota, the lanky, 6′6″ Shultz not only was an All-American basketball talent but also had played first base for the Brooklyn Dodgers. He had owned the first-base position with the club until the 1947 season, when Jackie Robinson took over. Branch Rickey had traded him to the Philadelphia Phillies, where he played one final season in the majors. Then he made basketball his sole vocation, as he melded into the run-and-gun style of Mendenhall's Packers.

"Murray was something else," Shultz recalled. "His theory was simple—outrun 'em and outgun 'em. Of course, a lot of the pro players thought that was the greatest way in the world to play. We really had a lot of fun playing for him. Murray was so excitable. We always kind of kidded him that he needed to get thick-soled, sponge-rubber shoes so that he wouldn't hurt himself when he was jumping up and down on the sidelines. He literally jumped and jumped like a kangaroo. It didn't matter whether it was a referee's call or a missed basket, or whatever. I can't remember how old Murray was at the time, maybe in his late forties. But his hair was totally gray. He looked much older than he was. I think coaching did that to him."

Holiday profiled the fiery Hoosier coach in an article on basketball's popularity in Indiana. "Mendenhall . . . is a silver-headed, hawk-faced athlete," the slick national magazine reported. "He is a quiet, bland man with an almost ministerial air away from the heat of the game, but when his fast-breaking [teams] begin to drive, he turns pure tiger."

Recruit Frankie Brian said Mendenhall "was a very emotional guy. He might not have been the wisest coach in professional basketball at the time, but he had so many other things going for him. He had the respect of every player on that team. Don't underestimate that. I mean, we all wanted to give him 110 percent on the floor every time. We'd run through brick walls for that guy. We probably beat a lot of teams we weren't supposed to, just because everybody wanted to play so hard for him." At 6′1″ with incredible speed and jumping ability, Brian was the perfect floor general for Mendenhall's fast-break attack. His aggressive, offensive-minded nature on the court, coupled with his broad Louisiana smile and friendly southern drawl, made him a crowd favorite in Anderson. "With Murray, it was Indiana basketball at its best," Brian mused. "Run and gun—lots of fast breaks. If we ever had the opportunity to fast break, we did it. And the fans loved it. Murray's biggest success was getting all of us to think alike. That's the true talent of a fast-break coach. . . . We were like a family. We really jelled, just like a machine. It was beautiful."

Mendenhall was an avid bridge player who demanded that all his players learn the intricacies and strategies of the card game. He often drew parallels between bridge and basketball. His theory was that to succeed in both, a player must be able to read his partner and anticipate many moves in advance. The card game also became a great way to pass the time on long road trips.

The Packers' recruiting stretched far south, where Mendenhall picked up not only Brian but also several stars from Texas, including Bob Kinney and Bill Closs from Rice University, Price Brookfield from West Texas State, East Texas's Bob Carpenter,

Jack Maddox from West Texas, John "Shotgun" Hargis, an All-American from the University of Texas, and Frank Gates from Sam Houston Teachers College.

In their NBL debut the Packers stormed out to an early 5-1 record. Their success packed the Wigwam. Howie Shultz recalled: "When the Packers came along, we really caught on right away. We became a pretty solid community project. And we drew well. The Wigwam might have held about 3,500 people, but there were probably about 4,000 people that would come out to our games. And those fans were so close to the floor. It was an intimate environment, and a tough place for opposing teams to come in and do well. The fans were very vocal." Ed Stanczak added: "I think our fast break offense created a real spirited atmosphere in there. We'd hit those 100-point games, and the fans would just love it. There was a real enthusiasm for it. The fans were so close that members of other teams would be taking the ball out of bounds, and the fans would get right up in their ears and yell 'Boo!' loudly. Make no mistake about it. Those fans loved their Packers."

Duffey's Midas touch, which he had cultivated in the business world, brought sudden success to the Packers. Stanczak's personal experiences with the boisterous team owner illustrate the shrewd business side that made Duffey a success. "Ike and I were close friends, and we both had the utmost respect for each other," Stanczak said. "But once the Chicago team called me to come play for them. At the time I was making $5,500 a season with Ike. I thought that was a pretty good salary, but I still went up to Chicago to hear what they had to say. They made me an offer of $6,000. So I came back to Ike to let him know about the offer in Chicago. Ike asked me, 'Do you want to go?' I just told him that Chicago was interested, and that they offered me $500 more a season. He asked me again, 'Do you want to go?' I said, 'I don't want to go. If you offer me the same amount, I'll stay.' And Ike said, 'Well, I'm not going to offer it to you.' And I asked him, 'You mean that $500 is going to make the difference between my staying or going?' And he said, 'If you want to put it that way, yes.' Then he told me, 'How do you think I got this money anyway?' I told him that I didn't realize he felt that way. He said, 'Ed, I'm a businessman, plain and simple.' So I thought about it, then told him that I'd stay in Anderson. He said, 'I'm glad I heard you say that. Now, if you prove yourself throughout the season, you'll get that extra $500.' And at the end of the year, I got it. That was Ike."

A mid-season slump hurt Duffey's club, and the team finished with a record of 24–20, two games shy of the 1947 playoffs. But Duffey was upbeat about the prospects for his newest business interest. "I am proud of our boys who have made remarkable progress during the past year," the jovial owner told an enthusiastic Kiwanis group in Anderson. "These players represent high types of men which will represent the Packers at all times. The team belongs to Anderson, and we feel we owe the city a great deal in being privileged to bring its fans major league basketball."

For the world-champion Zollner Pistons, the 1946–47 season would go down as one of the most pivotal and tempestuous in the club's history. Given the way the Zollners performed early in the season, no one could have predicted the impending storm. During their first seven league games player-coach Bobby McDermott and the Pistons machine cruised to a 6–1 record. Then the wheels came off. Fort Wayne dropped six of its next seven games. And in their annual preseason exhibition against the College All-Stars at Chicago Stadium, the Pistons let victory slip through their fingers in a heart-wrenching overtime loss. For the first time in the club's history, players harped on one another, fingered blame, and tore apart their team chemistry. Pistons publicity director Rodger Nelson termed the mood one of "simmering unrest in the ranks."[5]

Tensions came to a head on December 19. The Pistons had just completed a two-game swing to Rochester and Syracuse, losing both games. As the New York Central overnight train pulled out of the station, most of the players slumped into their seats for a long, sullen train ride back to Fort Wayne. McDermott sat over a few beers and stewed about the recent string of losses. When teammates Charlie Shipp and Milo Komenich, neither of whom had scored a single point in the Syracuse game, passed by him, McDermott confronted them on their lackluster performance. A fracas broke out.

Manager Carl Bennett recalled: "Curly Armstrong was in the room with those guys and noticed that McDermott was getting all over Komenich, because he made a couple errors during the game. Well, Bob probably had one-too-many beers, and so the two started pushing each other around. Well, the two of them kept arguing and pushing each other, and soon a fight broke out with those guys and Shipp. Curly ran back to the sleeper car where I was and got me out of bed. He yelled, 'Komenich and McDermott are going at each other!' So I ran back to their car, and Curly and I broke things up. The whole thing was a mess. McDermott had no right to handle his criticisms in that manner, with fists rather than discussions. When I got back home, I talked with Fred about it. We'd had some problems with McDermott's attitude in the past. He was very feisty. Well, Fred and I talked it over and decided to let McDermott go."

The *Rocket,* the Zollner company magazine, called it "one of the most sensational shakeups in the history of professional basketball."[6] All three players were suspended for insubordination. Zollner eventually reinstated Komenich but put McDermott and Shipp on the trading block. In a prepared statement to the press, Bennett explained that the Pistons' management "do[es] not wish to elaborate on the specifics of the insubordination, but I want to make it clear, however, that the move was not being made because of the team's losing streak, and also that it does not involve any violation of training rules or the playing condition of any of the men affected."

The day before Christmas, McDermott issued his own response in the *Fort Wayne Journal Gazette:* "In view of the events of the past few days, I feel free to make this statement. I have asked the club for my release, and they have agreed to give me my preference in selecting the team that I am to play with. There is no malice on my part, and I wish the Zollner organization continued success in sports. I am deeply grateful to the fans and to the friends I have made while playing in Fort Wayne." Ten days later, the Chicago American Gears signed McDermott as their new playing coach. Fort Wayne's "Mr. Basketball" was gone.

"The team didn't say much, because they didn't approve of Bob's actions," Bennett said. "But naturally the fans were upset. I mean, he was one of the greatest players on our team, as well as one of the top scorers in the league. It was certainly a lowlight in my career, because I always felt that my job wasn't so much to coach these guys as to work at player relations, to organize them, and to work with their personal relationships with each other. It was very disappointing."

The club persevered and finished the year at 25–19, a record that was good enough for second place in the NBL's eastern division. In the first round of the playoffs, the Pistons faced a new league entry, the Toledo Jeeps. The best-of-five series went the distance, with Fort Wayne taking the fifth and deciding contest at home. The Zollners lost to Rochester in the semi-finals, two games to one. To cap off the Pistons' gloomy season, the Toledo Jeeps forced Zollner's team to relinquish its three-year hold on the Chicago World Tournament with a 61–56 loss in the semi-final round.

One year earlier, Fred Zollner had stood at center court in Chicago Stadium and celebrated the Pistons' third consecutive world title. No doubt he had looked to the 1946–47 season with hope. Now the Fort Wayne manufacturer again gazed into the future. But this time he saw only question marks.

Since 1931 Frank Kautsky had fielded a professional basketball team in Indianapolis. He had built one of the most dominant forces on the midwestern circuit and was one of the founders of the National Basketball League. He had accomplished much, but not since his first amateur club captured the state tournament in 1931 had his team ever won a championship. But 1947 would finally be Frank Kautsky's year.

In the summer of 1946 business manager Abe Goldsmith retired, and Kautsky took on a new business partner, Paul Walk, a local radio personality, to handle the financial and promotional responsibilities of the team. Walk went to work immediately to secure several top players for the upcoming season. He signed new contracts with Arnie Risen, Bob Dietz, and Woody Norris, outstanding players from last season. Then he added several other Indiana luminaries, including Ernie Andres from Indiana University as the club's new player-coach, Herm Schaefer, the Fort Wayne Pistons veteran, Leo Klier from the University of Notre Dame, and Gus Doerner, an old Kautsky star from Evansville. This formidable combination inspired *Indianapolis News* sportswriter Angelo Angelopolous to pen: "With a new lease on life and the Butler Fieldhouse, a new bus, new faces, half-new management and an eighteen-piece band, the Indianapolis Kautskys will start their eleventh year in the National Professional Basketball League. . . . Kautsky's debut is one of promise. . . . At the moment it looks as if Frank Kautsky's nerves are going to have their quietest winter in years."

The Kautskys often attracted between 7,000 and 8,000 fans to Butler Fieldhouse for top league contests. What the multitudes saw pleased them greatly. Their team stormed to eight straight league victories and a spot atop the NBL's western division. Quarter-page advertisements in the *Indianapolis Star* hyped "the Fastest Basketball in the World," with the Kautskys featured in the first half of an NBL double-header or pitted against famed barnstorming clubs like the New York Renaissance. In January the temperature dipped to seven degrees above zero, yet crowds stood in long lines in the bitter cold to purchase tickets.

At the end of the successful season Kautsky's club prepared for what Angelopolous called "the playground for the pro cagers judged the finest in the land," the Chicago World's Tournament. The Kautskys had participated in the past eight World Championships but never advanced further than the first round. This season they drew a first-round bye.

Their first opponent was the Tri-Cities Blackhawks and their floor leader, William "Pop" Gates. "We always had great respect for Frank Kautsky and his teams," Gates recalled. "Those guys always gave us a good ball game. All those Indiana boys really knew the game. Even though we were competitors, it was a real treat to play against them." The Kautskys led throughout the tilt, but baskets by Gates and forward Mel Thurston brought the Blackhawks within two points late in the fourth quarter. Finally two nifty shots from Bob Dietz and another fielder from Herm Schaefer put the game out of reach for Tri-Cities. Indianapolis advanced to the semi-final round, 65–56.

Awaiting them were the Oshkosh All-Stars and their ageless all-star, Cowboy Edwards. Late in the NBL season, Oshkosh had slipped past Indianapolis to take the western division crown by a single game. But in Chicago that night, Frank Kautsky's men clearly were the better club. Schaefer was scintillating from the floor, where he popped 19 points. Teammate Risen added 10 more as Indianapolis charged into the final round with a dominating 59–38 win.

The final game was played on April 10, 1947, one day before Jackie Robinson first took the field for the Dodgers. The Toledo Jeeps was the only team standing between the Kautskys and the championship. The Jeeps were the surprise of the tournament—a young run-and-gun squad that upset the world-champion Zollner Pistons in their semi-final matchup. Indianapolis was a heavy favorite, but Toledo took charge of the tempo and the score early in the contest. The Jeeps led by one at the end of one quarter and trailed by only one at halftime. But in the third quarter, Kautsky forward Gus Doerner went to work. He hit on four consecutive shots to give Indianapolis a nine-point lead. For the moment Frank Kautsky stopped squirming in his seat. Toledo answered with a couple fast-break baskets, but Indianapolis responded like champions. The Kautskys never looked back. A balanced scoring attack by nine players gave Indianapolis the victory and the world title, 62–47.

More than 14,000 fans watched the victory celebration at midcourt. Doerner showed off the new gold watch he received from the tournament's sponsor, the *Chicago Herald American*. Leo Klier fired up a big black cigar. Ernie Andres boasted that he was getting a baseball jersey with the words "World Basketball Champions" emblazoned on the back so that Indianapolis Indians' fans along the third-base grandstand could read it when he reported to baseball training camp the following week. In a gleeful report in the *Indianapolis News,* Angelopolous quipped later: "The cynics who think professional athletes are incapable of pure joy at winning are hereby advised the Indianapolis Kautskys were the giddiest persons in Chicago's loop Thursday night. In a town that specialized in giddiness, that is an achievement."

Through the commotion, practically no one noticed Frank Kautsky. After 15 seasons in the professional ranks, he had finally brought a championship home to Indianapolis. As the flashbulbs popped and the crowd cheered, the pudgy team owner stood and watched the pandemonium that surrounded him, then broke down and cried. As he dried his tears he could utter only three words to the press: "God bless everybody."

This is the new National Basketball Association, the home of "big league" basketball. ... The men playing here are the best in all the world. ... When the evening's activity is over, the teams go to the locker room knowing they've given the fans their money's worth.

—From a 1950 promotional film,
The NBA: Big League Basketball

8. The Merger

In the summer of 1947 chaos broke out in the ranks of the National Basketball League. Maurice White, the unpredictable owner of the Chicago Gears, jumped ship and started his own midwestern professional circuit, the Professional Basketball League of America. The upstart league hosted 16 franchises from Chattanooga, Grand Rapids, Tulsa, Louisville, and other small cities. But most of these cities could not consistently support their teams at the gate. The league lasted only eight games, then folded. White lost $600,000 on the deal. His debacle forced him to sell off his players, including the highly celebrated George Mikan and player-coach Bobby McDermott.

McDermott went to Sheboygan. Another rising Chicago star,

George Ratkovicz, wound up in Anderson. The Minneapolis Lakers landed Mikan. For Lakers owner Max Winter, the contract with Mikan was the perfect foundation for a new basketball edifice he was engineering in Minnesota. That same summer, Winter also signed Fort Wayne Pistons standout Herm Schaefer and rookie Jim Pollard. Chicago's fiasco was the beginning of a dynasty for Minneapolis.

Meanwhile, in a press conference in New York, commissioner Maurice Podoloff commented on the inaugural year of the Basketball Association of America. "I have yet to hear a pessimistic note," he told reporters. "Some clubs did not do as good as they expected. Some did better." But when asked how the new league fared, Podoloff admitted a net loss of a half-million dollars. The BAA was in trouble. Despite the large venues and the promise of big-city dollars to support them, BAA owners could not keep professional basketball alive without top-shelf talent. NBL players like George Mikan attracted large crowds, sometimes as many as 10,000, in the smaller but more established NBL. By contrast, the BAA championship tournament averaged only 3,000 spectators. Podoloff bragged to the media that the BAA had recently acquired Joe Lapchick, the former Celtic, to coach the New York Knickerbockers. He stated that Lapchick's move was a sign of confidence in the new league. What Podoloff did not reveal was that the same day Lapchick joined the league, Providence coach Bob Morris resigned, as did coach Paul Birch in Pittsburgh. Podoloff knew that changes needed to be made quickly.

NBL commissioner Ward Lambert worked with the beleaguered Podoloff on an agreement that would prevent the two leagues from warring over players. "Our agreement," Lambert told United Press, "would . . . establish players in the leagues they are now in and prevent jumping around for higher bidders."[1] He also intimated that an eventual peace with the BAA might lead to a championship tournament between the leagues' top two teams. But one week after his announcement, Lambert was disturbed to hear of a "negotiation list" possessed by several BAA officials. One player on that list was Bob Davies, all-league forward for the NBL's Rochester Royals. Another was Don Otten, center of the Tri-Cities Blackhawks. Behind Lambert's back, the BAA's Boston

Celtics had courted the two NBL stars. Providence, Pittsburgh, and Philadelphia were also rumored to be calling on top NBL talent.

Player wars erupted between the two rival leagues. As the 1947–48 season got under way, the board rooms of professional basketball's top executives buzzed with activity as competing league teams sought to solidify new contracts with the game's top players. Both leagues vied for big-name drawing cards to attract greater fan support. But BAA owners found it difficult to entice NBL stars to jump leagues without proven stability and big-league dollars backing them. The players who did jump drained the limited pool of league funds. Podoloff had to find a more immediate solution to his problem. He called the Pistons' general manager, Carl Bennett, who was enjoying a rare evening at home.

For Bennett, the call was quite unexpected. "It was a call out of the blue," he said. "I knew that this was something that required some strong evaluation."

The next day Bennett had a clandestine meeting with Podoloff, who came in from New York. "Nobody knew Podoloff was in town," Bennett explained. "It was very secretive. We knew we couldn't talk about it, because he didn't want the press to know he was coming here. He wanted to come and talk to Fred [Zollner] and me and discuss how the two leagues could go forward together. Fred told me to evaluate the proposition, then come to him if the deal looked good."

Bennett added: "Podoloff told me that he knew [the NBL] had the key basketball players in the national circuit. He felt that the future of the game was in the big arenas. Podoloff knew that there were just four teams that were hanging in there financially in the NBL. He asked me, 'Would you consider getting these two leagues together? The BAA has seven, maybe eight, stable franchises. With your four, we could make a nice 12-team league.' He kept trying to sell me on the idea of the big arenas, saying that basketball has to grow, and we need to be prepared."

The next day, Bennett, Zollner, and Podoloff met in Bennett's living room for a day-long session to discuss the logistics of a proposed merger. "You couldn't meet in hotels about stuff like this. The media might get wind of it," Bennett stated. "The whole thing had to be pieced together with four NBL teams. We knew that Fort Wayne, Minneapolis, Rochester, and Indianapolis had to go together for the deal to work. Minneapolis was the real key. George Mikan was the biggest name in professional basketball. And Minneapolis had just picked up Mikan from Chicago."

Bennett successfully campaigned the teams one by one. "Minneapolis and Indianapolis were the first to come aboard," he stated. "Frank Kautsky's club wasn't as financially endowed as Minneapolis. But we knew Indianapolis was an important center for the game, revenue-wise and arena-wise [with Butler Fieldhouse]. Once those two signed, it was easy to get Rochester. They didn't want to be left with the rest of the old NBL teams. So they gladly came along. We knew that we had to keep the whole thing under our hat, because as soon as word hit about the merger, the other NBL teams would probably sue us. So the big question we tried to figure out was how to do this thing with the least amount of turmoil. After a short period of time, Podoloff called to tell me that he got the O. K. from the eight teams in his league. And our four teams were ready to make the move. So we decided to meet in Chicago at the end of the season."

On Monday, May 10, 1948, a historic meeting took place at the Morrison Hotel in downtown Chicago. Attending were Bennett from Fort Wayne, Kautsky and Paul Walk from Indianapolis, Les Harrison from Rochester, and Max Winter from Minneapolis. Representatives from the BAA included team owners Walter Brown from Boston, New York's Ned Irish, and Eddie Gottlieb from Philadelphia. In the center of the room stood a nervous little man in a dark suit and bow tie, BAA president Podoloff. The group convened at 10 in the morning. They did not break until well after midnight.

The *Chicago Sun-Times* was also there that day. After the exhaustive session, reporter Keith Brehm emerged with the group. The story broke the following day: "Professional basketball still had two leagues late Monday night, but there no longer were two of major classification. [The] Basketball Association of America, squaring away for the third season of its three-year experimental operation, Monday welcomed four former NBL teams—Rochester, Minneapolis, Indianapolis and Fort Wayne—into its fold, thereby effecting a 12-team circuit that stacks up as the strongest league ever organized in the pro cage sport."

As the news spread, *Indianapolis News* sports reporter Angelo Angelopolous noted: "Professional basketball . . . was feeling its way through the most important day in its history. The two major circuits were each holding their annual meetings, but by the end it was expected that one, the National League, would be decimated after eleven years of existence, and the other—the BAA—would be given the life blood it needed after two shaky, though promising, years of being. The acquisition [of Indianapolis, Minneapolis, Fort Wayne and Rochester] would be just what the BAA has needed and was looking for."

The merger capped a week of turmoil for the NBL. At its annual meeting, also held in Chicago, Lambert announced his resignation as league commissioner. His explanation was brief. He was stepping down "for health reasons." The National League also lost its president, Walk, when the Indianapolis Kautskys jumped leagues. And Bennett, a longtime executive committee member with the NBL, joined the BAA's new board of governors.

With no formal leadership in the NBL, the problem of the merger fell hard on the laps of Anderson's Ike Duffey and Tri-Cities owner Leo Ferris. On June 15, Duffey took over as NBL president. He, Leo Ferris, and other league executives chose as their new commissioner Doxie Moore, a former roundball star at Purdue University and the general manager of the NBL's Sheboygan Redskins. With their new officers hastily in place, the league prepared a formal statement regarding the events of the past week.

"There was some talk about the National League bringing a lot of lawsuits, but it isn't true," Doxie Moore assured the media. The team owners may have fully intended to sue the BAA and the four departing NBL teams, but the new commissioner gave no indication of bitter feelings on the part of the NBL. He urged peace between the NBL and the BAA. "The two leagues can operate side by side just as peacefully in the future as they have in the past," Moore continued. "There will be no war, no legal suits, and no contract jumping between the NBL and the Basketball Association of America."

But even as Moore spoke, the rival leagues were jockeying for the nation's top young talent. That very week, the BAA's Fort Wayne Pistons drafted Murray Wier, a University of Iowa graduate and most valuable player in the Big Ten. Then Wier revealed to Fort Wayne's Bennett that the NBL's Tri-Cities Blackhawks had already approached him. Bennett told the *Journal Gazette* that "if Wier has definitely signed a contract with [Tri-Cities], we will not disturb that status. It may be, however, that he has merely talked and negotiated with them, in which case we shall certainly do our best to get him for our club."

The dispute was a sign of impending conflicts that faced the NBL and the BAA. Both leagues feared that an all-out player war would escalate operating costs to astronomical proportions. Theoretically, new recruits would sit back as the bidding war began and wait to snatch the best offer. With both leagues struggling to keep their franchises stable and ticket prices low, officials in the NBL and the BAA knew that unbridled feuding would bring a quick end to both circuits. "Our fears came true when they threatened to sue us," Bennett recalled. "They said that the players signed NBL contracts, therefore they belonged to the NBL. We settled by agreeing that no one from either league would pirate the other's players. We would keep the two leagues separate. Well, that lasted all of about two months, then both leagues went after everyone they could get."

By June 1948 NBL commissioner Doxie Moore sent league president Ike Duffey to negotiate with the BAA in order to create a system of rules to prevent further warring. On July 30 Duffey went to New York to finalize the agreement with Podoloff. Podoloff's proposal was threefold: (1) each of the pro leagues will honor the other's reserve list (players on contract last season), (2) all players who have jumped from one league to the other will be returned, except player-coach Al Cervi of Syracuse (NBL) who shifted from Rochester (BAA), and (3) each league will honor the other's territorial rights for a period of one year (this prevented the NBL from creating a rival franchise in Indianapolis, which Duffey threatened to do). Podoloff not only hoped to harness the wild nature of the player wars, but he also thought his proposal might stem the tide of potential lawsuits by NBL team owners.

As the group wrapped up the last details of the meeting, Duffey stood up to leave with Podoloff's agreement in hand and proclaimed: "It's peace with honor." Podoloff turned to Bennett and other BAA officials and gave them a smile of confidence. The tentative agreement now seemed certain. But after the NBL president left the room, Bennett spotted a handwritten note on the table. It was from Ike Duffey—an intended telegram for Western Union. It read: "Members of the Executive Board, National Basketball League: No possible chance agreement with BAA—stop—Consider yourself free to operate as you see fit in contacting and signing any of their players—stop—Ike W. Duffey, President, NBL."[2]

"The two big pro basketball leagues, the Basketball Association of America and the National Basketball League, are on the outs again," the *Journal Gazette* announced the following day. "Maurice Podoloff, president of the BAA, and Ike Duffey, NBL prexy, issued statements today saying a two-day conference has resulted in a stalemate and that negotiations have been ended." Duffey declared to the press that the NBL and BAA faced "open warfare" with each other. Podoloff responded by calling the NBL a "minor league."

As the verbal battles played out, the threats of a player war became far more ominous than the reality of the situation. Since most clubs had solidified their rosters earlier in the year, only a handful of players actually jumped leagues. But with Minneapolis, Fort Wayne, Rochester, and Indianapolis now in the BAA, the two professional circuits took on a dramatically different look during the 1948–49 season.

The summer league wars in 1948 nearly overshadowed one of the biggest basketball stories to come out of Indiana that year. Trouble had been brewing in Indianapolis for nearly a year. Frank Kautsky's club had had a difficult time defending its reputation as world champs during the 1947–48 season, finishing the season 24–35, a woeful 18.5 games back of Minneapolis.

During the season, in a desperate move to raise fast cash, team manager Paul Walk had sold superstar Arnie Risen's contract to the Rochester Royals. The trade took away the Kautskys' most powerful scoring threat, as well as their foundation for the future. The news came as a surprising blow to Risen, who had been assured by Walk one week earlier that no trade was in the works. But after a successful performance against Rochester in Indianapolis, Walk called Risen into his office. The team manager looked up at the giant Kautsky center and said gruffly, "You now have a new home." He then excused himself, saying he had to make a long-distance phone call. Risen never saw him again.

Walk had never been successful in developing a rapport with the Kautskys players. Several former team members reported that immediately following the 1947 Chicago World's Championship, Walk had tried to deny the players their portion of the winnings, a sum Kautksy had promised them before the tournament began. Walk was in constant contract disputes with several players, including George Glamack, Herm Schaefer, Bill Closs, Leo Klier, and Risen. But the sale of Risen was the proverbial straw that broke the back of the franchise. "When [Waik] started selling everybody's contracts, it wasn't much fun anymore," Bob Dietz stated. "I knew that the time was coming for me and others to get out. It was too bad. I think if Frank had kept control of the team, we would have still been going strong."

The move deflated the morale of the team and incensed pro ball fans in Indianapolis. On several occasions, sports writer Angelopolous lambasted the Kautskys' front office in his weekly column. After the Risen deal he wrote: "The Indianapolis Kautsky management, Paul Walk executioner . . . that many times has broken faith with its ball players, yesterday broke faith with is fans. Often and long [the management] has said that they knew the heavy and faithful Indianapolis following deserved the best talent that money could buy. But in a tongue-and-cheek announcement, the Kautsky management told all listeners that the Kautskys sold Arnold Risen to Rochester 'for the betterment of the team.' . . . There stands a quote full of fallacies. . . . Risen was brought up here in pro ball. His leaving in his third year deprives Indianapolis of one of the nicest guys in athletics. . . . If Walk and Kautsky are wrecking the team to get fat prices for their high-salaried players and then maybe sell the franchise too, they don't deserve this fan." Angelopolous went on to describe Walk's recent moves as "baloney" and declared Kautsky "a puppet partner."

Owner Kautsky, who had always run his clubs on passion and ethics, now found the pressures of managing a professional basketball team too great. "My dad was always a fine gentleman," Don Kautsky recalled. "He always tried to be fair and honest with his players. . . . But he was getting older, and the time was coming for him to step down. He told me once, 'The game's getting too fast for me.' He meant financially. Then he said, 'It's time to get out.' I think it killed him to do it, because he loved the game and the players so much."

In July 1948 Kautsky and Walk sold the contract of the popular, high-scoring forward Klier to the Pistons. Then, on July 21, Kautsky sold his interest in the club to Walk. The following day Kautsky announced to reporters that he and Walk "could not see eye-to-eye on team matters" and said that their disagreements were the impetus for resigning from the pro game. "If you can't agree, it's time to break up," he muttered.

Kautsky's legacy was profound. His independent squad started in 1928 and took the state independent amateur title its first year. In the professional ranks Kautsky organized the National Basketball League in 1932 and the Midwest Basketball Conference in 1935. His efforts helped establish professional basketball as a dynamic institution during some of the game's darkest economic days. Kautsky shaped policy and structure in the NBL. He brought the game to one of the nation's premier venues, Butler Fieldhouse, and created mass appeal for the game throughout the Midwest. In 11 years the grocer from Indianapolis created an impressive athletic institution that had a significant influence on both the state and the nation. The *Indianapolis News* called him "the pioneer of pro basketball in Indiana." Now the team had to carry on without their longtime owner, cheerleader, and friend.

Sole owner Walk went to work immediately. He promoted Bruce Hale, the Kautskys' playing coach the previous season, to general manager and playing coach. He also needed a new name for the team. The club's new affiliation with the BAA required it to take a nickname other than the name of an owner or coach. Walk decided to hold a contest and let the fans name the club, hoping the contest would create excitement for his new BAA franchise and promote spectator participation. By mid-September the team had acquired three new players and a new handle, the Indianapolis Jets.

Walk's Jets kicked off their new BAA campaign with great promise. More than 7,200 fans poured into Butler Fieldhouse for the team's opening game against the St. Louis Bombers. As a promotional stunt, the club offered orchids to the first 3,000 women who walked through the gates. On hand for the occasion was BAA commissioner Podoloff, who sat and watched as his grand summer coup now played out before him.

Near the end of the contest, with Indianapolis leading by only two points, Hale drove toward the basket against Johnny Logan, the Bombers forward. "Johnny Logan on the floor probably wasn't wearing any more surprised a look than were some of the citizens in the seats," Angelopolous commented in his *Indianapolis News* column the following day. "Logan was chasing Bruce Hale down the floor, and Hale, who on a good night can talk to backboards, let fly a back-bending left-hand hook shot that went in. Logan wouldn't have been any more startled if Bruce's head had fallen off and rolled across the floor." His shot lifted Indianapolis to its first victory in the BAA, 84–80.

Initially, it appeared as though Walk had weathered the storm. Spectator interest was still high, and even skeptical sportswriters like Angelopolous seemingly enthused over the Jets and their prospects in the BAA. The DeSoto car company even featured Jets players in giant advertisements in the Indianapolis press. Each ad saluted the Jets Player of the Week, complete with a photo and background information on each team member. Underscoring the Player of the Week highlights were the names of several local auto dealers who offered "high grade used cars and top quality service."

But things turned south quickly for the Jets. The club won only two of its next 15 games and dropped to last place in the BAA's western division. In a scathing editorial on December 7, Angelopolous attacked the front office of the Indianapolis franchise: "None of the Jet fans, those who still bother to go to the Butler Fieldhouse, never have asked that the Indianapolis team be perfect, but from their recent comments a lot of fans are thoroughly disgruntled. . . . The reaction to the Jets reached a peak last Tuesday night when Ft. Wayne ran away from Indianapolis, and many a fan walked out of the Fieldhouse making audible comments, the nicest of which was 'That's terrible.'" The 77–62 loss to Fort Wayne was a telling sign that spectator support for Walk and the Jets was dwindling fast. Another sign came before the contest during the introduction of the starting lineups, when Fort

Wayne's Klier, the former Indianapolis star, took the floor to a standing ovation. The fans' reaction was in direct protest of Walk's decision to sell the popular player's contract to Fort Wayne earlier that year. To add further insult, the fans continued to cheer wildly for Klier each time he scored against Indianapolis.

Game after game the fans spoke out. Some sat behind the Jets' bench and emphatically screamed their disapproval of coach Hale. "What's going on?" asked one angry group of spectators who traveled south from Zionsville to see one game. "I'm going to quit coming," a waitress said disgustedly. One member of the Indianapolis Junior Chamber of Commerce snapped, "Walk is ruining basketball." Homemade banners posted at Butler Fieldhouse echoed the thoughts of many spectators: "Run Walk to the nearest exit!" In a game against Washington, fewer than 3,000 spectators came to the fieldhouse to watch Indianapolis defeat the Capitols. Walk lost nearly $2,000 on the game. The Associated Press inferred that the team was ready to fold. "I'm not a rich man," Walk told reporters. "And I can't keep taking it on the chin week after week."

Soon more troubles plagued Walk. A seedy element began to ooze its way into Butler Fieldhouse. The *Indianapolis News* reported: "[A] crowd of gamblers—petty and otherwise—grows with each game at the southeast corner of the Fieldhouse floor. More and more fans are objecting to the 'carnival atmosphere' surrounding the Jet games."

The BAA sensed that financially the Jets were a sinking ship. So the league sent Podoloff to address the recent developments with Walk's club. The BAA commissioner showed concern over a pressing issue in Indianapolis. For two weeks rumors had abounded that Walk was seeking to get out from under the tremendous financial burden. The *News* announced on February 3 that Walk had made overtures to Anderson's Ike Duffey to sell his franchise to the NBL president. Duffey had shown immediate interest. The Anderson millionaire described Indianapolis as "one of the best professional basketball towns in the country." While Walk emphatically denied the conversations with Duffey, he readily admitted that the club was losing money rapidly. He explained that the Jets needed to average more than 4,000 fans per game just to break even (a number they achieved only nine times that season). Podoloff fretted over the fact that his rival Duffey might actually buy out one of his BAA franchises. While he did not name Duffey, Podoloff snarled as he told reporters that "someone is trying to muscle-in and buy the club. . . . The BAA will not permit Indianapolis to suspend operations this season and, if necessary, will put money into the proposition."

But even Podoloff's iron will did not save the Indianapolis Jets. The club finished the season a woeful 18–42, dead last in the league. Its final game of the season at Butler Fieldhouse was a pitiful microcosm of their entire frustrating season. The *Indianapolis News* reported: "Continual yipping went on between coaches and players, with a goodly supply of swearing easily audible to the less than 1,000 fans present." The officials called seven personal fouls in the first minute and 40 seconds of the contest. The frustration level rose so high that one player even threw the ball at umpire Frank Scanlon and popped him in the face. Midway through the contest, new interim coach Burl Friddle left the bench and charged the stands to challenge an unrelenting heckler. The season finale was pure pandemonium. At the conclusion of the game, Walk turned on his heel and stormed off the court. It was his exit not only from the gym but also from the game. He and his Indianapolis Jets never returned to the ranks of professional basketball.

In the National Basketball League, Commissioner Doxie Moore and President Ike Duffey needed to act fast to replenish the vacancies created by the departure of Indianapolis, Fort Wayne, Minneapolis, and Rochester. They quickly established four new franchises in Hammond, Indiana; Waterloo, Iowa; Denver; and Detroit. The new clubs filled out a nine-team league with the NBL's old guard: Anderson, Syracuse, Tri-Cities, Sheboygan, and Oshkosh.

Instability was a hallmark of the NBL's 1948–49 schedule. The season was not a month old when news came that the Detroit franchise had folded under financial pressures. Moore and Duffey looked to fill the slot quickly, and in doing so helped the NBL achieve another milestone in sports history. On December 18,

Duffey offered the vacant franchise to the New York Renaissance. It was the first time professional basketball executives had allowed an all-black team to play as a unit in the lily-white professional leagues.

Duffey designated a slot for the team in Dayton, and the Dayton Rens debuted in mid-December as a member of the NBL's eastern division. William "Pop" Gates, back with the Rens after a successful season at Tri-Cities, coached the squad. Veteran Johnny Isaacs and former Harlem Globetrotters standout Sonny Wood were two top veterans for the NBL's newest entry. The club also featured the talents of George Crowe, a Franklin, Indiana, high school star who, in 1939, had earned the coveted title as the state's first "Mr. Basketball."

The NBL franchise in Hammond was the result of a careful orchestration by Duffey and some passionate basketball fans in the Calumet region of northwestern Indiana. During the summer of 1948 Duffey had seen that the NBL's Toledo Jeeps franchise was in serious financial straits. So the Anderson millionaire had bought the franchise, including every player's contract and draft rights. He then promised to transfer the team to Hammond if the city could muster the funds to support an NBL club. He approached Walter H. Thornton, a local businessman, with his proposition. Wally Thornton went to work immediately to organize a group of civic leaders from Region cities, including Hammond, Whiting, Calumet, and East Chicago. They in turn formed a corporation known as the Calumet Fans, Inc. The company went public on August 11, 1948 as 200 fans bought single shares of the new community team at $100 per share. They secured the 6,000-seat Hammond Civic Center for their home games and bought an NBL franchise for the city. A local jeweler donated a $100 gold wrist watch to the organization as a prize for the lucky citizen who won an areawide contest to name the squad. Joe Myers, Jr., was the winner with "Buccaneers."

The team featured NBL veteran Bob Carpenter as player-coach. Former Notre Dame scoring sensation George Sobek signed to play forward with the club, as did Clint Wager, a 6'5" rebounder. When Detroit folded 19 games into the season, Hammond also picked up the contracts of John Sebastian and Ollie Shoaf.

"Things were sort of iffy when we first started in Hammond," Shoaf laughed. "I guess you could say we were kinda like pioneers there. But the fans really supported our initial efforts."

Just as Calumet Fans, Inc., wrapped up its successful campaign for basketball funding, President Harry S. Truman's whistle-stop campaign tour chugged into the Region. With less than a month until the national election and Truman far behind Republican Thomas Dewey in the polls, the president delivered an impassioned speech to Lake County Democrats and encouraged them to "not give up the fight." Thousands crowded city streets to greet the president as basketball took a back seat to politics.

On November 3, Truman claimed an upset victory. So did the Hammond/Calumet Buccaneers. In their first NBL contest, the Bucs triumphed 58–39 over the Denver Nuggets. "Great first-nighters, the Calumet Buccaneers!" exclaimed the *Hammond Times* the following day. "They thrilled 3,500 opening game fans last night in the Civic Center with a smashing victory over the Denver Nuggets. . . . As they trekked smilingly to the showers, Coach Bob Carpenter and his fellow Buccaneers promised to make it two straight in their next contest."

Spectators throughout the Region came out to support their community-owned team. One section of the bleachers was reserved for the Little Bucs, a youth club whose members dressed as pirates for each home game. Also decked out in elaborate apparel were the Buccaneer Usherettes, eight scantly clad female cheerleaders who wore outfits that made them look as if they had just stepped off Treasure Island. Area high school bands also performed and added to the Civic Center festivities.

Early on, manager Thornton engaged in some player switching. Ollie Shoaf explained: "Players in the league really didn't have any loyalties in those days. You jumped around quite a bit, depending on who was paying you more. And teams didn't necessarily have loyalties to you, either. I remember one morning I woke up and grabbed the morning paper and read where I had been traded to Tri-Cities. Well, nobody in Hammond ever said anything to me. Of course, all the teams were grasping at straws in order to survive. They probably needed to sell my contract to get enough money to keep going. I recall just shrugging my shoulders and telling my wife that we'd better get packing. We were heading for Tri-Cities."

Shoaf did not end up in Tri-Cities, however. Instead, Thornton cut a deal to keep him in the Hammond backcourt with a new running mate, Bobby McDermott. "I was just a 'blue-collar worker' in the backcourt. McDermott was the real scorer," Shoaf said. The *Hammond Times* heralded McDermott's return to Indiana's professional hardwood: "Bobby McDermott, ageless, fearless, stormy petrel of many a professional cage brawl, today was signed to finish the season with the Calumet Buccaneers. . . . The fiery McDermott will add experience, competitive courage, and more importantly, basketball's greatest two-hand shot, to the Buccaneer offense. 'I'll give you everything I've got,' McDermott told [Manager] Thornton. 'I look forward to an opportunity to help the Buccaneers get into the National League playoffs.' "

The Buccaneers struggled through the remainder of their season. They finished the year 21–41, a record good enough, surprisingly, to earn them a spot in the first round of the playoffs. In a best-of-three series against Syracuse, the New Yorkers completely outclassed Hammond. In game one, Dolph Shayes and Al Cervi rained baskets all over the Buccaneer defense and dampened the enthusiasm of the overflow crowd at the Hammond Civic Center. The Nationals prevailed over the Buccaneers, 80–69. The next night in Syracuse, Shoaf's heroic 16-point effort was not enough to save Hammond from elimination as the Nationals marched to the NBL semi-finals, 72–66.

Awaiting Syracuse in the next round was the Anderson Packers. Coach Mendenhall's men were running and gunning their way through the league at an alarming rate. Their average of 72.1 points per game was nearly six points higher than second-place Syracuse. Mendenhall's rapid-fire style of play reaped great dividends. The squad won 76 percent of its games and finished the season nine games better than the rest of the league. Its 49 wins were nearly as many victories as Hammond, Dayton, Denver, and Waterloo had combined. In the semi-finals against Syracuse, Duffey's crew quickly disposed of the Nationals, three games to one.

In the championship series, Anderson's high-revving, offensive-minded machine faced a much slower Oshkosh club that had lost many top talents earlier in the season owing to financial straits. But owner Lon Darling's outmanned club fought valiantly against Brian, Shultz, Stanczak, and the rest of the Packers. Anderson won game one in Oshkosh, 74–70, then eked out a two-point victory the following evening. With Anderson up by two games in the best-of-five series, both teams headed to Indiana. "You just can't imagine the atmosphere around the town at that time," Brian recalled. "You couldn't ask for any better fans than we had. Wherever we'd go, they'd be patting us on the back and rooting us on. The momentum there was so great. When we came back to Anderson [for that final game], it was really special." The fan support must have motivated Brian, who found the mark on several long-range fielders and ended the game with 17 points. Ralph "Boag" Johnson, a Packer guard, added 13 more. Anderson conquered Oshkosh, 68–64, to claim the 1949 National Basketball League championship. "Everybody was very excited," Shultz recalled. "The city was thrilled. We were like heroes."

As president of the league, Duffey found it awkward to present the championship trophy to his own team. Instead, Shultz and forward Milo Komenich gladly marched the towering trophy over to Coach Mendenhall. An awards ceremony commenced. League commissioner Moore took the microphone to express his congratulations to Duffey's squad. "This is the greatest ball club I have ever seen," he exclaimed. The celebration continued. The owner of Sauter Shoe Store in Anderson presented each player with a new pair of Bostonians. Several members of the Packers front office, including the business manager and the ticket manager, took turns at the microphone to heap praise on the new NBL champs. The evening ended on a touching note. Isaiah Duffey, Ike's father, stepped to the makeshift podium at center court to congratulate his son for bringing a championship home to Anderson. "Our championship was a championship for the little guys, the little towns," Brian stated proudly. "After those teams moved from our league that year, I think it was important for us to win and show that a small town could produce a champion. Winning was special, but winning in Anderson was very special."

The National Basketball League went back to work during the off-season to secure new franchises for the coming year. Moore and Duffey got more aggressive in their fight against the BAA. They studied the possibility of having 11 new franchises in cities such as Baltimore, Milwaukee, Louisville, Cincinnati, and Des Moines. They also campaigned heavily to establish new squads in Rochester and Indianapolis, two BAA strongholds. Moore boldly told the media, "The NBL is definitely on the upgrade." But the truth was that several of the league's most stable franchises were tired of struggling with a circuit on the economic outs. At least three team owners—Magnus Brinkman, the cheese magnate who ran the Sheboygan Redskins club; Leo Ferris, top man at Tri-Cities; and even Ike Duffey in Anderson—made overtures to the BAA for a merger in the summer of 1949.

"Ike really kept the NBL going there for a while," Stanczak recalled. "He put up money for many of those clubs like Oshkosh, Hammond, Sheboygan, and others to keep them going. That was certainly one of his biggest contributions to the league. . . . Ike always had a tax man that walked around with him. And he just kept watching the money go out and out and out. Eventually the 'front money' was running out, and Ike got tired of carrying some of these clubs."

Fort Wayne manager and BAA executive committee member Bennett said "the NBL clubs were running out of steam. They were in the midst of suing us at that time. Podoloff knew that they were barely hanging on financially, and they probably wouldn't make it in the BAA." To end the litigation, Podoloff agreed to take them all in. "Just like that, no more lawsuits," Bennett said. "I think Podoloff thought that he'd rather do it this way than continue fighting in the courts."

On August 3 Duffey and Ferris traveled to New York to finalize the merger. Flanked by Ned Irish and Walter Brown of the BAA's executive committee, Podoloff was all smiles at the bargaining table. In a tip of the hat to the NBL, Podoloff named Duffey to chair the new league's executive board and awarded Ferris a spot on the executive committee. The following day the *Indianapolis Star* reported: "Professional basketball's costly three-year war came to an end yesterday in the biggest post-war merger involving sports enterprises—the joining forces of the Basketball Association of America and the National Basketball League. . . . The new loop will be known as the National Basketball Association."

"It was wild—unwieldy," Bennett recalled. "We now had 17 teams in the league. Some divisions had six teams, others had five. There were a lot of weird schedules. We didn't even play the same number of games that season. But Podoloff knew that this strategy was the perfect way to solve a long-term problem in a very short time."

During the past two decades I have covered more than 2,000 basketball games.... All that time I've wanted to see just one team on which every player was recognized as a star of national magnitude. Alex Groza, Wallace Jones, Ralph Beard, Joe Holland, and Clifford Barker showed me that team.... Never before in the history of modern day sports has a cooperative team proved so successful.

—Indianapolis radio announcer
Luke Walton, in *The Fabulous Five:*
The Indianapolis Olympians

9. In the Tall Cotton

One month before the National Basketball League teams made their big jump to the new National Basketball Association, the faltering league made a business deal that had far-reaching influence on the new NBA. It was perhaps the biggest coup in the old circuit's history. In the summer of 1949, four of the starting five players from the University of Kentucky team that had dominated the National Collegiate Athletic Association tournament for the second consecutive year and captured the gold medal at the 1948 London Olympics made a deal with the league and the city of Indianapolis that was unprecedented in the history of professional basketball. The players joined the league as a unit, formed their own team, and bought ownership rights to their own franchise, the Indianapolis Olympians.

NBL vice-president Leo Ferris explained the deal to the local media. The NBL and the city had agreed to loan the University of Kentucky players $30,000 as working capital to start their franchise. The players were to be the majority shareholders in the club, with a minority business interest available for several top bidders in the city. Ferris told the *Indianapolis Star* that "the players picked Indianapolis over two other cities as a 'home,' because they are convinced that the Hoosier capital has the greatest basketball possibilities."

One of the five was Ralph Beard, Jr., of Hardinsburg, Kentucky, whose grandfather, Marvin Beard, had been a baseball and track luminary at Vanderbilt University and whose father was a golf professional and pro baseball player for a team in Evansville, Indiana. Ralph was the typical all-American boy with a real passion for basketball whose dedication and hard work paid off. He was named to Kentucky's All-State high school team his junior and senior years and led Male High to the state championship in 1945.

At the University of Kentucky his coach was Adolph Rupp, a stormy pit-bull type who demanded nothing less than perfection from his players. Kentucky fans revered him as "the Baron of the Bluegrass." A student of the game under University of Kansas coaching legend Phog Allen, Rupp had taken over the helm at Kentucky in 1930. A brilliant strategist, he guided his Kentucky Wildcats to one winning season after another.

Beard and Rupp were perfect for each other. Rupp demanded precise execution on the floor and maximum effort at all times. Beard supplied both. Former Beard teammate Cliff Barker recalled: "Ralph wasn't very big. But he was a 100 percent player, a 110 percent player, all the time. He could run. He could shoot. Ralph was one helluva player, period." Leo Barnhorst, former professional teammate of Beard's, recalled: "Ralph was very intense—incredibly fiery. And he was so doggone fast. I used to always joke that Ralph Beard was the only guy I've ever seen that could throw a pass, then go and catch it. I mean, the guy was quick."

The 1945–46 Wildcats compiled a 28–2 record heading into the National Invitational Tournament in New York City. Beard stormed into Madison Square Garden with a full head of steam, seemingly unaware that he carried the fate of his team on his 18-year-old shoulders. Rupp's Wildcats faced a strong Rhode Island team. The two squads were evenly matched and the score was knotted at 45 apiece with only seconds remaining, when a Rhode Island player fouled Beard. The pride of Hardinsburg stepped to the free throw line with the crowd screaming wildly and the national media scrutinizing every move. Blood ran from Beard's knee from an injury earlier in the game. He eyed the basket, chewed on his five-pack wad of gum, then calmly and coolly sank the free throw. Kentucky won, 46–45.

Back in Lexington, Ralph was a hero. Wherever he went local fans gave him hearty pats on the back and offered to buy him dinner. Young children asked him for autographs. During a special appearance he made at a March of Dimes radio benefit, a listener called in with a $25 pledge if Ralph would sing "Rock-a-Bye Baby" on the air.[1]

In the fall of 1946 Rupp and his point guard got help from new recruits who took the Wildcats—and college basketball—to a whole new level. The top recruit was Alex Groza of Martins Ferry, Ohio. Alex had twice made the Ohio All-State basketball team and scored a state record 628 points in his senior season. Groza's success came purely from hard work and determination. He had no natural basketball skills to speak of. He was tall and awkward, 6'5" and only 165 pounds. He had an unusually large nose that accentuated his gangly appearance. His friends called him "the Beak."

Alex had his heart set on joining his brother, Lou, a football hero at Ohio State. But no Buckeye recruiters came calling. Neither did anybody else. Groza's high school coach could not stand to watch his star center's talents go unnoticed by college recruiters, so he invited Rupp to speak at a high school banquet in Martins Ferry. Groza's coach used Rupp's trip to hype his senior all-star, and Rupp granted the gangly youth a tryout. Groza made the cut and joined the Wildcats in 1944. He played in a handful of games during the 1944–45 season, but then enlisted in the Army during the final stages of World War II.

The military did wonders for Groza's basketball career. He served with the infantry, which toughened up his strength and his attitude; he grew two-and-a-half inches and gained more than 40 pounds; and he honed his basketball skills with the service team at Camp Hood, Texas. Following V-J Day Groza received his honorable discharge and returned to the University of Kentucky a stronger, more aggressive player.

Another serviceman who returned from the war to join Beard and Groza on Rupp's UK squad was Cliff Barker. A waist gunner whose plane had crashed over Germany, Barker had spent 16 months as a prisoner of war. He hailed from tiny Yorktown, Indiana—population 1,000—and had gone through his freshman year at the University of Kentucky before joining the Air Force.

"I was 28 years old when I decided to go back to college," Barker recalled. "And I was so thrilled to hear Coach Rupp say that my scholarship was still waiting for me. When I came back to the team, I got quite a ribbing. I was by far the oldest guy on the team. Everybody called me Dad." He joined Beard in the Kentucky backcourt in 1946. His sharp passes and ball-handling skills helped create openings for Beard on the outside and Groza on the inside.

With his backcourt duo in place and Groza in the middle, Rupp looked to fill the forward spots on his team with two bruisers who muscled in for rebounds and created openings for Groza under the basket. He found a talented tandem in Wallace Jones and Joe Holland. "Wah-Wah" Jones, from Harlan, Kentucky, had set a national high school scoring record in football, pitched Harlan High to the state baseball tournament two years in a row, and earned All-State high school basketball honors three out of four years. Holland, from Birmingham, Kentucky, was a model of discipline. In one basketball contest early in his college career, he leaped for a long rebound when an opposing player intentionally cut him at the knees and sent him sprawling. Holland jumped to his feet with fire in his eyes. With a clenched fist drawn, he took a step back, then relaxed, extended his hand, and gave his opponent a wink and a hearty handshake.

Beard, Groza, Barker, Jones, and Holland—these five fireballs filled out Rupp's starting roster. Sportswriters throughout the country called them "the Fabulous Five." As sophomores these Wildcats compiled a 34-2 record and reached the NIT finals, losing by four points to Utah. Beard and Groza both made the All-American team that season.

The four-point loss nagged at Adolph Rupp all summer. He knew that with Beard and Groza he had the top two college talents in the country; 1947-48 was going to be his year. That season the team won both the Southeastern Conference and the NCAA tournament, then represented the United States in the 1948 Olympic Games in London against the top teams in the world.

In their final year in the collegiate ranks, the Fabulous Four (Holland had graduated the previous spring) had their best season ever, with only one loss. But at the National Invitational Tournament in Madison Square Garden, where Kentucky was a heavy favorite to win the championship over Loyola of Chicago, something went woefully wrong. On the offensive end, Groza seemed to have a difficult time getting open under the basket. Beard too had an off night, managing only two points in the first half. But in the second half, Beard came to life. Slashing inside and popping long shots from outside, he tallied 13 second-half points in a desperate attempt to keep the Wildcats alive. But Beard's effort was in vain. In what the national press called "the greatest upset in college basketball history," Loyola toppled mighty Kentucky, 67-56.

In the press room following the game, Adolph Rupp sat with his head in his hands as reporters fired questions at him. "Why was your team so far off form?" one asked. "Well, sir, I can't figure that out," Rupp answered. "I never could figure out why teams go flat. You go out and get the answer to that and you'll get the Academy Award, or whatever they give for basketball."

In the NCAA championship the following week, every opponent that faced Kentucky in the tournament felt the wrath of Rupp's fury over the NIT loss. Kentucky destroyed its opponents and won the championship for the second consecutive year.

"As soon as we were finished with our college careers, we started our own exhibition circuit," Barker recalled. "Joe [Holland] joined us again, and we'd go barnstorming around together. We had a sportswriter in town named J. R. 'Babe' Kimbrough. He acted as our business manager. We traveled around to all these little towns in Kentucky, to folks who never got a chance to see us play in college. We also traveled to West Virginia, Tennessee, and Indiana. We played in a lot of small towns in those states.

Pro scouts contacted each of the players to sign individual contracts with various outfits in both the NBL and the BAA. But NBL vice-president Leo Ferris had a perfect suggestion to inject new life into the sputtering National League. Beard explained: "Ferris approached Babe Kimbrough and asked him if the Kentucky boys would want to enter the league as a unit and play professionally. And Kimbrough said, 'Absolutely!' Later we found out that the leagues merged, so now we were part of the new NBA. There were 17 teams in the league. It was a wild setup, but we were glad to be a part of it and stay together as a unit in the pros."

Their name, the Indianapolis Olympians, reflected their gold-medal performance in London in 1948. Decked out in bright red, white, and blue uniforms, they were professional basketball's first and only all-rookie team. Historian Ron Newlin reflected on the start of the new Indianapolis franchise: "I think the Indianapolis Olympians are one of the greatest stories of all times in professional basketball. It's like a classic American myth. Five college buddies go out and form their own team so they can stay together. . . . and they were incredibly successful. They really took the city of Indianapolis by storm."

Beard said that the players "borrowed $30,000 from the league and the city of Indianapolis and went there to form our team. We rented the Butler Fieldhouse for $800 a night. We loved it. That was widely considered the greatest floor in the league at that time. And the fans really embraced us. Whenever we'd play Minneapolis, or Anderson, or Fort Wayne, we'd pack that Butler Fieldhouse—15,000 fans. Boy, we were really in the tall cotton then. We were rolling. By the end of our first year in the league, we had paid off our $30,000 debt to the city, we'd paid ourselves the generous salary of $5,000 each for five months, we'd given ourselves a $5,000 bonus each, and had $28,000 in the bank to boot."

The team appointed former *Lexington Herald* sportswriter J. R. "Babe" Kimbrough as president of the Olympians. Groza, Beard, and Barker were vice-presidents. Holland acted as treasurer, Jones as secretary. Kimbrough and the quintet owned the majority shares of the team, but public shares were offered to the community at a heady $1,000 per share. Through negotiations with the NBL's Ferris, 30 business and professional men in Indianapolis agreed to invest in the team and give them the working capital they needed to begin operations.

A week before before the start of the NBA season, Indianapolis officials held a special ceremony to celebrate the city's newest basketball team. Mayor Al Feeney presided. Sporting a bow tie and a broad smile, Feeney proclaimed October 12–18 "Basketball Week" in the city. At his side were Barker, Groza, Beard, Jones, and Holland. It seemed fitting for Feeney to pose with the team for news photographs. Feeney had pioneered professional basketball in the city with the Indianapolis Em-Roes in 1913.

Indianapolis radio station WISH covered the Olympians' games. The staccato cadences of veteran broadcaster Luke Walton punctuated the airwaves with exciting action of the Indianapolis Olympians at Butler Fieldhouse. Walton called them "the Runnin' Rookies" and peppered his broadcasts with such spirited lines as "Here come the Olympians, running right down the middle of Meridian Street!" Walton's relationship with the players and their families grew as they traveled together through the NBA schedule. "He knew what a big fan I was and how closely I followed the team," Barker's wife, Meredith recalled. "I was keeping statistics on the guys from my seat in the stands. So a lot of times Luke would call me down at halftime and ask me to go on the air and report first-half statistics."

Walton, Meredith Barker, and the rest of the fans had much to cheer about in the Olympians' inaugural NBA season. The "Runnin' Rookies" compiled a 39–25 record and won the NBA's western division. Beard and Groza made the NBA's first All-Star team, and Groza finished second in the league scoring race to George Mikan. Beard also amassed some impressive individual statistics for the season—ninth in total scoring, seventh in total assists. The franchise was successful at the box office, too. Owing to the spacious Butler Fieldhouse and their wildly popular fast-break style of play, the Indianapolis Olympians amassed one of the highest total attendance figures in the NBA.

The Olympians easily qualified for the 1949–50 NBA playoffs. Sportswriter Angelopolous penned: "Having demonstrated convincingly enough that sometimes they'd rather play basketball than eat, the Indianapolis Olympians begin a series that in professional sports is designed to see that its members do just that— eat. The playoffs begin with Indianapolis and Sheboygan at Butler Fieldhouse."

In the series against Sheboygan, Groza was scintillating. "The Beak" averaged 23 points in the three-game series to push Indianapolis over the Redskins, two games to one. In the next round they faced the Anderson Packers, their intrastate rivals. "Those games were so heated," Barker recalled. "We filled the gym for those games. You couldn't hear yourself think out there, it was so wild."

Game one of the NBA western division finals took place at Butler Fieldhouse. After the game, Angelopolous reported: "You see a lot of ball games when you write sports. You enjoy some of them; you'd rather be somewhere else at others. You watch so many you don't excite easily. And sometimes when someone asks why you write sports, you don't know. Then one evening you reach for the score book just like hundreds of other times, and you start making marks and notes, a little bit detached from the whole scene. But this evening turns out to be the one when you know the answer, and at the end you're up, too, and you're shaking a bit, and you choke up and giggle a little incoherently, sillily. For this evening there has passed before you that glimpse of the human spirit in full flight. It touches you, too, and you are glad you are there. When the question comes again about why write sports, Indianapolis' conquest of Anderson last night could be an adequate answer. It's a lofty nickname, the Olympians, the Indianapolis rookies have carried in this, their first year of professional basketball. But you and 8,054 other spectators . . . today can say no one could have carried the nickname more nobly."

Anderson led 69–60 with only five minutes remaining in the game. The Packers tried to stall out the clock, but Indianapolis continued to whittle away at the Duffeys' lead. Then, with only two minutes remaining and the score tight, anarchy broke out on the floor. Ed Stanczak recalled: "Wah Jones and I were really get-ting into it underneath the basket. I kept trying to go down low near the hoop, and he kept trying to hold me down. He kept grab-bing my shorts until once he grabbed in a place where the shorts were the shortest, if you know what I mean. Well, I told him to back off. 'You're getting too personal,' I told him. Well, he just kept after me and didn't stop. The first time he grabbed me I was in the low pivot. They tried to throw me the ball, and I lost it out of bounds. [Coach] Murray Mendenhall started yelling at me and getting on me about the missed pass. I told him that Jones was grabbing me, and he said, 'Well, do something about it.' So I did something about it."

Beard picked up the story: "Jones was really working over ol' Stanczak, grabbing him, pulling on his jersey, you name it. Well, I overheard Stan yelling at him, 'Listen, rookie! One more time and you've had it.' Sure enough, the next time down the court, we're running our fast break when I look over and there's Jonesy over there on the floor holding his right eye with blood gushing out. I guess that was a lesson for a rookie real quick." Barker recalled: "Stanczak really peeled Wah across the face with an el-bow—knocked him out cold. It took eight stitches to fix him up." And Stanczak added: "I got thrown out of the game. But Jones was out of the game, also. Some people might say that was dirty pool, but there's only so much a guy can take. It was real com-petitive out there. I just wanted him to know that just because he was an 'Olympian,' he couldn't get away with that kind of gar-bage with me. It's rough out there—a jungle. You had to earn respect."

After Stanczak stomped off the floor and Jones was carried off, the game resumed. Jones's plight seemed to inspire teammate Groza to some last-minute heroics. He laid in three quick baskets to give the Olympians their first lead since early in the first quar-ter. Indianapolis held on to win, 77–74, as the heated rivalry moved to Anderson for game two.

Unfortunately for Indianapolis, the Olympians made the 45-minute journey to Anderson minus two of the Fabulous Five. With Jones still nursing his injured eye, Beard fell victim to a severe stomach virus. Their forces depleted and facing a hostile crowd at the Wigwam, Indianapolis stood little chance against the more experienced Packers. Four Anderson players scored in double figures as Ike Duffey's crew sailed past Indianapolis, 84–67.

Game three at Butler Fieldhouse set an NBA attendance record. A standing-room-only crowd of 14,461 nudged shoulder to shoulder as the rivalry resumed. Beard and Jones were back in the Olympians' lineup, though neither was in perfect health. But even with the partisan crowd rooting for their rookies, Indianapolis could not manage another last-minute victory. Sportswriter Angelopolous lamented: "Having failed to pull off one of their patented miracles by no more a margin than the seam of a molded ball, the Indianapolis Olympians consigned their basketball season to those who deal in retrospect. . . . The crowd that literally clung to the rafters and spilled onto the sides of the playing floor may not have been happy with the outcome, but they should have no quarrel with how the Olympians played the game."

Groza's 26-point effort kept Indianapolis close throughout the contest. But with less than 20 seconds remaining, Anderson still held a two-point lead. In a desperation move, Barker seized an inbound pass and heaved it 80 feet across the court. The shot drifted long and bounced into the overflow crowd. The Indianapolis Olympians' title hopes disappeared along with the ball.

But the playoff loss did little to dampen the popularity of the Olympians. Professional basketball was back and stronger than ever in Indianapolis. That spring broadcaster Luke Walton wrote a book about the city's newest sports sensation. *Basketball's Fabulous Five: The Indianapolis Olympians* hit the bookstores just before the team's initial run through the NBA playoffs. Walton wrote: "In a time when Democracy is striving to protect its ideals and its very life, these five boys score a definite point for the side of free enterprise. Five American kids rolled a ball and a barrel hoop into a thriving business! Where else in the whole world could you find it?"

In the beginning the Olympians were just a terrific shot in the arm, both for the league and for the city of Indianapolis. I don't think anybody could have imagined the shocking developments that occurred. It was a shame ... a crying shame.

—Leo Barnhorst,
Indianapolis Olympians, 1950–53

10. A Ten-Foot Pole

In the board room on the 80th floor of the Empire State Building in New York, the NBA board of governors convened for a historic meeting in the summer of 1950. At the forefront of discussion was the issue of allowing African Americans into the league. Fort Wayne general manager Carl Bennett was an early proponent of the idea. He explained: "We had had discussions in our executive meetings a year earlier. Walter Brown [Boston], Ned Irish [New York], and myself decided to take the vote to the entire board of governors. But the rule did not pass that first year."

Bennett continued: "The vote really wasn't that close the first year, in 1949. Most of the resistance came from those clubs who scheduled the Harlem Globetrotters in their arenas. They didn't want to upset Abe Saperstein, who, at the time, had the exclusive market on African American talent. Scheduling the Trotters was big business back then. They were big at the box office. So no one wanted to anger Saperstein and lose their contracts with him. After all, if the NBA started bidding for blacks, Saperstein's payroll costs would skyrocket, because he'd have to pay them more to keep them on his team."

Bennett explained the series of events that took place prior to the second vote in 1950: "The person who deserves the real credit for getting blacks into the NBA is Ned Irish. Even back in 1949 Irish was complaining that the Knicks were having a hard time winning ball games in New York. He just wasn't attracting enough fans to Madison Square Garden. He felt he needed some quality black players to help make his club more competitive. So he approached me and some of the others about his aspirations to purchase the contract of Nat 'Sweetwater' Clifton, the Globetrotters star."

Clifton, whose nickname blossomed from his love for sugary colas and other soft drinks, was a giant, soft-spoken athlete who led the Globetrotters in scoring and rebounds. "Ned Irish was adamant about getting Clifton to New York," Bennett recalled. "He campaigned heavily to get the vote in his favor. But the majority of the league representatives felt that the Trotters were too valuable an asset to risk losing. So they turned Irish down. All season long Irish kept telling us that he couldn't stay in business without Clifton."

Irish was a fiery team owner with a flair for the dramatic. When the board of governors convened, he was nowhere to be found. As Commissioner Maurice Podoloff called the meeting to order, Irish stormed into the room. Bennett described the scene: "Ned always had a habit of doing crazy things in our meetings in order to get his point across. But this time he was really mad. He stood and pounded his fist on the table and shouted at us. 'I'll tell you one thing,' he said. 'I want to have approved the right to have black ballplayers in our league. If I can't get Sweetwater Clifton on the New York team, then New York will no longer be a part of this league.' That's just the way he said it. Then he turned on his heel and walked out of the room, just like that."

Bennett continued: "Everybody in the room knew that New York was the grandaddy of basketball at that time, so we all listened to him. I think Irish acted that way because he thought he could get away with it. . . . And he could, too. New York carried a lot of weight in the league. They may not have had the best team, but Madison Square Garden was a major venue for the league."

Irish's brash actions stunned the group. But even with the New York owner's impassioned speech, ambivalence still filled the board room. Podoloff called for a vote. The tally was tied at 5–5, until Bennett cast the deciding vote. By a slim margin of 6–5, African Americans were finally allowed to compete in the NBA.

Bennett recalled: "When we walked out of the meeting, Eddie Gottlieb, the owner of the Philadelphia Warriors, came up to me. He told me, 'Carl, you sonuvabitch. You just ruined the league. In five years, 75 percent of the league is going to be black. We won't draw crowds. People won't come out to see them.' Well, Gottlieb was right about the first part, but very wrong about the second part. In five years or so, the league indeed was 70–75 percent black. But the fans really came out to support our teams after we allowed blacks into the league. I didn't notice any dip in league attendance. The shift didn't stop the fans from coming at all. In fact, I think they really appreciated the talents of these wonderful athletes."

On May 25, 1950, a headline in the *New York Times* read: "Clifton, Negro Ace, Goes to Knickerbocker Five." Irish kept his promise. Another outstanding African American athlete, Chuck Cooper, a 6′5″ forward from Duquesne University, signed as a first-round draft pick of the Boston Celtics. In a later round, the Washington Capitols recruited Earl Lloyd, a 6′6″ forward from West Virginia State. Lloyd earned the distinction of being the first African American to play in the NBA, since his Washington team opened its schedule a day early against Rochester. Cooper and Clifton both made their NBA debuts on the hardwood in Fort Wayne, Cooper on November 1, Clifton on November 4. Cooper's start with Boston against the Pistons was also the NBA debut for another Boston Celtics rookie, Bob Cousy.

Clifton, Cooper, and Lloyd faced the hardships of racial prejudice on their NBA road trip. Even though the three owned contracts worth in the neighborhood of $10,000 each, they still could not eat in many Indiana restaurants when their teams traveled to the Hoosier state. Apparently the game advanced faster than midwestern society in 1950.

In Anderson, Ike Duffey found it increasingly difficult for his small-town team to compete financially with the big-city NBA clubs. Midway through the 1949–50 season the Packers led the league's western division by two games, but attendance at home games averaged only about 2,500. Duffey's heated battles with Podoloff were over. But life as a professional basketball executive grew too burdensome.

Ike's nephew Martin Duffey recalled: "Ike's real passion was railroading. That was a reflection of his dad. So finally in 1950 Uncle Ike just decided to devote his whole life to trains. He sold the packing plant and went to work as president of the Indiana Central Railroad for a salary of one dollar a year. I think those days on the railroad were the happiest of his life."

On December 4, 1949, the *Anderson Herald* announced that Duffey and his brother had sold their interest in the packing plant for $3 million. "In addition to purchasing the packing firm here," the paper reported, "the Emge Packing Company signed a 50-year lease with I. Duffey and Sons Co., for the operation of seven Indiana stockyards or marketing centers, located in Anderson, Elwood, Fairmount, Flora, Warren, Montpelier, and Hartford City. . . . Discussing the Packers professional basketball team, sponsored by the firm, Ike Duffey . . . said an important announcement regarding the team would be made at the Anderson-Sheboygan game here Monday."

Before about 1,500 fans at the Wigwam the following week, Duffey announced that the Packers would stay in Anderson, at least for the rest of the NBA season. "Unless we take a terrific beating this year, the Packers will remain in Anderson. We are asking each fan present to bring along another friend to the games," he pleaded to the tiny crowd. With the 1949–50 season only two months old, Duffey already had lost $14,000 on the Packers.

In January businessmen from Toledo offered Duffey $25,000 to take the costly franchise off his hands. But rather than snatch up the Ohio offer, Duffey turned to the citizens of Anderson. Duffey proposed to sell the team to the city "lock, stock and barrel" if they raised enough funds in the following week. A local civic group formed to keep the Packers in town. On January 4, approximately 50 community leaders convened at the downtown YMCA in an effort to sell $10,000 worth of season tickets that remained for the rest of the year.

Local businesses, from Sears Roebuck to privately owned drugstores, barber shops, and even a camera repair shop, pooled their economic resources and formed the Packers Civic Committee. Full-page advertisements ran in the *Anderson Herald*: "Do You Want to Keep Pro Ball in Anderson? . . . Be a Packer-Backer." In one week's time, the committee proudly presented Duffey $10,000 in paid season ticket receipts. The team now belonged to the city of Anderson.

The community found new enthusiasm for its Packers. Attendance averages more than doubled, and the team responded. "Our salaries dropped off quite a bit after that," explained Packers forward Ed Stanczak. They could only pay us $50–$75 a game. But we respected their spirit. It really says something about the fans in Anderson to try to keep the team going without major corporate sponsorship."

Anderson finished second in the NBA's western division, only two games back of the "Runnin' Rookies," the Indianapolis Olympians. In the playoffs, the Packers defeated Tri-Cities two games to one, then edged past Indianapolis in a thrilling two-point finish at Butler Fieldhouse. They reached the NBA semifinals before bowing out to the Minneapolis Lakers in two straight games.

During the off-season the "Packer-Backers" worked hard to raise more funds to keep their NBA franchise alive. However, in mid-April 1950, the NBA declared that all clubs must provide a $50,000 performance bond to keep the franchise status active. Through attrition, Podoloff whittled down his unwieldy group of 17 teams.

The required bond dealt a lethal blow to most of the small-town teams in the NBA. Anderson, Sheboygan, Waterloo, and Denver dropped out, as did two larger markets, Saint Louis and Chicago. "Big city operators in professional basketball put the squeeze on small towns at an executive committee meeting in New York," wrote Russ Lynch, sports editor for the *Milwaukee*

Journal. According to Lynch, the league planned to drop the clubs anyway, even though several showed a small profit for the season. "Even in Anderson, they stayed out of the red," Lynch noted.

But the Packer-Backers still had fight left in them. Even though their club had no NBA franchise, professional basketball continued in Anderson. In the summer of 1950, Doxie Moore, the old NBL commissioner, reorganized a group of former NBA, NBL, and BAA clubs to form a new league, the National Professional Basketball League, or NPBL. Four NBA rejects, Anderson, Sheboygan, Waterloo and Denver, joined clubs from Louisville, Grand Rapids, Kansas City, and St. Paul.

The *Anderson Herald* had a call to arms, or rather a call to pocketbooks, to get Hoosier fans to support their newest business interest. "The people of Anderson have been concerned over the loss of the Anderson Packers basketball team," one lengthy ad read. "This is our chance to bring them back for some good, clean basketball this season. . . . Enthusiasm has indicated that Anderson wants to join this league, but the effort needs YOUR help. This undertaking is to be owned and operated by the people of Anderson. You can help by becoming a contributor. . . . No one is asked to give a lot. Everyone is asked to give a little. Will you give a dollar?"

Bob Myers, chairman of the Packers Civic Committee, named popular Packers player Frank Gates to coach the community squad. The team included some Packer holdovers, such as Charlie Black, Milo Komenich, and Richie Niemiera. Former Indianapolis Kautsky luminary Leo Klier also joined the squad and was one of the leading scorers in the new league.

The Denver franchise had difficulty in financing the team's long trips to all its eastern and midwestern counterparts. Financial pressures forced the organization to fold. Bill Butterfield, an office supply store manager in Evansville, bought the franchise midway through the season and moved it to the Hoosier state. He dubbed the new team the Evansville Agogans, a nickname which meant "those with intense interest and excitement."

The Agogans featured the talents of former local high school athletes, including Butterfield's son and Norm McCool, both outstanding players from Evansville Bosse High School's state championship squad. The team included players with professional experience, including Ollie Shoaf, the former Hammond Buccaneer guard, who drove from his home in Norris City, Illinois, to join the Agogans for many of their contests.

"We didn't have contracts," Shoaf recalled. "And we really weren't playing for all that much money. We just played for the fun of it. We'd go out to play, then split the proceeds. Sometimes we'd book the Harlem Globetrotters and other barnstormers to come to the Evansville Central High School gym. We even beat the Trotters one time, 66–59. That was one of our better nights, on the floor and in our pocketbooks, too."

It was a valiant effort to revive the old National League. But without major corporate backing the new National Professional Basketball League had little hope of survival. In December the St. Paul franchise attempted to "jump ship" and approach Podoloff for admission into the NBA. Scheduling was also a nightmare. Most teams didn't even play the same number of games. Sheboygan, which owned the best record in the eastern division, compiled a 29–16 record. Meanwhile, the western division leader, Waterloo, totaled a 32–24 season mark. The league was so discombobulated and so deep in debt by the end of the year that the two divisions never organized a tournament to determine the league champion. The season and the league ended abruptly with both teams staking claim to the NPBL title.

In Anderson the city's grassroots campaign fought hard to keep the Packers alive. But by the end of the season, even the never-say-die Packer-Backers saw the end in sight. A government audit in March revealed that the organization owed Uncle Sam $1,119.87 in taxes. The franchise had only $428.80 in the public coffers. As soon as it became evident that the Packers were not in the running for the league championship, the corporate officials of Anderson Basketball, Incorporated decided to forgo the rest of the season and settled with the players for the remainder of their season's wages.

The spirit of the city could not compete with the ever-increasing costs associated with running a professional basketball franchise. On March 24, 1951, the Anderson Packers defeated a team of college all-stars at the Wigwam. As the last Packer-Backer walked out of the arena, the lights turned out on the gym and on the legacy of the Anderson Packers.

On April 23, 1954, the NBA board of governors ushered in the modern era of professional basketball by instituting the 24-second shot clock. The mandate was the brainchild of Danny Biasone, owner of the Syracuse Nationals. Biasone and other league officials felt that deliberate stall tactics too often slowed the game to a painfully plodding pace. The 24-second rule ensured that the team in control of the ball had to make an attempt to score within 24 seconds or lose possession. No longer could a team hold the ball for minutes on end to run out the clock in a close game. Now both teams had to play aggressive offense from beginning to end—a full 48-minute game.

When the NBA voted to approve the new rule, it drew upon several cases from the league's past that illustrated how slow and ineffective pro ball had become. The two most egregious instances had occurred within weeks of each other during the 1950–51 season. Each involved teams from Indiana. And each pushed the very limit of what the league could expect fans to endure in a professional basketball game.

The first was a reflection of the wildly unpredictable nature of Coach Murray Mendenhall. In April 1949 Mendenhall returned to a triumphant welcome in his hometown, Fort Wayne. That season he took over the head coaching responsibilities of Fred Zollner's Pistons after three successful years in Anderson. General manager Carl Bennett discussed game strategies with Mendenhall before each contest. On November 22, 1950, Mendenhall and Bennett conceived an outrageous plan for their tilt with the perennial league power, the Minneapolis Lakers, which was in the midst of a 29-game home winning streak.

"We were on the northwestern train from Fort Wayne to Minneapolis," Bennett recalled. "As I was walking through the car, Murray Mendenhall pulled me aside and said, 'We're going to have a hard time keeping up with them. So we're just going to have to sit on the ball and pray for a miracle.' Well, that's just what we did. We got the opening tip of the game and just stood there with the ball. They didn't come out after us, and we didn't go after the basket. There was no rule that said that you had to shoot. So we just stood there and stood there."

From the sidelines Pistons' radio broadcaster Hilliard Gates brought the play by play, or rather the lack of play by play, to the audience back home in Fort Wayne. "The Lakers were in a zone defense," Gates recalled. "And they just stood back in that zone and didn't guard the Pistons players who had the ball on the outside. Most of the game there was nothing to report. No one moved. By the end of the first quarter the score was only 8 to 7." Bennett laughed: "Poor Hilliard! He tried to make it sound like there was really a great game out there. He always had a gift for that. But he was really searching for things to say, because, after all, nothing was going on out there on the court."

At halftime the Lakers held a 13-11 lead. The fans erupted in disgust over the Pistons' deliberate stall tactics. "There were more than 7,000 fans there in Minneapolis that night," Bennett recalled. "And they were booing and throwing things on the floor. It was a madhouse." Gates added: "One lady got so irate that she turned around and hit me on the head with her purse. I guess she thought that since I was from Fort Wayne, I must have had something to do with all this."

Mendenhall asked the players during the halftime break if they wanted to continue the stall. Without exception, all enthusiastically voted yes. The waiting game continued. With four minutes remaining in the game, Minneapolis held a 18-17 lead, when Fort Wayne regained possession. "He told them to hold the ball for the last shot," Bennett explained. "We called a play for our center, Larry Foust. He broke away from [Minneapolis center George] Mikan, ran down to the corner of the court, and nobody picked him up. He waited until the last possible second, then let it fly. It hit the backboard at an angle, and swoosh! It went in, and we won, 19 to 18." Gates said: "As soon as the shot went in, we all made a mad dash for the locker room, because the fans came out of the stands after us. We just barely made it into the locker room. We had to stay there for more than an hour and a half before we were able to get out of that arena."

At the Pennsylvania Station in Fort Wayne hundreds of loyal fans stood for hours in the cold to greet their triumphant Pistons. In New York City, however, NBA commissioner Podoloff was far less enthused. Bennett explained: "Podoloff called us the next day. Several officials from Minneapolis protested the game. The press and the rest of the league were really on him to do something about all of this. Podoloff was irritated, but I don't think he really planned on doing much. He just told us that he thought what we did showed disregard for the fans. He said that he expected us to never do it again."

It was—and, because of the introduction of the 24-second clock, will forever be—the lowest-scoring game in NBA history. Minneapolis coach John Kundla said the game "gave pro basketball a great big black eye." One outraged Minneapolis fan told a reporter that the game was " . . . stinko basketball, and I'm toning down my comment so you can print it." The *Fort Wayne Journal Gazette* termed it "the most weird game in modern professional basketball." Bennett told of the repercussions: "Being on the NBA board of governors, I really heard it from the rest of the league representatives. It wasn't long after that game that talks began on how to eliminate those stall tactics."

But before the NBA's board of governors had the opportunity to discuss the ramifications of the Fort Wayne–Minneapolis contest, Indianapolis and Rochester squared off in another unusual record-setter. The date was January 6, 1951, just five weeks after the Fort Wayne–Minneapolis game. Before 3,790 rabid fans in Rochester, the Royals and the Olympians played to a 65–65 tie at the end of the 48-minute regulation time.

As they huddled on the sidelines before the first overtime period, both squads came up with the same strategy. "It was pretty simple, really," Olympians guard Cliff Barker recalled. "If we got the ball, we were going to hold it for the entire overtime period, then take a final shot in the last second or two. Ralph [Beard] or I would take the ball out on top and just hold it. They didn't come out after us, so we kept working it around to wait for the last shot. Apparently they had the same strategy, because when they got the ball, that's exactly what they did, too."

Both teams stalled through one extra session, then two, then three. One team scored with only seconds left, then a quick basket at the other end left the score tied again as the final buzzer sounded. In the fourth overtime neither team even attempted a basket. As the game wore on, nearly 200 irritated fans got up and marched out, all the while growling such comments to reporters as "I didn't pay to watch grown men stand around all night."

The score was tied at 73 at the end of the fifth overtime. Barker recalled: "We were really getting worried. We had another game to get to in Moline at two in the afternoon the next day. Because this game went so long, we were missing our train connections to Chicago to get to the next game. We finally sent five players out of the game, so they could catch the train to Chicago and make the connections. Only half of us finished the game in Rochester, while the other half headed to Moline."

With depleted forces, the Indianapolis Olympians began their sixth overtime session. Rochester snagged the opening tip and again held for the final shot. With only four seconds left, a Rochester player heaved a hook shot at the basket. The ball smacked hard against the rim and bounced long into the arms of Olympians guard Paul "Lefty" Walther. Ralph Beard sprinted to the other end of the court at full speed. Walther tossed the ball three-quarters of the court. The ball arced high and landed neatly into the hands of the speedy Beard. He flipped the ball off the end of his fingers as the buzzer sounded. The ball banked in, and Indianapolis survived the six-overtime marathon, 75–73.

Six overtimes set a new NBA record. The *Rochester Democrat* cried foul. "Fans Irked at Freezing Tactics Used in Royal-Olympian Marathon," the banner headline read in the sports page the following day. "More than 26 of the 30 overtime minutes, the ball stayed neatly tucked away under an arm of a Royal or Olympian player. One or another player just stood there with the score tied, waiting out the clock for a last-second, 'nothing-to-lose' shot. . . . Customers who complained were burned up at the unchallenged freeze. For the Olympians, it sure wasn't good basketball, but it paid off."

Three years later at the NBA board of governors meeting, Biasone and Podoloff revisited the Fort Wayne–Minneapolis low-scoring contest and the Indianapolis-Rochester six-overtime battle. These two record-setting performances encouraged NBA officials to implement new rules aimed at eliminating strategic stalling. The results of these two contests inspired the changes that ushered pro ball into the modern age.

May 17, 1949, was Leo Barnhorst's birthday. Indianapolis Cathedral High School's most valuable player and leading scorer at the University of Notre Dame, Barnhorst stood at the threshold of an uncertain future on graduation day. Barnhorst received an offer from Phillips 66 Oil Company to earn a steady wage and play basketball with the corporation's champion AAU squad. But before Barney accepted the offer, he received a call from Walter Kennedy of the National Basketball Association.

Kennedy was Podoloff's assistant commissioner. "He was interested in having me sign a professional contract with what was the BAA then," Barnhorst explained. "At the time we had territorial draft rights, so I was to be assigned to the Indianapolis Jets in my old hometown, which I loved. But then the Jets folded and the two leagues merged. Things were still up in the air, so the NBA drafted me as a 'league draft' and told me they would find a place to put me. I told him I was concerned about having a stable job, since I was just finishing school and didn't have any money saved. So he offered me a $9,500 contract, which was one of the 10 or 15 biggest contracts in the league at the time. He then asked if I would be interested in a bonus if I signed—a new car. Well, I could see that I was not going to be heading to Phillips 66 after that."

Barnhorst continued: "I was worried. I told Kennedy I wasn't sure if I was good enough to make the pros. He assured me that I would be O.K. I asked him if he would be willing to guarantee to sign me to a 'no-cut' contract for the first year. He said, 'Oh, sure. No problem.'" That day the NBA gave Barnhorst an unexpected birthday present, signing him up for the first "no-cut" contract in professional basketball history.

"When the Kentucky boys came along and formed the Olympians, it only seemed natural that I would go there," Barnhorst remarked. "But they didn't want to pay the salary the league promised me. So Podoloff called me up and told me I was going to Chicago to play for the Stags. I really didn't have a say in the thing. We didn't have agents in those days. Podoloff just said, 'If you want to play, go to Chicago. If you don't go to Chicago, you don't play.'"

Barnhorst started for the Stags as a yeoman forward and played in all but one of Chicago's games, averaging nearly seven points a contest. Leadership and management in the Windy City were unstable, and by the end of the season, Barnhorst's fears came true. The Chicago franchise folded. For nearly six months his contract was up for grabs. One week before the start of the

1950–51 season, he finally received some good news. "Barney Signs with Olymps," the headline read on the sports page of the *Indianapolis News*. "General manager J. R. 'Babe' Kimbrough announced that Leo Barnhorst . . . would join the team this weekend. . . . Barnhorst is expected to give the Olymps aid on the backboards, where he shone at Notre Dame."

During his first year with the Olympians Barnhorst played in every league game, upped his scoring average to eight points per game, and eventually earned a spot in the starting lineup. Barney's teammates also had another good year. Alex Groza garnered a spot in the top 10 in league scoring, field goal percentage, and rebounds. Ralph Beard earned top 10 honors in both scoring and assists.

The Olympians made the NBA playoffs that season but narrowly lost in the playoffs to former league champion Minneapolis. But pro ball fans in Indianapolis were not discouraged. *Indianapolis News* reporter Angelo Angelopolous echoed the feelings of the spectators in his column following the Olympians' last playoff game, "There were, no doubt, a house full of coaches and others who could see bright futures for Al and Ralph." Groza and Beard were both 23 years old and on top of the world. Both made top money at a sport they loved. Beard exclaimed: "We were on our way, man. We were on our way." But the two all-stars never again played in a professional basketball game.

In January 1951, Manhattan College basketball player Junius Kellogg made a stunning announcement to his coach, Ken Norton. Gamblers had approached Kellogg with a $1,000 bribe to shave points in Manhattan's upcoming game at Madison Square Garden against DePaul University and to stay under the spread on the game.

"The spread" was an idea conceived by bookies to make sporting events more enticing to gamblers. No gambler would bet against a champion squad with superior athletes in a game against the last-place team in the league. But if, for example, bookies placed a 10-point spread against the champion squad, then the champs would have to win by 11 or more points to be considered the "winner" in the gambler's world. Only then would those who bet on the champions receive their payoff.

The offer to "fix" the DePaul game by deliberately staying under the spread had shocked Kellogg. He and his coach reported the attempted bribe to Frank S. Hogan, New York's district attorney. Hogan immediately arrested the gamblers involved. Kellogg became a hero on the Manhattan campus. Coach Norton openly condemned the "fixers" within New York's gambling element. And Hogan dedicated himself almost exclusively to pursuing and prosecuting gamblers and game fixers in college basketball.

One month later Hogan uncovered another long-running series of fixes at City College of New York. Next to be uncovered was Long Island University. Players on both teams were directly tied to gamblers operating out of Madison Square Garden, which had a reputation as a haven for gamblers, game fixers, and underworld figures.

The arrests drew nationwide attention and even provoked a response from J. Edgar Hoover. The head of the Federal Bureau of Investigation called the scandals "hypocrisy and a sham." Newspaper reporters throughout the country sounded out in disgust. Max Kase, sportswriter for the *New York Journal-American* who broke the original story of Kellogg and the Manhattan scandal, penned: "A first blush of sympathy for the corrupted weaklings has given way to a cold rage because of their lack of loyalty to their school and a callused greed for their Judas pieces of silver."

Back in Indiana, fear that the scandals might spread to the Midwest echoed loudly in the opinion pages of the *Indianapolis News:* "Having shown what they can do to corrupt college basketball teams, the gamblers are not above trying to fix contests at the high school level. Fortunately, Indiana high school basketball is a clean and highly competitive sport which home town loyalty protects from corrupting influences. It is well, however, to forestall temptation. . . . Let every law enforcement official be on the alert for the insidious influences that have given the eastern college game a black eye. Enforcement officials should watch the gamblers; the rest of Indiana will watch the games."

One of the most outspoken critics of gamblers and game fixing at Madison Square Garden was University of Kentucky coach Adolph Rupp. The coach himself was often seen in the company of known gamblers in the Lexington area, but at a speech on August 15 in Lincoln, Nebraska, Rupp boldly refused to be intimidated by those who dared to corrupt college basketball's top players. "Imagine what going to the big cities means to my boys," he said. "And it's all poppycock about them being contaminated by the gambling element at the Garden. In the first place, they're always under my wing. And in the second place, college boys of the type who play in the [Southeastern Conference] aren't easily tempted. At least I'll vouch for my 'Cats."[1] Before he left, Rupp jutted a finger into the air and declared: "Gentlemen, I'll guarantee you this: Gamblers couldn't touch my boys with a ten-foot pole." His words made headlines on sports pages throughout the country.

In October 1951 the Indianapolis Olympians prepared for another season of excitement and promise. The Fabulous Five had proved to be outstanding citizens, as well as outstanding basketball players. The highly visible Olymps were in peak demand at civic gatherings and corporate promotional events. Beard and Groza held annual summer basketball camps to help area youth develop their roundball skills. They also sponsored many charity fund-raisers, such as the annual press versus radio basketball benefit for polio research.

On October 18, just before the start of the season, *Indianapolis Star* sports columnist Bob Stranahan was standing on a street corner when he spotted Beard driving by in his car. The All-American flashed his broad Kentucky smile. "Hiya', Bob! . . . We're goin' swell," he hollered enthusiastically from the car window. The next day Beard and several of his Olympian teammates headed to Chicago to watch the Rochester Royals faced a team of college all-stars in a preseason exhibition at Chicago Stadium. The all-stars were coached by the mentor of the Fabulous Five, Adolph Rupp. The Olympians had their own preseason exhibition game set for the following night in Moline but had decided to take the detour through Chicago to enjoy the all-star game and visit with their old friend Rupp.

Leo Barnhorst recalled: "We all gathered at Butler Fieldhouse. We were going to take two or three cars up to Chicago together. When I got to the parking lot, I saw some of the guys reading this newspaper article from the *Chicago Tribune*." The article stated that New York district attorney Frank Hogan had "the goods" on several former players from the University of Kentucky in regard to gambling and point shaving. "I remember Alex just pushed the article aside and said, 'Well, there's nothing to that.' But I remember Ralph reading that thing pretty intensely. Of course, everything Ralph did was intense. So we didn't think a thing about it. We just tossed it aside and headed to Chicago."

After watching the contest at Chicago Stadium, the Olympians walked out together. Cliff Barker recalled: "Some guys grabbed us by the arm and said, 'You're coming with us.' We didn't know what the hell was going on. We came to find out that they were detectives that had come to pick each of us up."

The Chicago police held four Olympians: Beard, Groza, Barker, and Joe Holland. They also commandeered the Olympians' new coach, Herm Schaefer. Officers took them to separate rooms at the Cook County Courthouse, where the Chicago arm of Hogan's investigative team questioned them for more than seven hours without the benefit of legal counsel.

"They really didn't spend much time with me," Barker recalled. "They wanted to know if gamblers had ever approached me to fix games back when I played at Kentucky. I told them no. Nobody ever approached me. . . . You see, I could never really control the game. Gamblers always want the guys who can control the game. On our team, that was Beard and Groza." Barnhorst recalled that when other team members "finally got the call very early in the morning, we found out that they were releasing Holland, Barker, and Schaefer. But they were holding Groza and Beard. Apparently the two of them attested to the facts surrounding a game from 1949."

The game in question was Kentucky's 1949 first-round NIT tournament game against Loyola at Madison Square Garden in New York. The day before the contest, Nick Englisis, a small-time gambler and a former University of Kentucky student, had visited three Kentucky players in their hotel room: Dale Barnstable, a talented junior guard, and Beard and Groza. Englisis described how he engineered the fix in an exclusive article for *True* magazine in March 1952. At the time the article was published, Englisis was serving prison time for bribery and conspiring to influence the scores of college basketball games. Nick "the Greek," as he was known, played on the University of Kentucky football team briefly when Beard was on the freshman team. Englisis used this tie to reintroduce himself to the Kentucky All-American. After a successful performance in an SEC battle earlier in the year, Englisis congratulated Beard and handed him a $20 bill.

During the early 1950s, it was common practice for a fan or alumnus to financially reward college players for outstanding games, particularly if that same fan or alumnus had bet a large amount of money on his favorite team to win. The National Collegiate Athletic Association had yet to come of age as a powerful governing body. Rules against such practices were not well defined. After a well-played game, an All-American talent like Beard or Groza would not be surprised to extend his hand for a congratulatory handshake and find his palm greased with a $10 or $20 bill. A gift from someone like Englisis was commonplace.

But Beard, Groza, and Barnstable found nothing common about Englisis's next move. With his loose ties established, the Kentucky gambler asked them to meet briefly with a few influential friends. The group consisted of Nick and his brother, Tony, their sidekick, Saul Feinberg, and Nat "Lovey" Brown, the "heavy" of the group. They took the athletes to meet Eli Kaye, a New York underworld figure who supplied the front money for Englisis's operations. According to Englisis's article, he offered Beard, Groza, and Barnstable $1,500 to shave points and stay under the 11-point spread against Loyola in the 1949 NIT tournament. The group's proposition stunned the three Kentucky ball players. They resisted. But the gamblers' sales pitch overwhelmed them.

In Charles Rosen's *Scandals of '51*, Barnstable described the conversation: "Those guys were smooth talkers. They should have been salesmen. They took us out for a stroll, treated us to a meal, and before we knew anything, we were right in the middle of it. They said we didn't have to dump the game. They said nobody would get hurt except other gamblers. They said everybody was doing it. . . . We just didn't think. But if somebody who suspected what was going on at the Garden had warned us that things like that were against the law, we'd never have done it."

Barker commented: "I don't think Beard, Groza, and Barnstable ever did throw the game. I think it's just the way the score came out. I don't deny that they took the money. But I don't think they tried to lose the game on purpose. They were just poor country kids who weren't used to seeing a bunch of money fanned under their noses like that."

After the game, in the parking lot at Madison Square Garden, the three met Nick Englisis to receive their $1,500 payoff. Englisis, who had bet heavily on Loyola, reaped a hefty $6,000 profit.

Two and a half years later, Hogan's investigative army caught up with Beard and Groza. Much later, in a 1992 public television interview, Beard stated: "As long as I live, I will never forget October 19, 1951. The whole thing was so confusing to me at the time. But I told all those policemen the truth, which was that I never did anything to adversely influence the score of a basketball game. As God is my witness, I can tell you that. Yes, I took the money. But I never shaved points or did anything like that. I just couldn't. I wanted to win too much. I know some people may call me a liar, and I guess God and I will only know the truth. But the money meant nothing to me. I would not, and could not, shave points in that Loyola game."

In his *True* article, Englisis painted a dark and seedy portrait of deceit among the ranks of the University of Kentucky's basketball team. According to Nick "the Greek," Beard, Groza, and Barnstable also fixed other Kentucky games with Englisis's help. The NIT tournament was to be their grand coup in New York's gambling circles. "We [the other gamblers and I] thought the tournament was the spot where we were going to hit the real big money because Kentucky was entered and favored to win," Englisis stated. "We got a room in the Hotel Paramount in Manhattan so we could be close to the situation all the time. That's where Madison Square Garden puts up most of its tournament teams. Groza came into our room with Beard and Barnstable the day they arrived. By now they were anxious guys. They had the whole tournament planned. They were going to make a bundle the whole way. We agreed to pay them $500 apiece for the Loyola game. But the entire affair backfired. . . . Groza realized everything was wrong—that Kentucky might lose—and he'd lose his chance to make money all the way through the tournament. In the NIT, one loss eliminates you. . . . Alex started to get active, but the first thing he did was to foul. . . . He fouled out. That was it. The crowd roared when he fouled out, because now they knew that Loyola was a cinch to win. Groza walked to the bench and buried his face in a towel. . . . Beard and Barnstable tried to make up the deficit late in the game, but then Beard fouled out and walked off the court chewing his gum like a piston. He sat down and kept his head on his chest. I guess he was counting the dough he lost out on [because he could not continue shaving points in other NIT tournament games]."

Beard and Groza vehemently denied Englisis's allegations in an *Indianapolis News* report the following week. "This article is filled with black lies intended to throw the blame on us," they stated. Beard pointed out: "I didn't even foul out in that game. I played all but two minutes." In Englisis's article, the gambler mentioned that Groza showed up on campus one day in a new car: "I know he didn't buy it with pennies from his piggy bank." To that quote, Groza replied: "I borrowed more than $1,000 from my brother, Lou, to buy that car."

One of the biggest points of dispute the two players had with Englisis's article was that the gambler claimed to have arranged fixes on nine Kentucky ball games during the 1948–49 season. Beard emphatically denied the claim but openly admitted that he, Groza, and Barnstable did take money on three separate occasions: the Loyola game, a game in Chicago against DePaul, and an SEC contest against Vanderbilt in Nashville.

"Bribes Rock Olympians"—the headline screamed across the front page of the *Indianapolis Star* on the morning of October 20, 1951. Photos showed Beard and Groza in the company of Chicago's undercover police force. The *Star* described the scene: "The Olympian stars, unshaven, rumpled, and tired after a night of questioning by Attorney Vincent A. G. O'Conner of New York and his aides, stood silently as their bond was arranged by Coach Schaefer. Then the fiery little guard, who has thrilled thousands of Hoosier pro fans with his sparkling play, turned to Groza and said quietly, 'What an ordeal.' The big six-foot-seven-inch center just nodded."

"The city was stunned," Barker recalled. "Everybody was, even Rupp. He once said that gamblers couldn't touch his boys with a

10-foot pole. But now folks were saying that gamblers must have found an 11-foot pole. But none of us, including Rupp, had any idea that this type of thing could happen."

The fate of the two stars was swift and stunning. While officials in Chicago released Beard and Groza on $1,000 bond each, NBA commissioner Podoloff ordered an emergency meeting of the board of governors. He then flew to Chicago to carry out the league's order. First, the league forced the two stars to surrender their stock in the club. Then came the most stunning mandate of all. "They told us that we were banned from the league for life," Beard lamented. "And that was it. Just like that, it was the end of my career. I was ruined at 23 years old. Can you imagine how that'd make you feel at 23? All I ever wanted to do was be a professional basketball player. And, of course, Alex and I were. We owned our own team. We were on top of the world. Now it was all gone. I'd lost everything. I was humiliated. I was ridiculed. I was branded a criminal. You know, stuff like that just never goes away."[2]

Podoloff stood stern and solemn before reporters. "You must remember we have a definite interest in the spectators who are paying the freight," he said. "We are morally bound to present a sport that is beyond any criticism of conduct on the playing court. This would not be so if we allowed these players to return. We can survive the loss of a number of players, no matter what their status is, but we cannot survive doubt of the honesty of the sport." Podoloff thanked the New York police department for its help in "cleansing professional basketball from the taint of fixes."

Beard's 22-year-old wife, Marilyn, gave a tearful statement to reporters: "I can't quite make myself believe it. I haven't any idea what we'll do now." In Cleveland, Groza's brother, Lou, the famed football place kicker, broke down and cried. He was too overcome to talk on the phone with reporters and had to be excused. Wallace "Wah-Wah" Jones commented: "I hope it isn't true and can't believe it is. All I know is that if it is true, I had nothing to do with it. I don't know what will happen to the Olympians. We'll go ahead without the two boys . . . but we surely will miss them."

Indianapolis Star columnist Bob Stranahan commented that

"those stinking gambling dollars weren't even a gamble. The fixers weren't even gamblers enough to take a chance. They had to have a sure thing, even if it meant wrecking the futures of some kids along the way. This should be a lesson in greed to all of us. It just doesn't seem possible."

The value of Olympians stock plummeted from $10,000 to $1,000 a share overnight. Fans searched for answers. "Say It Isn't So," read one editorial in the *Indianapolis News*. "Those weeping words from a small boy admirer must have been the bitterest pill of all for Shoeless Joe Jackson when he was accused of selling out his team, and the faith and ideals of the patron's youth in the 1919 Black Sox baseball scandal. And it must be bitter, indeed, for Alex Groza and Ralph Beard, stars of the Indianapolis Olympians, to know that the first reaction of Indianapolis basketball fans, young and old, to the news of their arrest for basketball 'fixing' was the same as that disillusioned Chicago boy: Say it isn't so."

Barnhorst recalled: "It was really tough when we first got back into town after the news broke. No one in the city really knew how to react. But then the most extraordinary thing happened. Luke Walton, our play-by-play radio announcer, came on the air one night with a five-minute editorial that examined the whole affair. He said that while what Beard and Groza did was wrong, he wanted everyone listening to realize that this gambling thing happened when they were just boys—college boys. He explained that they were young, poor, and tempted by some smooth-talking gamblers. After all, when someone lays $1,000 or so in front of them and tells them that they can go ahead and win the game, just don't win by more than 10 points, anyone can see how confusing it can get for a couple of 21-year-olds. Well, after Luke's editorial went on the air, it seemed as though the attitude changed toward Ralph and Al. They were just victims in the whole thing."

Barker stated: "The city accepted us afterwards. But I'm sure it was tough on Al and Ralph. It's hard to believe with all the players in the league that Al and Ralph were the only two 'caught,' supposedly. There were rumors of a list of names the NBA was checking into, but they really singled out Al and Ralph. I don't know what the league was thinking."

Decades after the scandal, the wounds still cut deep into Beard's soul. In the public television documentary, he shrugged: "I guess you can say that I was pretty bitter. We knew, and the league knew, that several players on other NBA teams were betting on games, shaving points, etc., etc. Podoloff just used us as scapegoats."

It was common knowledge among NBA insiders at the time that point shaving and gambling was a growing plague in the professional ranks. It was even rumored that Podoloff had a short list of names of players under close internal scrutiny in the NBA. Ironically, not a single player from the Indianapolis Olympians was on Podoloff's alleged list. Groza said: "I know that all the Olympians' games were strictly clean. There's nothing that has been crooked in professional basketball."

Podoloff's young league was in jeopardy of its own widespread gambling scandal. In the turbulent wake of the current college arrests, the repercussions of a public, police investigation in the pro ranks would most likely ruin the NBA. Many observers felt that the college scandals produced two perfect targets in Beard and Groza. By banning the two NBA all-stars for life, Podoloff could send a harsh message to the league's gamblers and game fixers. "These fellows have got to disassociate themselves from the league immediately. If not, I will vacate entire franchises," he sternly told the press.

Rupp attempted to lessen the impact of the Beard-Groza scandal in the Bluegrass state. "The Chicago Black Sox threw games. But these kids only shaved points," he pleaded to a bank of sportswriters. "College teams go to New York and find odds for the basketball games in the newspapers. If we allow newspapers to print odds for guttersnipes who infest the sport, I think it's time we checked up on some of the newspapers. Why condemn kids for one mistake in a lifetime? Let's be more lenient toward them."

But neither the players nor the University of Kentucky basketball program found much leniency. On March 29, 1952, Judge Saul Streit sentenced Beard, Groza, and Barnstable to indefinite probation and suspended sentences. Beard exclaimed in the courtroom: "I'm guilty. Let me out of here. Let me die." Streit used the sentencing as a forum to lambaste Rupp's basketball program. In a 67-page report, Streit noted that "the University of Kentucky is the acme of commercialism and overemphasis. I found undeniable evidence of covert subsidization of players, ruthless exploitation of athletes, cribbing on examinations, illegal recruiting, a reckless disregard for the players' physical welfare, matriculation of unqualified students, demoralization of the athletes by the coach, the alumni, and the townspeople. . . . It is the most fruitful racket yet invented to destroy the amateur code."

That same day the NCAA announced an investigation into the University of Kentucky's entire athletic program. Beard echoed Streit's remarks when he commented to the *Indianapolis Star:* "Recruiting, that's the start of it. They went out and got us to play. It got so big. We got big—too big." In August the NCAA banned the Kentucky basketball program from Southeastern Conference play for one year. The university later estimated that the revenue lost by that one-year ban equaled nearly $100,000. Several university officials pressed President Herman Donovan to investigate Rupp. The coach responded: "No one has fought for cleaner sports and tried harder to keep them free from gambling than I have, and if anyone had anything on me, I would not be sitting at this desk, and I would not embarrass the university by remaining here."[3]

No evidence ever surfaced that Rupp was involved in any way with gambling on games or conspiring to manipulate the final scores of games. "I would rather lose a million dollars than lose a basketball game," he told reporters. On the surface, he was as tough as ever. But underneath, the scandal wounded him deeply. He did not speak to Beard or Groza for more than two decades.

In Beard's bungalow home on Haverford Road in Indianapolis, the phone rang off the hook for weeks after the scandal broke. Some called to express their sympathies. Others, mostly reporters, unleashed an unending series of questions. Groza stayed mute on the subject. But Beard's words spoke adequately for both Olympians stars. "I know I made a mistake, and I was wrong," the All-American guard told the *Indianapolis News.* "I don't want anyone's pity. I want a chance to do something about it. Maybe it'll help for others to realize what a mistake it is to take that kind of money. It's been a terrible burden. I haven't been able to eat, sleep, or think. We couldn't talk about it, and we just had to sit tight and hope it would blow away. But I always knew deep down in my heart it wouldn't."

With Beard and Groza facing Hogan's investigative army, the rest of the Indianapolis Olympians forced themselves to focus their attention on the coming 1951–52 season. Doubts loomed. The *Indianapolis News* commented: "The Olymps now go on without two of the greatest basketball players ever—Al Groza and Ralph Beard. . . . Even without the morale implications, the loss of those two, both of whom were elected to the NBA all-star team last year, would stun any basketball team."

Podoloff responded to the Olympians' plight by ordering each of the other NBA clubs to surrender one player to a list of potential recruits for the beleaguered Indianapolis squad. Some new faces joined the club, including Ralph "Buckshot" O'Brien, a 5'9" gunner from Butler University, and Bill Tosheff, a versatile guard from Indiana University. Barnhorst recalled: "We didn't have any superstars. We were surviving with a bunch of blue-collar workers. We even won a few games we shouldn't have, simply because some teams underestimated us. But attendance was dwindling. We even managed to get into the playoffs that year, but we only averaged less than 5,000 at each of our games. We just weren't as competitive as we were before."

The club limped along for two seasons without their superstars. Barker explained: "It was just like anything else. The world loves a winner. After the scandal, we really didn't have the kind of talent to attract fans. Our attendance fell off quickly, and we disintegrated. Somebody came up one day and offered us $250,000 for the franchise. We got together and decided that if it meant that much to someone else, it would mean even more to us. So we didn't sell the team. But we were going under fast."

"We just couldn't survive," Barnhorst shrugged. "So the only thing to do was throw in the towel. That was it. After the 1952–53 season, the Indianapolis Olympians went out of business."

One year after the scandal, District Attorney Frank Hogan puffed on his pipe as he stood above his littered desk in Manhattan. Slowly and patiently he mulled over piles of legal documentation regarding the indictments in the college basketball scandals. In all, the web of illegal gambling and game fixing entangled 32 players in eight major universities. The scandals virtually annihilated the spectator's trust in college basketball. University officials nationwide quickly nixed the once wildly popular college double-headers held at Madison Square Garden. As the sordid details of each and every bribe came out in the papers, basketball fans drifted further and further away from the college game.

Professional basketball became the direct beneficiary. A new, larger audience sought a different type of entertainment on the court. Podoloff's NBA gladly supplied it. Even with the controversy in Indianapolis, Podoloff reasoned that Beard and Groza's indiscretions had occurred while they were still in college. According to Podoloff, the world of professional basketball still was clean.

In 1952 Beard and Groza signed contracts to play in a rival pro organization, the American Professional Basketball League. The league was, in essence, the old East Coast–based American League, which had formed in 1925. Beard and Groza joined the New Jersey Titans, along with former Long Island University star Sherman White, another player involved in the scandals of 1951. A team from Elmira, New York, signed Bill Spivey, a former University of Kentucky center who had alleged ties to gamblers in a separate incident in the Bluegrass state. But before the league embarked on its inaugural season, APBL president John O'Brien put a halt to the signing of those involved in the scandals, telling reporters: "In all its history, our league never has been tainted and I wouldn't want it to start now. Why, in years gone by, we have banished players who were even suspicious. We didn't need proof. If a player was seen in the company of a gambler, his contract was not renewed. That's the only way to keep basketball clean."

New Jersey and Elmira pulled their franchises from the league in protest, and the APBL fell apart before the season even started. National sportswriter Red Smith was outraged: "At the age of 24, the American Professional Basketball League has died of a rare ailment—acute prison pallor. In an expression of policy which ought to go ringing down the corridors of sports, two clubs decided that if they had to use nothing but players who had never dumped a game, they wouldn't play. When they withdrew in a gold-plated huff, the five other teams quit, throwing everybody out of work. So now the fixers who destroyed basketball at Long Island University and dealt the amateur game mortal damage all over the country, have put a professional league out of business."

Slowly Beard and Groza began to forget the pain of October 19, 1951. It took 16 years and a new league before the two got involved with basketball again. In 1967 the American Basketball Association ushered in a new era of professional ball, as well as a new team from the Bluegrass state, the Louisville Colonels. The business manager of the team was Groza. Beard joined the club later as a weekend scout to supplement a successful career in pharmaceutical sales. Both former Olympians bounced back after a tragic time of severed glory and unfulfilled dreams.

For Groza, the years following the scandal were difficult. Much later, Barker's wife, Meredith, recalled: "Just a few years ago Alex called us out of the blue and asked Cliff and I to come to meet him in Denver. We didn't know it at the time, but he was very, very ill. And he knew it. I'm sure he did. And that's why he wanted us to get together. He kept asking Cliff if he was all right. He asked Cliff and I if we were going to be O.K. financially. We asked him why. And he started to tell us about the scandal. He felt that he might have ruined our lives by his actions, and he wanted to get it all off his chest. We told him he didn't have to say a word to us, but he insisted. He told us about the meeting with those gamblers and how he took the money. Then he said to us in confidence, 'Never did I throw a game. . . . Never!' It must have been such a release for him after all those years. He wanted us to know what happened and wanted to be sure that Cliff and I were all right. He kept calling Cliff 'Dad,' which was his nickname in college. 'I'm so sorry, Dad. I'm so sorry.' He kept saying it. Cliff and I were stunned. It was really something. After we said goodbye, Cliff and I came back to Indiana, and Alex went to his home in California. That was the last time we saw him. Six months later he died."

Beard, in his television interview, admitted that he continued to live with the pain every day. "Nowadays I'd rather be playing golf than watching a professional basketball game. It's just too tough. You know, there are days I go maybe 10 minutes without thinking about it, especially during basketball season. It just brings back too many painful memories."

> I was totally shocked. Move the Pistons
> to Detroit? I hated the thought of that....
> nothing was near as nice as Fort Wayne,
> particularly the fans.

—George Yardley, Hall-of-Fame
Pistons player, 1953–59

11. The Fateful Seventh Game

Asked to reflect on his professional basketball experiences in Indiana, former Anderson Packer and Fort Wayne Piston Frankie Brian exclaimed: "Our rivalries with the other teams in the state were really strong. Back when I played, Indiana had more teams in professional basketball than any other state. It was really unheard of in the league at that time. That's why I've always felt that Indiana was the home of basketball." He was right. In the early postwar years from 1946 through 1953, professional basketball in the Hoosier state underwent a whirlwind of change unmatched in basketball history. Not since the old NBL's inaugural year in 1937 had a single state produced more franchises in a professional sport at any one time. The league wars in 1947–48 destroyed some Indiana franchises and gave rise to others. In all, seven different Indiana teams took the court during that seven-year span. But at the start of the 1953–54 season, only the Fort Wayne Zollner Pistons remained. Through the turbulence of player wars, league mergers, and public scandals, Fred Zollner proved that the National Basketball Association's smallest franchise still had the deepest pocketbooks and the most stable organization.

During the NBA's inaugural year in 1949, Zollner had primed his Pistons for the new league by hiring away Coach Murray Mendenhall from the Anderson Packers. Mendenhall's legacy in Fort Wayne's high school ranks, his congenial nature, and his loose, fast-break style of coaching made him popular among players and fans. Mendenhall had gone to work right away. He aggressively recruited some of the top college athletes, and Zollner gladly shelled out the money to lure them. The organization's 1949–50 recruits featured the tallest front line in the NBA. Two rookie forwards, 6'5" Fred Schaus and 6'9" Larry Foust, joined lanky seven-footer Don Otten in the starting lineup. When the Anderson Packers folded in 1951, Fort Wayne picked up the contracts of several seasoned pros, including Charlie Black, Frankie Brian, and Boag Johnson.

Another Mendenhall recruit in the summer of 1950 was George Yardley, a highly-talented, 6'5" forward from Stanford University. During his career with the Pistons, he became the first professional basketball player to score 2,000 points in a single season. The *Los Angeles Times* National Sports Award Board named him the Outstanding Amateur Basketball Player of the Year in 1953. He was the third player chosen in the draft. Fort Wayne general manager Carl Bennett notified the Stanford star via telegram: "Fort Wayne of the National Basketball Association drafted you. Please call me collect late Tuesday or Wednesday at Harrison 9426 or Anthony 3264. Also advise [Stanford] Coach Dean of our choice."[1] Yardley recalled: "When I got the telegram, I had to laugh, 'Fort Wayne?!' I'd never heard of such a place. I'd heard of Indianapolis before, and I knew where Indiana was on the map, but what kid from California had ever heard of Fort Wayne, Indiana?"

Yardley, who was born in Hollywood and grew up in Newport Beach, was a multisport athlete, but because of his lanky, 6'5" frame, he gravitated toward basketball. At Stanford he broke the school's career scoring record set in the 1930s by jump-shot artist Hank Luisetti.

Initially Zollner offered a $6,000 contract to Yardley. But

Yardley stalled. According to Rodger Nelson in his book *The Zollner Piston Story*, Yardley despised training camp and saw no rush in signing. He spent the extra time in California playing beach volleyball and biding his time. Zollner, misinterpreting Yardley's intentions as a holdout for more money, upped the ante to $9,500. Yardley finally signed. By spending his summer on the beach, Yardley came to Fort Wayne $3,500 richer.

"My wife and I didn't know what to expect when we got to Fort Wayne," Yardley recalled. "We had a hard time adjusting to the weather in Indiana. We had never seen snow before. So that first winter was pretty rough. Of course, in Fort Wayne, the Pistons were the only game in town. They didn't have professional football or baseball teams. So major league sports to Fort Wayne was the Pistons. And the people supported the team very well. They were great basketball fans. But more importantly, they were great people. They wanted you to know that Fort Wayne was a great place to live, and they did everything they could to illustrate that to you. To this day I believe that Fort Wayne has some of the coldest weather and the warmest people in the country."

Teammate Frankie Brian recalled Yardley's arrival in Fort Wayne: "We could see from the onset that he was just a terrific basketball player. Plus, he was just a great fella. George was one of those guys that you just liked to be around. He had an energy about him. He really added a lot to our team chemistry." Yardley was also a man of many hidden talents, as Brian pointed out: "Something very few people know about George is that he is quite a tailor. And I'll tell you, in an hour's time he could make you one heckuva shirt. It would look just like a shirt you'd buy at the store. He made a lot of stuff. He made a lot of his wife's clothes. We'd often go out shopping when we weren't playing, and George would buy all this material. Can you imagine a big guy like that going into a store and buying all this material? I mean, the clerks would look at us like we were crazy. They obviously didn't know what George could do with a sewing machine."

Yardley fully expected to come to Fort Wayne to play for Mendenhall. But the team had been struggling of late, and even the popular Mendenhall could not escape the tough scrutiny of Zollner. The owner bought the remaining year on Mendenhall's contract, and after 29 seasons during which Mendenhall had built a coaching legacy in the Hoosier state, he was sacked.

Zollner felt that the Mendenhall-led Pistons were too loose—not enough discipline. So he hired the strictest, hardest-nosed basketball strategist he could find, former Piston point guard and New York Celtic Paul Birch. "That Paul Birch was a tough one!" exclaimed Frankie Brian. "I mean, you did what Paul Birch told you, or you could expect to hear about it. Whatever he told me to do, I knew I'd better do it *now*. I remember once we played a game in Baltimore, and we didn't play up to his expectations. Well, after the game we were all sitting around this table, and he stormed in there and hauled off and kicked that table. Well, it knocked that table right over and all of us with it. We just toppled over backwards. He could get pretty upset. He was something else. I knew that I'd better perform the way he wanted me to, or I'd surely hear about it."

When Yardley arrived, he found Birch to be a superb coach. "He taught me a lot about basketball," Yardley commented. "But he was a real loony. He was very demanding—kicking and throwing things and going nuts. He was very physical and loud, just a really tough guy. But he really knew the game. He was a defensive-minded coach who knew that a good defense wins championships. If he hadn't had all his personal hangups, we might have had a strong team for many years."

Birch unleashed his hard-nosed, dictatorial coaching style on the Pistons at the start of the 1951–52 season. Rodger Nelson, former sports information director for the Pistons, said of Birch: "For him, coaching was no popularity contest."[2] Once when the team lost a game on the road, the brooding Birch made his players sit in the dark on the plane all the way back to Fort Wayne. He often ate oranges or other kinds of fruit during the game. When a Piston player made a mistake, the coach might chuck a peel at him across the locker room. Birch also had a knack for drop-kicking everything in sight, including gym bags, towels, and once an oxygen tank the team's trainer kept on hand in case of emergencies.

Birch's defensive-minded play pushed the Pistons to the league's second-best defensive record, but also the NBA's second-worst offensive record. The club won only six games in its first 24 starts.

Birch shrugged off the season as a time of rebuilding, calling it "our sacrifice year."

Fort Wayne fans seemed less enthused about this new defensive style of play. Mendenhall's old run-and-gun strategy had generated more points and more excitement on the court. Attendance figures in Fort Wayne remained lower than in the rest of the league cities, partially because of the slower, more deliberate play and partially because North Side gym held only a third the capacity of other large NBA venues.

Then, on September 28, 1952, the city of Fort Wayne cut the ceremonial ribbon on its newest attraction, the spacious Allen County War Memorial Coliseum. Fred Zollner was one of the driving forces behind the arena, which held nearly 10,000 spectators. The Coliseum not only played host to Pistons basketball games but also featured Fort Wayne Komets hockey matches, musical performances from such popular artists as Gene Autry, Holiday on Ice exhibitions, and the American Bowling Congress national tour. Just months after its opening, the *Fort Wayne Journal Gazette* reported that 373,708 patrons had passed through it. Zollner's Pistons were the facility's best tenant. Nearly 100,000 pro basketball fans poured into the Coliseum during the first two months of the 1952–53 campaign.

For the past two seasons the NBA had staged an annual All-Star game. Celtics owner Walter Brown hosted the first two All-Star contests at the Boston Garden. With the new arena as an attractive drawing card for the league, the Pistons' Carl Bennett, now athletic director, petitioned to hold the 1953 All-Star Classic in Fort Wayne. His request met with resounding approval. On January 13 pro basketball's main officials and top players headed to the Summit City for a two-day NBA promotional extravaganza.

One day before the game, on January 12, George Craig took the oath of office as governor of Indiana. At an official ceremony at the Indiana State House, Craig announced his first order of business. He declared the week of January 12–18 as "Indiana Basketball Week." The proclamation read: "WHEREAS the National Basketball Association has awarded the All-Star Game to Fort Wayne to be played at Allen County War Memorial Coliseum on January 13, 1953, and, WHEREAS the members of the

All-Star team, composed of the Eastern and Western Division, are selected by sports writers and sportscasters; and, WHEREAS each team will be represented by outstanding basketball players of the nation, which will be a tribute to the great State of Indiana, which, by the performance and participation of the citizenship of our great State, demonstrates that Indiana is known as the basketball center of America; and, WHEREAS the City of Fort Wayne was one of the pioneers in the State to further this great sport of basketball having been represented previously by professional, college, high school, and independent basketball; and, WHEREAS the Zollner Pistons, by virtue of its sponsor, Fred Zollner, are now recognized as the oldest team in continuous operation in the world today in organized professional league competition having started to play professional ball in the National Industrial League in the year 1940; and WHEREAS this outstanding event will be held in the Allen County War Memorial Coliseum, erected as a living memorial in honor of the men and women of Allen County who gave their lives in World War I and II for our Nation, so that we might live; therefore, BE IT RESOLVED that the Governor of the sovereign State of Indiana declare the week of January 12–18 as 'Indiana Basketball Week,' and that the Governor extends to the participants, the citizens of the State of Indiana, his best wishes for a successful event, and may the best team win."

Zollner and Fort Wayne mayor Harry Baals hosted a civic luncheon on the playing floor of the Coliseum for the 20 All-Star participants, the NBA board of governors, the Zollner Pistons, and about 900 fans. In a special ceremony Baals presented NBA Commissioner Maurice Podoloff with the key to the city. Several leading national newsreel organizations, including Movietone News, Paramount News, and Pathe News, brought film crews to Fort Wayne, and two national television services, Telra of Philadelphia and Telenews from New York, also covered the festivities. Bennett recalled how Zollner rolled out the red carpet for the press: "To ensure maximum national news coverage, Fred Zollner ordered his DC-3 airplane to fly to each of the major market clubs, pick up their respective media representatives, and fly them to Fort Wayne, free of charge, to report on the All-Star game.

Zollner set up a palatial press headquarters at the Van Orman Hotel in downtown Fort Wayne."

The NBA assigned veteran broadcaster Marty Glickman, the "Voice of the New York Knicks," to call the play by play for national radio broadcast. He chose as his color commentator Hilliard Gates, the Pistons play-by-play man. Gates recalled: "The Mutual Broadcasting Company bought rights to that game. It was the first NBA game to be broadcast from coast to coast. Marty was going to be the eastern division representative and I was going to represent the western division. It got me a lot of attention nationally that I might not have gotten otherwise. It ended up being a great break for my career, as well as a tremendous honor." Gates's skillful commentary and his well-researched insights during the game made a favorable impression with the national media. Several seasons later, he was offered the head sports anchor job for the Boston Celtics Radio Network but opted to stay in his hometown of Fort Wayne.

In all, 73 newspaper and radio representatives flooded Fort Wayne. In addition, seven camera operators perched themselves on bulky equipment on the crowded sidelines. Executives from Dumont, a national television organization, were so impressed with the results that they offered NBA Commissioner Maurice Podoloff pro basketball's first television contract for the following season.

On game day, *Journal Gazette* columnist Bob Reed reported: "Tonight's crowd looms as the largest ever to see a sport event here, definitely the largest indoors and probably anywhere. Extra seats have been installed. . . . We expect near 10,000 [spectators]. . . . Fort Wayne moves up still another notch in the world of sport with the staging of the National Basketball Association's annual All-Star Game here. It is rather ironic that the city which was referred to just a few years ago by a New York writer as a 'whistle stop' in comparison with other cities in the NBA should be staging the league's mid-season classic and in only the third year of its inception."

The Pistons' Larry Foust and Andy Phillip, a former member of the University of Illinois "Whiz Kids," earned spots on the West All-Stars. They joined George Mikan and Vern Mikkelsen of the

Lakers and Indianapolis's Leo Barnhorst, among others. Boston's "Easy" Ed McCauley and Bob Cousy as well as Syracuse's Dolph Shayes led the East squad. During the introduction of the players, the lights dimmed and a large spotlight spilled onto the floor. As each All-Star ran into the spotlight, Norm Carroll, the Coliseum's organist, played a few bars of each player's college alma mater.

The *Fort Wayne Journal Gazette* reported that 10,332 "bug-eyed spectators" enjoyed "one of the best basketball exhibitions ever staged anywhere, any place." It was the largest crowd to attend an All-Star game to that point. All cheered wildly as Podoloff presented Zollner a ball autographed by each player and each member of the NBA's board of governors.

In the contest Mikan paced his squad with 22 points to lead the West All-Stars to a 79–75 victory over the East. Foust reached double figures with 10, and Phillip added nine points and eight assists. The *Journal Gazette* stated: "Fort Wayne fans, seeing their first National Basketball Association All-Star game, came away from the Coliseum last night feeling they had witnessed a great ball game. Players, too, felt it was a corker, and those who have played in all three agreed this was the best of them all. It was truly an awe-inspiring spectacle. . . . "

The *Journal Gazette* was not alone in its praise of the festivities in Fort Wayne. Ike Gellis from the *New York Post* penned: "There may be as good an all-star game in the future, but the third one staged here last night will never be surpassed. For a city of only 135,000, Fort Wayne gave the pro game a big-time touch. It was Phillip's feeding of his Western mates that made the difference." Matt Jackson of the *Rochester Times-Union* echoed: "It was a Hollywood production, big league from start to finish. Anyone who inherits next year's All-Star contest will find it like singing after Caruso to match the efforts of the hard-working Zollner crew. Not a trick was missed in presenting the world's greatest basketball stars to the record turnout. . . . It was the greatest shot in the arm professional basketball has had since the inception of the sport. Every player lived up to all the glowing advance reports. It was a great show, performed by outstanding artists and staged in a perfect setting by the perfect host, Fred Zollner. It did a lot for the cause of pro basketball."

Several new recruits gave Fred Zollner reason to lick his chops in anticipation of the 1953–54 season. Six-foot six-inch forward Mel Hutchins provided the height and talent to make the Pistons competitive against taller foes like Minneapolis. Word finally came from California that Yardley, who had just completed a two-year military stint, was ready to sign. And then, in the spring of 1953, Zollner pulled off one of his greatest coups of the year by signing the Pistons' number one draft pick, Columbia University's Jack Molinas. The *Journal Gazette* reported on April 25: "Coach Paul Birch of the Fort Wayne Zollner Pistons nabbed the collegian he was seeking . . . in the annual professional draft of college stars by the National Basketball Association. He's 6'6" Jack Molinas of Columbia University, proclaimed the outstanding college star of the recent nationwide Harlem Globetrotter tour." In his weekly column, *Journal Gazette* reporter Bob Reed commented: "Who will be 'Rookie of the Year' in the National Basketball Association? As the season gets underway, it is believed that there has never before been such an array of young talent in the pro league. Fort Wayne is certain to make a strong bid for the honor with George Yardley and Jack Molinas as candidates."

Molinas, who grew up in the Bronx the son of a Coney Island restaurant owner, had attended Stuyvesant High School, where he starred on the basketball team. In college he had led Columbia in scoring, and the school had enjoyed its best season ever during his collegiate career. The Pistons signed Molinas for $9,500. At the time he and Yardley were the highest-paid players in the franchise's history.

Frank Brian was Molinas's roommate. "Jack was new to the club," Brian recalled. "Because he was a rookie, the coaches wanted him to room with a veteran player. So they put him with me. . . . I remember watching him play in practice. He was such an outstanding ballplayer. He could do it all, both inside and outside. He was big, but he could do a lot with the ball. I knew he had quite a future in pro basketball."

Molinas was a flashy maverick on the court. Some players complained that his showy, individualistic style interrupted the flow of team play. But no one doubted his raw basketball ability. Carl Bennett recalled: "I scouted Molinas. I watched him play. I knew he could really help our ball team. He had long arms and big hands. And his basketball savvy was incredible. I knew he was going to be one of the greatest players to ever play the game."

In one of his first outings with the Pistons, Molinas found his team down by 20 points to Syracuse entering the third quarter. Almost singlehandedly, the Piston forward brought his club back from the brink by racking up 20 points in the third quarter alone. He finished with 24. Six nights later against Milwaukee, he tallied 22 points, then repeated his performance with 22 more against Baltimore three nights later. With the season only a month old, he led the Pistons in shooting percentage with a 46.7 average, the second best in the entire league.

Early in the season, the *Journal Gazette* asked readers to select their all-time Pistons team. Rookie Molinas was one of the top vote-getters. He joined such Piston greats as Bobby McDermott, Paul "Curly" Armstrong, Larry Foust, and Buddy Jeannette. By early January, Molinas had earned a spot on the West All-Star team, alongside his teammates Mel Hutchins and Foust. The future looked bright for young Jack Molinas, but just days before the All-Star classic his career came to a sudden halt.

On January 10, Carl Bennett was in Miami Beach exploring possibilities for Pistons exhibition tours through the Sunshine State when he got a phone call. "I got back to my hotel and found out that Maurice Podoloff had been trying to get in touch with me," Bennett recalled. "When I finally talked with him, he was very short and to the point. He wanted to set up a special meeting with Fred Zollner right away. That was it. He wouldn't elaborate at all. So I called Fred and set up a meeting. But I wasn't allowed to be a part of it. The meeting was held behind closed doors, with only Podoloff and Fred in the room. I found out later that they were talking about Jack Molinas."

For several weeks Podoloff had headed an internal investigation of Molinas's activities with known bookies in the New York area. The bookies had been friends and associates of Molinas when he attended Columbia. Through wiretaps Podoloff had discovered that Molinas had been engaging in gambling and game fixing on the professional level. The NBA had notified Zollner in mid-December that an investigation was under way. The Fort Wayne owner sat tight until he received word from Podoloff that the league was ready to proceed with public charges against Molinas.

Podoloff summoned Molinas to New York. With Zollner and several investigators present, Molinas was questioned from 7:30 in the evening until well after 2:30 in the morning. In a signed confession, the Pistons rookie admitted placing bets on his team to win in several contests during the first two months of the 1953 season. Molinas listed 10 separate incidents, including his spectacular 22-point performance against Baltimore in November. Molinas swore that he had never shaved points, thrown games, or bet against the Pistons and the spread. He told Podoloff he had received about $400 in total winnings. With his chin sunk to his chest, the 21-year-old Molinas repeated a sullen mantra: "I've never done anything dishonest in my life."

The statement was far from the truth. Molinas had had a discipline problem dating back as far as high school. At Stuyvesant, he often missed the team bus and blew off games to hang out with his friends in Coney Island. He was a renegade at Columbia and missed several games owing to disciplinary measures. He had known connections with Joe Hacken, a bookie from the Bronx. And while he was never formally charged with shaving points or throwing games in college, New York State Supreme Court Judge Sarafite, in reviewing the basketball career of the Pistons' recruit, referred to Molinas as "a master fixer."[3]

"Jack was a sick man," Carl Bennett recalled. "He had some real gambling problems. Molinas caught on to the fact that the NBA was tapping his phone line, but he continued to place bets anyway. He had his opportunities, both before and after the Pistons, to get some help. But he didn't, or maybe couldn't, do anything to stop the problem."

Molinas's roommate Frank Brian exclaimed: "To think that he was betting on games. . . . That was the last thing I ever would have thought. When Fred called us together to tell us that Molinas was betting on games and that his career was over, it was a real shocker to me. Nothing ever really tipped me off that he was placing bets. Whenever we were in a hotel room together, he would always tell me that he was going to call his girlfriend. Well, I didn't want to be around when he talked to his girlfriend. So I tried to give him some privacy by going to one of the other guy's rooms. Of course, I discovered later that he was really talking to his bookie. Looking back now, I can see how he maybe used certain code words to communicate, so as not to give anything away to me or the other guys. He would always say things on the phone like 'I feel really good tonight' or 'Everybody's just fine here.' That meant that all bets should be placed on Fort Wayne to win. Or if he said something to the opposite effect, like 'I just don't feel very well,' that meant to place bets on the other team. At the time, it all seemed innocent enough."

The Pistons and the league suspended Molinas indefinitely for gambling on games involving the Fort Wayne team. In 1957 he opened a law practice in New York and played and coached semi-pro ball in the Eastern League. On March 17, 1962, he was arrested on gambling charges. New York district attorney Frank Hogan pinpointed Molinas as the prime conspirator in a new ring of college fixes. At the hearing in New York, Judge Sarafite called Molinas "a completely immoral person, and the ringleader of groups that corrupted college ballplayers to dump games for money." He was sentenced to 7–12$^1/_2$ years at Attica prison. Molinas's prison term did little to stem the tide of illegal activities by the former Pistons standout. On February 25, 1970, his parole was transferred to California. In Los Angeles, Molinas was instrumental in setting up a pornography ring, Jo Jo Productions. The FBI, as well as other organized crime task forces, kept taps on Molinas's phone line. The Mafia also kept a close eye on Jack Molinas for large gambling debts he owed in Las Vegas. In the summer of 1975, he was found outside his Los Angeles home with the bullet of a .22 through his head.

The Molinas case was the NBA's first official instance of a player gambling on the pro level. Commissioner Podoloff assured the media that the case was an isolated incident that involved only one player. Both Podoloff and Zollner proclaimed that no one else on the Fort Wayne team was implicated in the scandal.

In the wake of the scandal, the *Journal Gazette* ran an editorial entitled "The Case of Jack Molinas." The article concluded that, Fort Wayne "is a nationally known basketball center. It likes that reputation and wants to keep it unsullied. Everyone who loves or plays the game should learn something from the unfortunate experience of Jack Molinas. Basketball fans are sorry that this young man violated an essential rule of the NBA. They never like to see an athlete offend against rules of sportsmanship. But the game is more important than any individual who can't keep his hands clean. The game will go on without him."

The game did go on without Molinas. So, too, did the Fort Wayne Pistons—but not with Coach Birch. Birch resigned in 1954, citing the Molinas scandal as the prime handicap that prevented the Pistons from performing better. But it was no secret that Zollner had grown unhappy with his team's style of play under Birch. If during the Mendenhall era his team had lacked discipline, under Birch the Pistons were not loose enough.

Zollner tinkered with his team to find an effective combination to win an NBA championship. Gone were veterans Fred Schaus, Ken Murray, and guard Freddie Scolari. New to the Pistons lineup were Bob Houbergs, a veteran from Baltimore, Paul "Lefty" Walther from the defunct Indianapolis Olympians franchise, and Dick Rosenthal, the Pistons' number one draft pick of 1954. Rosenthal had rewritten many scoring records at the University of Notre Dame. The NBA had instituted territorial draft rights for its franchises to help keep local stars and local interest in the region. Because of his ties to Indiana, Rosenthal became Fort Wayne's hottest new prospect. "As a rookie coming into the league, it was awesome to recognize just how talented the people were who were playing professionally," Rosenthal recalled. "It was amazing to see how much everybody had to elevate their game in order to compete against this handful of players deemed the greatest in the country."

Zollner thus assembled a team he believed could compete for the 1954–55 NBA title. Now he needed a coach to replace Birch. When faced with key decisions in the past, Zollner had always relied on the steady advice of his top people, including Carl Bennett. This time the Fort Wayne owner decided to fly solo. He retreated from the public for three weeks to contemplate his choices. No one, not even the players or his closest advisers, knew what he was going to do. In the end, his choice befuddled everyone. He took the biggest gamble in his club's history and hired Charley Eckman, a veteran college and professional referee with absolutely no coaching experience. Zollner had once overheard Eckman boast that he had seen and experienced more basketball than many coaches in the league. The boisterous official had theorized: "You don't have to teach these pros anything. Just give 'em the ball and let 'em play." Because Zollner was concerned that the Birch-led Pistons were "a little over-disciplined," the choice of a the happy-go-lucky Eckman seemed appropriate for his club.

Zollner told the shocked media: "In all of my business activities, I'm a nonconformist. I do what in my own mind I think is right."[4] He added: "Charley Eckman was my number one choice from the very beginning. . . . He meets all the qualifications for the position. He has a thorough knowledge of basketball as it is played in the National Basketball Association because of his firsthand association with all the teams in the league over a seven-year period. . . . He has developed a keen and analytical knowledge of players in the league which will be invaluable to us in the coming seasons. His college officiating over a 12-year period will be extremely helpful in developing rookies for the NBA's caliber of play."

Eckman told reporters: "I know I haven't had much coaching experience, but I know I can get along with both the players and the fans. That's the big thing in coaching anyway, getting the boys to play together and keep them in a happy frame of mind. How much can anybody teach these players today? Everybody is an All-American and knows the game backward and forward."

Bob Reed, sports editor for the *Fort Wayne Journal Gazette*, wrote in disbelief: "Searching for the proverbial needle in the haystack might present a comparatively easy task compared to putting a finger on the person who knew all along that Charley Eckman would be the next Zollner Piston basketball coach." Bob Renner of the *Fort Wayne News Sentinel* pointed out that "Eckman's only coaching background was as a recreational director in the Air Force during the war."

Several members of the team were not impressed, either. George Yardley recalled that Eckman had a likable personality but said of Zollner's decision: "We were awestruck. Had Zollner lost his mind? Eckman was a good official, but he knew nothing about coaching basketball. Fred Zollner had put together the best talent in the league that year, then he blew it when he hired this oddball as our coach. We were successful that year strictly because of the talent on our team. But Eckman got the credit as a great coach. It's hard to imagine how much more successful our team would have been with a real coach. It was a joke."

Mel Hutchins described Eckman's coaching strategy: "If you need a basket, give the ball to Yardley or Hutchins."[5] Yardley elaborated: "On the floor, Eckman never gave us any indication of anything we should do. If we were down by four or five points during the first few minutes of the game, he'd say, 'Well, you guys just lost another one for me,' or something to that extreme. He just didn't understand coaching at all. It was very easy for him to lose confidence in us, and he never set up any plays for us. His one command was, 'Just go in there and do something.'"

Eckman faced a difficult situation at Fort Wayne. Team morale was at an all-time low, and team members were skeptical of Eckman's leadership abilities. The Eckman PR machine went to work immediately. His first move in the off-season was to visit each new recruit and every player on the past year's squad at their homes. He covered more than a thousand miles in a week, stopping along the way for interviews with the press and broadcast media.

One of Eckman's most successful decisions was moving Yardley into the starting lineup. Under Paul Birch, Yardley had been relegated to a substitute's role. In his rookie season he had averaged nine points and 6.5 rebounds per game. Now under Eckman, Yardley's career rocketed. During the 1954–55 season the former Stanford star averaged nearly 16 points and nine rebounds per contest. In fact, Yardley, Mel Hutchins, Larry Foust, and Frank Brian all had double-digit scoring averages during the season. Andy Phillip, who shared the backcourt responsibilities with Brian, was one of the league's leaders in assists. Bob Houbergs, Dick Rosenthal, Don Meineke, Max Zaslofsky, Jim Fritsche, and Paul Walther each provided solid support from the bench.

On November 6, Fort Wayne faced New York at the Coliseum in the first nationally televised regular-season game in pro basketball history. The Pistons defeated the Knicks, 90–83, before only about 1,000 paying customers. Apparently the fact that the Pistons were on TV excited Fort Wayne fans so much that they decided to stay home and watch their club on the tube.

It had been a decade since Bobby McDermott and Buddy Jeannette led the Pistons to three consecutive professional basketball titles. The 1954–55 squad, completely handcrafted by Zollner, seemed to be the owner's opportunity to recapture the glory. As the *Journal Gazette* noted, "This is the Piston's strongest bid for the title in its NBA history."

The Pistons compiled a 43–29 record for the year, three games better than Minneapolis in the western division. In January, Yardley, Andy Phillip, and Larry Foust made the West All-Star team. Eckman was named coach for the West All-Stars, making him the only man in history ever to referee and coach in All-Star games. By the beginning of March, it was clear that the Pistons were guaranteed a spot in the playoffs. When Milwaukee defeated Minneapolis on March 6, the Pistons secured first place in the NBA's western division.

In the playoffs Minneapolis faced Rochester in the division's semi-final round. Fort Wayne awaited the winner. Minneapolis no longer had George Mikan, who had retired a season earlier. But Jim Pollard, Vern Mikkelsen, Slater Martin, and Clyde Lovellette still gave the Lakers plenty of firepower. Minneapolis churned out two wins over Rochester to advance in the tournament but ran out of steam against the mighty Pistons. Fort Wayne prevailed, three games to one, to earn a spot in the 1955 NBA championship against the Syracuse Nationals.

As both teams prepared for the tournament, Fred Zollner discovered that his relentless pursuit of a "major league" operation might have actually backfired on him. The Allen County War Memorial Coliseum, one of his pet projects, had become a bustling promotional hub in the Midwest. For two years rumors had spread that the American Bowling Congress (ABC), the nation's largest bowling tour, might choose the Coliseum as a Midwest tournament sight. On March 6, the same day the Pistons clinched first place in the western division, the city celebrated as Mayor Robert E. Meyers confirmed the rumors. In a prepared statement, he welcomed ABC tournament officials and thousands of tourists to Fort Wayne. The *Journal Gazette* stated: "Fort Wayne will start playing host . . . to one of the nation's blue ribbon sports events, the American Bowling Congress. The 'world series' of bowling has taken over the Allen County Memorial Coliseum for a run of 73 days, with the sound of falling pins to reverberate through the huge arena daily through June 5."

For Zollner the news was bittersweet. The Pistons owner had fought hard to make the Coliseum a large commercial center. But the dates for the ABC tour directly clashed with the 1955 NBA tournament. The Pistons had their best opportunity in years to win a national title. But his talented club had no gym in which to play their home games. As Coliseum crews tore out the basketball floor to make way for 38 bowling alleys, Zollner and the Pistons sought new "home" quarters 120 miles southwest of Fort Wayne at the Indianapolis State Fairgrounds Coliseum.

Sports historian Ron Newlin reflected: "Even as late as the mid-1950s, professional basketball had not come into its own, so to speak. Today it's unfathomable that a bowling tournament could take priority over the NBA finals, but that's what the Zollner Pistons had to deal with in 1955. Fort Wayne had one of the best teams in professional basketball, but they still couldn't take priority over a group of bowlers. It was just an indication that pro ball hadn't yet arrived."

The *Journal Gazette* recognized the challenges facing Zollner's club in the NBA championship: "Fort Wayne's Pistons, in the final playoff series in the NBA for the first time in history, are getting a bit of the rest from their strenuous winning battles against the Minneapolis Lakers and preparing for the final effort against the Syracuse Nationals, Eastern Division champions. . . . Syracuse gets a big advantage in home floor even through the Pistons tied them in the overall standings, because the Nats won seven out of nine during the season. On top of which the Pistons' 'home court,' the Indianapolis Coliseum, is virtually a strange one."

Although Commissioner Podoloff bragged that his NBA featured the largest venues in the biggest cities, the 1955 NBA finals featured the two smallest markets in the league. The New York media once joked that Fort Wayne was a "whistle stop" in the Midwest and Syracuse a "truck stop" in the East. Now these two towns boasted the best teams in the NBA.

The Pistons, having never beaten Syracuse on its home floor, battled the odds as well as the Nationals. Despite a valiant effort by the Hoosier club and magnificent individual performances by Frank Brian and George Yardley, the Pistons lost the first two games of the series by narrow margins. *Journal Gazette* columnist Reed noted: "No matter what happens to the Pistons the rest of the way in their series with Syracuse, you must hand it to them for the way they fought back in the first two games when it appeared as if they were hopelessly beaten. . . . The present series has seen some of the best basketball imaginable from a spectator's standpoint, with the issue in doubt right down to the final buzzer. . . . The Pistons' chances are admittedly slim, but a couple wins in the first two games at Indianapolis would radically change the situation, and the way they came back in the two losses may be an indication that they are going to keep fighting."

The Pistons did keep fighting. During the third game at the Fairgrounds Coliseum, Brian put on another spectacular show, aggressively pushing the ball up the court for basket after basket and ending the game with 16 points. Fort Wayne held off a late Syracuse rally and finished the game on top, 96–89.

On a balmy Indianapolis evening two nights later, Fort Wayne squared the series with Syracuse. A balanced scoring attack (seven players in double figures) powered the highly charged Pistons machine to a 109–102 victory. The *Journal Gazette* proclaimed that the Pistons played "their most brilliant basketball of the season. . . . You never would have known tonight that Syracuse was the team that had won nine out of eleven from the Pistons this season. In tonight's performance, the Pistons outplayed the Eastern Division champions in every department of the game."

Just one week earlier, after Fort Wayne fell behind Syracuse by two games, the *Journal Gazette* had bleakly noted that the Pistons' chances were "admittedly slim." Now columnist Bob Reed changed the tune: "The series now stands at two each, but as someone remarked, Fort Wayne's deuce looks a little bigger just now than does Syracuse's. That's because the Pistons are coming stronger every game, and the general opinion is that they have the Nats on the run."

Game five in Indianapolis was a nail-biter. With only 12 seconds left in the contest the Nats had the ball, down by only a point. Syracuse guard Dick Farley, a standout from Indiana Uni-

versity, broke loose under the basket as the clock wound down
. . . :11 . . . :10 . . . :09. The ball left Farley's hand . . . :08 . . . :07
. . . :06. The short-range shot rolled around and around the rim
. . . :05 . . . :04 . . . :03. The Pistons and 4,111 fans gasped. Then
the fans cheered as the ball rolled off the rim and into the hands
of Fort Wayne guard Frank Brian. Syracuse fouled Brian with :01
left to stop the clock. Brian sank two free throws to ice the game
for Fort Wayne. The final score: Fort Wayne 74, Syracuse 71.

As teams throughout the nation competed for the American
Bowling Congress tour crown in Fort Wayne, the Pistons completed their "home stand" in Indianapolis. The Pistons needed
only one more victory to seal the championship. The Nats had to
win the final two contests at home to claim the title. Momentum
seemed to favor Zollner's team, but Syracuse preserved its perfect
home court record against the Pistons with a high-scoring victory
in game six, 109–104. The Nationals' win set up a seventh and
deciding game at the Onondaga Memorial Coliseum the following afternoon.

It was Easter Sunday, April 10, 1955. At noon, three-and-a-half
hours before tipoff, several Pistons players sat and relaxed in a
coffee shop outside the Onondaga Hotel. NBA Commissioner Podoloff, enjoying his lunch several tables away, spied the players
and went over to their table. "May the better team win," he
smiled, as he gave the players a hearty pat on the back. He turned
to leave, then leaned back and added: "That doesn't always happen."

From the opening tipoff, Fort Wayne was determined to win on
the Nats' home floor and overcome what the *Journal Gazette*
called "the Syracuse jinx." The Pistons stormed out to an early
17-point lead in the first half. Hutchins and Foust led the charge
as the Zollners hit more than half their shots from the field. But
the deficit merely strengthened Syracuse's resolve. In the second
half, the Nats slowly chipped away at the Pistons' large lead.

Taped radio broadcasts of live sporting events were extremely
rare in 1955. But during the second half of the game, radio station WKJG in Fort Wayne recorded the cheers of 6,697 wildly
screaming Syracuse fans and the urgent play-by-play calls of Fort
Wayne announcer Gates. With 83 seconds remaining in the game,
Fort Wayne held a one-point lead, 90–89. Here is a transcript

of Gates's commentary from that audiotape of the final thrilling moments of play.

There are 83 seconds to go. Superlatives escape me here. Adjectives cannot be found to describe this ball game, the "world series of professional basketball," the championship game, here in Syracuse, New York. Both teams are tied at three games apiece. It's the fateful seventh game, folks, and the Pistons are leading, 90–89.

Dolph Shayes, the great Syracuse forward, who scored 196 points in the playoffs, 120 against Fort Wayne, is stepping to the line to shoot two free throws. The first shot is in the air . . . it's good. Now it's 90 to 90. Shayes aims, shoots, and scores again. Syracuse leads, 91–90.

Brian brings the ball up the court. He passes to Yardley, guarded by Lloyd. Yardley drifts to the left side. There's 13 seconds to shoot on the 24-second clock. Yardley passes to Phillip who tries to get the ball into Larry Foust. Seven seconds to shoot! A pass to Brian, who jump passes to Yardley. Yardley gets some room. He jumps, shoots, and misses, but a foul will be called before the shot. Give the foul to King [of Syracuse].

George Yardley now on the line for the Fort Wayne Zollners. It's a one-shot foul. He shoots. He scores! It's tied at 91 to 91. Fifty-nine seconds to go! The ball goes down to [Syracuse's] Earl Lloyd. Lloyd passes to King. King driving into the lane. Fifty seconds! It's back to Lloyd. Lloyd's at 25 feet. He passes to King. Eight seconds to shoot on the 24-second clock. Forty-five seconds to go in the game. Back to Lloyd. Lloyd shoots. It's bounding around, and . . . it's no good! The rebound is to Andy Phillip of Fort Wayne! There's 36 seconds to go, twenty seconds to shoot. It's 91 to 91.

Andy Phillip drives into the attacking zone. He's holding . . . 28 seconds to go! He has 14 seconds to get a shot away. This is almost unbelievable. You couldn't write a script like this with the score deadlocked. Hearts are thumping. Phillip passes to Yardley, who passes back to Phillip. Phillip's along the left side trying to set up Larry. Pass to Foust, over to Yardley. He has to hurry to get a shot. Yardley goes under . . . and . . . the whistles are blowing. Oh!! Traveling on Yardley?! Eighteen seconds to go. Now only 17 seconds left in the ball game. Yardley had the ball batted away, then picked the ball back up again. Then apparently he traveled. They say he shuffled his feet when he tried to grab the ball. Syracuse has called a timeout.

The auxiliary clock, the 24-second clock, is not running now, of course. The master clock is the all-essential clock now, because Syracuse can move it around here and wait for a last shot, a last drive. It's 91 to 91, with exactly 17 seconds to go. The Nationals take the ball out of bounds. The crowd begins to break into a scream here. They pass the ball in right here in front of our microphone. King throws the ball into Kerr. Kerr back to King. The clock's winding down . . . 15 . . . 14 . . . 13 . . . 12. The whistles blow. Brian fouls! Brian fouls! Brian fouls George King! There's 12 seconds on the clock, and the referee says that Frank Brian has fouled George King.

It's only a one-shot foul, just a one-shot play. There are 12 seconds to go. Fort Wayne and Syracuse are tied. This is the last quarter. Police are sitting on either side of the Fort Wayne bench. King with one throw. Twelve seconds to go. King aims. He shoots. He scores!

Fort Wayne's ball out of bounds. It comes in to Phillip . . . ten seconds . . . nine . . . Phillip is going into the corner. He . . . has the ball stolen! King took the ball away! Four . . . three . . . two . . . one. The game is over. Syracuse wins. (Long pause as crowd cheers wildly) Syracuse has won the world's basketball championship, 92–91, in an almost unbelievable basketball game. There are thousands of spectators out on the basketball court. This is the first time in history an eastern division team has ever won the title. King, as Phillip pivoted, moved in and pulled the ball away from Andy, and that was the ball game. Syracuse has won, 92–91.

Fans, I want to say one thing in congratulating Coach Al Cervi and the Syracuse Nationals. They have a great basketball team. But I want to add one thing. We hope that when the Pistons land in Baer Field tonight at around 10:00, that we see a large throng welcoming them, because this was the most courageous stand of their career, and they were eked out here by one point, 92–91. Dame Fortune—Lady Luck—has the pendulum swinging against Fort Wayne in the last 11 seconds of the ball game, and Syracuse won. My hat is off to Charley Eckman and the gallant Pistons, who refused to be subdued here.

More than 4,000 fans welcomed the defeated Pistons upon their return to Fort Wayne. For weeks after the game, players, sportswriters, and fans argued and replayed the last seconds over and over. *Journal Gazette* columnist Reed, in an article entitled "May the Better Team Win," told his readers about Podoloff's remarks to the Fort Wayne players—"May the best team win. . . . That doesn't always happen"—and commented: "We wonder if he remembered that about five hours later as he was presenting the championship trophy to the Syracuse Nationals. Because his words turned out to be strangely prophetic, for the better team didn't win."

Gates recalled: "The seventh game, that fateful seventh game, was a real heartbreaker for everybody, especially Fred Zollner. The fact that we couldn't play our home games in Fort Wayne was a particular sore spot with him. I think Fred always thought that if he'd had the Memorial Coliseum for home court advantage, his team would have been the national champions of 1955." Yardley contradicted him: "I don't think the fact that we couldn't play our home games in Fort Wayne made much of a difference in the outcome of the tournament. After all, we won the three games we played in Indianapolis. The only thing that was really tough was that we were all young, and the enthusiasm of the crowd is very important to young athletes. We maybe didn't get quite the support in Indianapolis that we might have had in Fort Wayne. Of course, when it really comes down to it, games are won or lost on many more factors than whose court you're on or the calls the officials made. The simple fact of that final game in Syracuse was that we were ahead by 17 points, and we just let down emotionally. We became complacent. If we hadn't, we'd have won. We just didn't finish the job." Carl Bennett shrugged: "It's hard to think back and speculate whether we would have done better in the tournament if we'd played at home. There are so many factors that it's hard to pinpoint just one aspect of the game that made the difference. We did have good crowds at home, and we played very well at the Coliseum. So who knows?"

The Pistons' loss in the 1955 NBA finals obviously broke the hearts of the players and fans of Fort Wayne. But the defeat was to have a far greater impact than anyone could have imagined. The rumors began to fly the following season.

"Fred always wanted everything for his team to be 'major

league,'" reflected Hilliard Gates. "To be booted off your home court in the most important series in professional basketball and be replaced by a bowling tournament was a real disappointment to him. Had we played in Fort Wayne, had we won, well, then, I think Fred wouldn't have given it another thought. But I think losing that tournament ignited Fred to start looking at other venues in other cities to continue his drive for a 'major league' sports team."

Since the early 1920s the city of Fort Wayne had been the Midwest's hotbed for professional basketball. Now it seemed that the Summit City's basketball tradition was in jeopardy. Eastern newspapers started fleeting rumors at the end of the 1955–56 season. They claimed that the NBA would become a major league sport only when each franchise relocated to a major league venue. Despite Fort Wayne's recent success, the New York media still considered the northern Indiana city a "whistle stop."

Reporters tried to corner Zollner on the issue. The millionaire owner assured the local press that "if the fans prove they want us, we have no plans to move." But on December 13, 1956, Coach Charley Eckman completely rattled Zollner's lulling reassurances. At a speech in Indianapolis, Eckman said "there is a good chance the club may be relocated in another city by next season." It was the first hint of a move from inside the Pistons organization.

Zollner acted quickly to quell the storm of questions. "Professional basketball has arrived as a big-time sport," he told the media. "Metropolitan thinking is that three franchises in the National Basketball Association, including Fort Wayne, should be transferred to larger cities. We have made no commitments and sincerely hope the loyal fans in this area, through their interest and attendance, will help us keep Fort Wayne on the map to occupy the same position in professional basketball that Green Bay does in professional football."

Zollner got some public relations help from Maurice Podoloff, who also likened Fort Wayne to the tiny but highly successful Green Bay. "I have never heard any sentiment at all among the board of governors of the NBA about Fort Wayne being asked to drop out to make way for a larger city," Podoloff stated before a live television audience during a Pistons home game. "The NBA looks at Fort Wayne as the Green Bay of professional basketball. Fred Zollner has been of much help in recent years in making the league stronger, and he can have a franchise in Fort Wayne just as long as he wants to have one."

On camera, Podoloff was reassuring. But behind the scenes it was another story. George Yardley speculated: "Certainly the Allen County Memorial Coliseum was a much smaller facility than in other areas, such as the Boston Garden or Madison Square Garden in New York. But many other places, like Syracuse, St. Louis, or Minneapolis were about the same size as Fort Wayne. I really think what precipitated the rumors about the move had nothing to do with the size of the facility or the fan support. I think Fred was really pressured by the league to make the move. In all those other cities, it was much easier to get to those places. Airports and train stations were more accessible. We were probably the hardest place to get to in the entire western division. So I think Fort Wayne was inconvenient for the league. I think Podoloff was putting some pretty heavy pressure on Zollner to move his club to a major metropolitan area."

Zollner asked Fort Wayne fans for their support. On December 23 they responded. More than 8,100 spectators filled the Coliseum to catch their first glimpse of the Boston Celtics' heralded rookie, Bill Russell. Yardley played a sensational game against the much taller Russell, pouring in 22 points and holding Russell to only five. The fans thrilled as Fort Wayne beat Boston, 95–87.

But the crowds were inconsistent during the opening months of the 1956–57 season. Carl Bennett explained: "I think we always had decent crowds in Fort Wayne, but by the time we moved into the Coliseum, we were bringing in an average between 4,000–4,500 fans into an arena that seated 10,000 people. We were playing about 40 home games a season, which was about two games a week. It was hard to consistently draw large crowds for that many games in a small city like Fort Wayne. I mean, we only had 178,000 people in the entire city at the time. Boston, New York, and some of those other places had millions of potential fans to draw from night in and night out. But in Fort Wayne, even with our loyal support, it was very difficult to keep the Coliseum full for our games."

By January 1957 more rumors spread. This time Zollner allegedly had explored NBA franchise opportunities in Cincinnati, Louisville, and Milwaukee. Ben Tenny, outspoken columnist for the *Fort Wayne News Sentinel*, wrote in a January 18 article: "You know there is really no actual need for the team to be moved. The NBA won't insist that Fort Wayne do so. It might even in time okay the move here of some other franchise holder who might believe he could get along on the attendance Fort Wayne furnishes. You know, as do so many others, that the failure to break even in the promotion here is not too costly, because tax setups being what they are, much of the loss can be written off and value received in the way of advertising and good will in public relations. You wonder what player reactions will be and know, since some of them have told you, that the Pistons themselves had hoped all this move talk would die down. They enjoy playing here for what Coach Charles Eckman has termed 'the hard rock 3,000 fans,' the ones who will be the most unhappy if he and his top bossman do go through with their projected move."

That same week the *Journal Gazette* announced new developments on the potential move. "Zollner Piston Officials 'Explore' Detroit as Possible Site for Team," the banner headline read. Columnist Reed reported: "The possibility that the Zollner Piston basketball team will be moved from Fort Wayne loomed more strongly last night than most fans realized when it was learned that two Zollner officials were in Detroit 'exploring' the prospects of that city as the site of an NBA team." It was the first time Detroit had been mentioned as a possible site for the Pistons.

Reed's article continued: "Otto Adams, treasurer of the Zollner Corporation, who is close to the basketball situation, and R. J. Roshirt, a former resident of Detroit and now assistant to President Fred Zollner, were the officials who visited the Motor City. . . . 'Nothing definite has been done,' said Adams. 'We have no commitments and not even any offers from anyone in Detroit. We talked to a number of people and inspected Olympia Stadium and the University of Detroit Fieldhouse.' . . . In discussing a possible Piston move, Adams said it is not considered for the immediate future. 'Of course,' the Zollner spokesman said, 'it will not happen during the present season, but we are looking ahead. You don't make moves like this overnight.' "

There may not have been any plans for an overnight move, but discussions and decisions transpired in a matter of days. One week later, at the NBA All-Star festivities in Boston, Zollner confirmed reports that he was looking favorably to Detroit. The *Journal Gazette* wrote: "It was expected before the NBA All-Star game that Charley Eckman, coach of the Zollner Pistons, would make a trade. Now it appears as though the only trade will be the Memorial Coliseum for the Detroit Olympia." The deal seemed certain when Podoloff gave the NBA's blessing to the potential move. The *Detroit Free Press* quoted Zollner: "If it was a 50-50 bet that we would bring pro basketball to Detroit when we opened business negotiations, it is a 75-25 proposition now."

Still, questions remained. Detroit had a dismal history with its professional basketball franchises. The Detroit Falcons had lost $50,000 in one ill-fated season in the BAA. The NBL had fared just as poorly with the Detroit Gems, a team that lasted only one season and lost $30,000. *Detroit Free Press* columnist Tommy Devine commented: "If Fred Zollner does move here, he had better come in with both his eyes and purse wide open."

Carl Bennett explained: "Fred always had his eye on the future. He always had a great vision. All of the automobile manufacturers were heading up to Detroit, so it was only natural for Fred to look to Detroit as the future of the piston plant, as well as the team. Fred never minded losing money on the team. He wrote off many of his expenses as advertising costs associated with the plant. But he had to be practical about the future of the company. So a move to Detroit seemed logical."

On February 14, 1957, in a double-header billed as "a real sweetheart," the Coliseum hosted a Valentine's Day twin bill, with the Pistons facing Boston in the opening game and New York squaring off against Minneapolis in the nightcap. More than 5,700 fans came out to enjoy the contests. But one fan was conspicuously missing. Zollner was in Detroit for final negotiations with the Olympia Stadium management.

The Pistons celebrated the holiday with a 112-106 victory over the Celtics. But Fort Wayne's love affair with the Pistons was over. At a brief press conference in Detroit, Zollner announced that he had signed a six-year contract to play 22 nights a year at Olympia Stadium. The new contract would take effect at the start of the 1957–58 season. "The move was inevitable," Bennett commented. "Fred's drive and his vision had simply outgrown Fort Wayne. It was a real disappointment for the city, though."

The *News Sentinel* wrote that Zollner "said that he has a 'gentleman's agreement' with the Olympia owners that he can void his contract there at any time, adding, 'But I don't think we will ever want to move.' That statement, of course, reminds Fort Wayne fans of the statement he made less than two years ago, when thousands turned out at Baer Field to welcome the team home from the heartbreaking loss at Syracuse in the playoff finals, 'I will have a pro team in Fort Wayne as long as I make this city my home and have a business here.' But today the city finds itself without one starting with the next campaign. Time changes everything."

George Yardley recalled: "I was very depressed to hear the news. I hated to leave Fort Wayne. The fans just didn't take us to heart like they did in Fort Wayne. We knew our days of family enjoyment in a small-town environment were over. When we finally made the move, we had a real difficult time there. It was obvious that we were in a city that really didn't care if we were there or not. Detroit already had the Lions, the Tigers, and the Red Wings. They didn't need the Pistons. Attendance wasn't anywhere near what it was in Fort Wayne."

The announcement upset many Piston loyalists, including Ben Tenny of the *News Sentinel*. In one article the columnist snapped that Zollner had "washed Fort Wayne out of his curly hair." But in a subsequent piece, a more reflective Tenny offered a respectful and thoughtful look at the Zollner organization: "The ones who are sore are venting their feelings in no uncertain terms. Around some, it's not popular now to even mention the names of Zollner, Eckman, or others connected with the move. At the risk of having some of that ire directed my way, I would like to point out, however, that the industrialist who is ending the long era of athletic promotions here, does not deserve only condemnation at this time. It was his right to call it quits here any time he so chose, though most of us had thought he would do so only when he tired of being a pro team sponsor. What should also be remembered are these facts: He did give Fort Wayne a lot of entertainment, a lot of valuable publicity, through the sponsorships of softball and basketball. . . . On top of that, it might be pointed out that thousands of dollars have been used to give hundreds of Fort Wayne youngsters pleasant hours in swimming, skating, and playing through the extensive Knot Hole Gang setup the organization has sponsored. That alone deserved the city's thanks. Chances are those projects long will be part of his program here, even though he has decided to try to be 'big time' in a 'big city' in his basketball venture."

On March 19, the Pistons closed the season with a 110–108 loss to Boston at the Allen County War Memorial Coliseum. The loss eliminated the Pistons from the playoffs. The season, as well as a longstanding professional basketball heritage, drew to a close that day. The *News Sentinel* called the contest "a fantastic finish . . . to a fantastic era in Fort Wayne sports history."

On April 1, 1957, the day the gates opened on the Pistons' new headquarters in Detroit, the doors closed on an epoch in Indiana sports history. When the NBA ushered in its 1957–58 season, not a single team from Indiana was on its schedule.

Fred Zollner's move to Detroit was not an easy one. Ten years after the move, *Sports Illustrated* featured Zollner and "his misfiring Pistons." The article examined the auto parts manufacturer's difficulty in getting the city of Detroit to embrace his club. "'Piston games,' said one Detroiter, 'were known as a place where you could take your girl and sit upstairs for 50-cents and neck in privacy.'" *Sports Illustrated* columnist Myron Cope noted: "Zollner has remained something of a mystery man to the city of Detroit ever since he moved his club in 1957. Fort Wayne, he had concluded, could not support pro basketball; Detroit, Zollner soon learned, was damned if it would."

After an inauspicious start in 1941, the Fort Wayne Pistons had captured three national championships, three world tournament titles, and six division crowns. One season before Zollner's team left for Detroit, the Pistons had compiled a 37–35 record and held a two-year reign as the NBA's western division champs. After the move to Detroit the Fort Wayne entrepreneur enjoyed only one winning season in 17 years. In 1974, Zollner ended his long tenure as a professional basketball owner. He sold the Pistons to Bill Davidson, a Detroit businessman.

Forty-one years after their first professional basketball championship, the Pistons regained their glory. In 1989 and again in 1990, Isiah Thomas, an Indiana University product, led Detroit to national championships. Zollner never saw the city of Detroit celebrate its first NBA title. The corporate maverick from Fort Wayne had passed away on June 21, 1982. "He was a man with a vision," Dick Rosenthal noted. "Fred nurtured professional basketball from a very iffy proposition to a major business venture. He embodied the soul of the organization and the league. Professional basketball has come a long way. The game owes a great deal to the pioneer spirit of an owner like Fred Zollner."

Carl Bennett summed it up with a smile: "My life working for Fred was a dream. If somebody would have asked me when I was a kid what I wanted to do with my career, I would have told them exactly what I did for Fred Zollner's organization. It was fun and extremely rewarding. He was just a man who was committed to doing everything he could to develop the game of professional basketball. His motto was his life. Everything he did was 'Major League.'"

Though the Pistons' move left Indiana with no pro basketball team to call its own, the state continued to be a big contributor to the world of professional basketball. The same year the Pistons moved to Detroit, former Crispus Attucks star Oscar Robertson completed his freshman year on the basketball court at the University of Cincinnati, five-year-old George McGinnis learned to bounce a rubber ball in his parents' Indianapolis home, and Joe and Georgia Bird of French Lick celebrated the recent birth of their third son, Larry.

A new era of professional basketball began ten years later, in 1967, with the birth of the American Basketball Association. Included in the league was a new entry from the Hoosier state, the Indiana Pacers. Once again Hoosier hoops fans thrilled to the excitement of pro ball in the state. The Pacers won three ABA championships in the league's first seven years. They then joined three other ABA franchises in a merger with the National Basketball Association in 1976.

The game changed dramatically in the decade between the Pistons' departure in 1957 and the Pacers' entry in 1967. Commercialism and showmanship began to take center stage in a realm where superior athletics merged with Hollywood glitz. For Indiana, the ten-year hiatus served as a silent bridge between professional basketball's pioneers and the high-flying athletes of today's NBA.

Epilogue

In an interview with the *Dallas Morning News* in November 1994, Dick Ebersol, president of NBC Sports, called professional basketball "the world's premier television attraction." Before the interview, Ebersol had inked a four-year broadcast contract with NBA Commissioner David Stern for $750 million over four years. Cable news giant Ted Turner paid the NBA another $352 million for cable rights to league contests. For the first time in history, television network executives declared that televised professional basketball was a more popular national pastime than major league baseball.

Television is not the only financial tributary pouring into the National Basketball Association's overflowing reservoir of money. The *Dallas Morning News* reported that a league-approved product line brought in more than $3 billion in 1993, an increase of 400 percent in six seasons. More than one-third of the sales were foreign. By the year 2000, the sale of basketballs internationally is expected to exceed the number sold in the United States. And players' salaries, product endorsements, and movie contracts make the NBA one of the most lucrative business ventures in all of sports. Professional basketball is not only big business, it's good business.

In the midst of this current financial free-for-all, it is easy to overlook the colorful and turbulent history of professional basketball's pioneers. William "Pop" Gates, a Hall-of-Fame member of the legendary New York Renaissance barnstormers of the 1930s and '40s, commented: "Many of the ballplayers of our generation, prior to the NBA, white and black, really made the game what it is today. I think pro basketball has yet to honor many of its founders. It's not a matter of money, but just a matter of recognition for the old-time players who shaped the professional game and made it what it is today. . . . They gave their lives to the game. They gave their blood and their bodies just to try to make a living playing the game they loved. After all, if you don't have a good foundation on your building, the building will collapse. For the NBA, we were that foundation."

The foundation was a rough and rugged one. The cornerstones were laid by many defining moments: when a bloody Al Feeney charged topless onto the court in Columbus, Indiana, after angry fans tore his Indianapolis Em-Roes jersey from his back; when Indianapolis Kautskys players John Wooden and Bill Perigo braved a blinding snowstorm in a dilapidated jalopy to play a game two states away for a mere $50; when members of African American touring squads like the New York Rens and the Harlem Globetrotters earned lavish applause from midwestern spectators, only to be denied service in local hotels and restaurants later that same night; when visionary owners like Frank Kautsky and Fred Zollner sacrificed bottom-line profits to feed their burning passion for professional basketball; and when players competed for the love of the game, with little regard for financial compensation.

"Nobody ever got rich playing professional basketball in the 1920s, '30s, and '40s," noted Dale Ogden, sports historian and curator of history for the Indiana State Museum. "Many games in the early years were put together whenever and wherever they could be arranged. Some teams had success in league play. But most of the leagues, as well as the teams in them, were financially unstable. Other teams had a certain degree of success on a barnstorming tour. But in that situation there were so many unpredictable circumstances, such as the other team not showing up or inclement weather preventing travel. Plus, with barnstormers profiting only from gate receipts, low fan turnout meant a slim paycheck. There was never any guarantee when these men went out on the court. So they had to be playing for something other than money. There must have been a real passion for the game that fueled the early success of professional basketball."

Was it just a game to professional basketball's pioneers? Hardly. Passion fills the voices of pro basketball's forefathers as they reflect on the memories and meaning the game holds in their minds and hearts. Former Fort Wayne Pistons player Carlisle "Blackie"

Towery said: "God only knows where I would have been if it hadn't been for basketball." Towery continued with the game long after his professional career as a recreational director for a maximum-security prison. The game was such an important factor in Towery's life that he passed on this positive influence to others throughout the years.

"You really had to love basketball to play at that time," said Ollie Shoaf, a guard for the Hammond Buccaneers and the Evansville Agogans. "There just wasn't any money or stability in the game at that time. You really didn't know from one day to the next what was going to happen. The payroll was never guaranteed. So you'd just keep going and hope that all the expenses would take care of themselves out on the road. It was always impressive to me that the guys were all out there simply because they loved the game."

Indianapolis Kautskys player Frank Baird echoed: "Since it wasn't a full-time job, you had to love it. I mean, you'd have to love basketball to drive all the way to Oshkosh in the bitter snow to play a basketball game. You see, it wasn't the money that took you up there. It was the competition and just the fun of playing against the best and playing with the best."

For some, Hoosier Hysteria, that special brand of Indiana basketball, made a profound impression on their early adult lives. Frank Brian, an outstanding shooting guard for the Anderson Packers and the Fort Wayne Pistons, reminisced: "Whenever I hear the song 'Back Home Again in Indiana,' I get real nostalgic, because Indiana was like a second home to me. The fans were so congenial and really loved their basketball. They really embraced me. Basketball was its own special culture there. It will always hold a special place in my heart. When anybody ever asks me about the fans in Indiana, there's only one word I can say—unbelievable. Yes, sir—unbelievable. It was great." Hall-of-Famer George Yardley, another Pistons player, agreed, "If it's wintertime, and it's Indiana, it must mean basketball. The fans there were really wonderful. I loved it, truly loved it. It was the greatest experience in the world."

Camaraderie among team members fueled the passion of many who participated in pro basketball. Leo Barnhorst, the University of Notre Dame forward who had a successful career with the Indianapolis Olympians, the Fort Wayne Pistons, and the Baltimore Bullets, reflected: "We really lived as a family. I know that sounds corny, but we really did. The game of professional basketball allowed me to share some great times with a great bunch of guys. I've always considered myself very lucky to have been able to participate in such a wonderful game. That's all I can say—just very, very lucky."

The game pushed many of the players to greater personal heights. Rough and tough Anderson Packers star Ed Stanczak noted: "Basketball was a real character builder for me. It was a rough, physical game, and you had to prove you could hold your own. It was gratifying to me to know that I could make it—that I could compete with the best and hold my own out there. It really boosted my confidence and gave me the tools I needed to succeed in other endeavors throughout my life."

The game also sparked a social revolution in the world of athletics. William "Pop" Gates, captain of the great African American touring squad the New York Rens, stated: "I can't say that it was hard. Looking back, who knows? Maybe it was. But honestly, I can say that touring and playing professional basketball was enjoyable. I'm glad I had the chance to meet many people who respected us. Color was not an issue with them. They respected us not only because we were successful basketball players, but also because we were successful people with strong personalities—strong wills. After they saw that, I believe, they respected us as equals in every way—not just on the floor, but as human beings, as well."

Hall-of-Famer John Wooden, star of the Indianapolis Kautskys and the Hammond Ciesars, summarized the sentiments of Indiana's professional basketball pioneers: "I never did it for the money. I don't think any of us did. We did it purely because we loved the game. It was fun. The game enabled us to keep close with some other people who were also interested in basketball. And when other players from other parts of the country came into town for the games, we shared a special bond with each of them, also. There were just so many wonderful associations and friendships that we were able to develop and continue long after our playing careers were over. To me, that's what playing professional basketball meant. Those were good times—great times."

References

1. Dividing Up the Nickels

1. Joe Lapchick, *Fifty Years of Basketball* (Englewood Cliffs, N.J.: Prentice-Hall, 1968), p. 26.
2. John G. Dale, "The Golden Era of Montgomery County Basketball" (Crawfordsville, Ind.: unpublished), p. 2.
3. *Indianapolis News,* November 18, 1937, p. 4.
4. Dale, "The Golden Era of Montgomery County Basketball," p. 4.

2. The Golden Age

1. Lapchick, *Fifty Years of Basketball,* p. 28.
2. Arthur Ashe, Jr., *A Hard Road to Glory* (New York: Warner Books, 1988), p. 50.

3. The Unanimous Choice

1. *Fort Wayne Journal Gazette,* December 20, 1926, p. 10.
2. Dwight Chapin and Jeff Prugh, *The Wizard of Westwood* (Boston: Houghton Mifflin, 1973), pp. 53–54.
3. *Fort Wayne Journal Gazette,* March 24, 1928, p. 7.

4. The Grocer and the "India Rubber Man"

1. *Indianapolis Star,* April 10, 1947, p. 13.
2. Chapin and Prugh, *The Wizard of Westwood,* p. 44.

5. A Bunch of Palookas

1. Zander Hollander, *The Pro Basketball Encyclopedia* (Los Angeles: Corwin Books, 1977), p. 27.
2. *Indianapolis News,* February 1, 1937, sect. 2, p. 4.
3. *Indianapolis Star,* April 10, 1947, p. 13.
4. Robert Peterson, *Cages to Jump Shots* (Oxford University Press, 1990), p. 129.
5. Bernice Larson Webb, *The Basketball Man: James Naismith* (University Press of Kansas, 1973), p. 325.

6. Major League

1. "The Big 'Z' and His Misfiring Pistons," *Sports Illustrated,* December 18, 1967, p. 28.

7. Wheeler-Dealer

1. *Indianapolis Star,* April 10, 1947, p. 13.
2. Eric Nadel, *The Night Wilt Scored 100: Tales from Basketball's Past* (Dallas: Taylor, 1990), pp. 21–22.
3. Ocania Chalk, *Pioneers of Black Sport* (New York: Dodd, Mead, 1975), p. 105.
4. *Holiday,* "Hoop Happy Town," February 1951, p. 76.
5. Rodger Nelson, *The Zollner Piston Story,* Allen County Public Library Foundation, 1995, p. 147.
6. Ibid., p. 147.

8. The Merger

1. United Press, April 1, 1947.
2. Robert W. Peterson, *From Cages to Jump Shots* (New York: Oxford University Press, 1991), p. 164.

9. In the Tall Cotton

1. Charles Rosen, *The Scandals of '51* (New York: Holt, Rinehart, and Winston, 1978), p. 169.

10. A Ten-Foot Pole

1. Russell Rice, *Kentucky Basketball's Big Blue Machine* (Huntsville, Ala.: Strode, 1976), p. 213.
2. Todd Gould, producer, *Pioneers of the Hardwood,* PBS documentary, WFYI-TV, February 1993.
3. *Kentucky Basketball's Big Blue Machine,* p. 234.

11. The Fateful Seventh Game

1. Rodger Nelson, *The Zollner Piston Story,* Allen County Public Library Foundation, 1995, p. 171.
2. Ibid., p. 214.
3. Neil D. Isaacs, *The Great Molinas* (Johnson City, Tenn.: WID Publishing Group, 1992), p. 163.
4. "The Big 'Z' and His Misfiring Pistons," p. 28.
5. Nelson, *The Zollner Piston Story,* p. 221.

Index

Todd Gould is Senior Producer for public television station WFYI in Indianapolis. His production of "Pioneers of the Hardwood" was a 30-minute special for the statewide public television series "Across Indiana." The National Academy of Television Arts and Sciences has recognized his work with five Emmy Awards.